DON'T WASTE YOUR TALENT

The 8 Critical Steps To Discovering What You Do Best

Revised Second Edition

BOB MCDONALD, PH. D.
DON E. HUTCHESON

Second Edition with Revisions
By
Lazar Emanuel & Thomas N. Tavantzis, Ed. D.
The Highlands Company

Published by
THE HIGHLANDS COMPANY
1328 Boston Post Road
Larchmont, NY 10538

Printed in the United States of America.

ISBN: 0-9755112-1-1

CONTENTS

WE HIRE
PEOPLE
FOR THEIR **SKILLS**
BUT
THE
WHOLE PERSON
SHOWS
UP
FOR
WORK.

— CHESTER I. BARNARD

INTRODUCTION

Using Your Talent

We know two things for sure about success. You have to know what you do best, and you have to find the right fit between yourself and your job. We founded a company over fifteen years ago with the idea of helping people do just that. That company is The Highlands Company.

We are not alone in our thinking. Peter Drucker, a widely respected management consultant and insight-provider about modern business, a man Fortune magazine called the "most prescient business-trend spotter of our time," agrees. Drucker has said:

> *Success in the Knowledge Economy comes to those who do two things: identify and articulate their talents, and place themselves in positions to use them.*

But how do you go about identifying your talents? As Peter Drucker has also said:

> *Most people think they know what they are good at. They are usually wrong.*

How well do you know your own talents? Can you describe them? How do they manifest themselves at work? At home?

This book is about identifying and using your talents. It is about The Highlands Program and The Highlands Personal Vision Factors – the structure and process we developed because we believe that people deserve to be on higher ground in their lives and careers. We created The Highlands Program to do two things: First, to help you identify and articulate your natural gifts and talents. Second, to help you figure out the right fit between you and your career. You do this by creating your own Personal Vision— a comprehensive map of what you're hard-wired to do. A Personal Vision opens the doors to your creative insight, energy and talent and puts you on the clear, smooth road to success and satisfaction.

Every one of us is born with unique talents and gifts. They are hard-wired into us. We don't learn them and we can't ignore them. They are just part of who we are. For some, talents are specialized and particular – a gift for music or design, for instance, or a gift for theoretical thought. For others, talents are more generalized – as a talent for leading teams, or the abilities that make teaching, selling or writing easy. Some talents are mutually exclusive—talents that make you a naturally gifted manager are nearly the opposite of talents that make you an insightful consultant or a creative designer.

The first step in using your talents is to identify what your talents really are. Your talents are not something you necessarily know about yourself. You have to discover them in a purposeful way. With the right tools, this is relatively easy and straightforward.

Knowing *what* your talents are is a huge accomplishment in itself, but it's not enough. After you know what you're naturally gifted to do and how you're hard-wired, you have to place yourself in a position to use your talents. This means finding the right fit, and it can be a somewhat larger problem.

We discovered that most Programs designed to help People figure out their best Careers look with too small a Perspective. We determined to create a program that would look not only at one or two dimensions of people, but would instead treat them and their careers holistically and honor their complexity.

In 1990 we started wondering how people could be helped to discover work in which they could succeed and which they would find enjoyable at the same time. We were right at midlife, and had enjoyed successful, satisfying careers. One of us had been a psychologist for eighteen years and built a strong and lucrative practice. The other had been an entrepreneur, starting and running two profitable advertising agencies. But at this midlife turning point we both wanted something different. As with most people at midlife, we wanted to use talents that our previous careers had ignored.

The psychologist quit his practice and the entrepreneur sold his last agency. We embarked on what would turn into two years of research on two questions—How do you figure out what you are good at? How do you get into a position where you can do that very thing every day?

We discovered that most programs designed to help people figure out their best careers look at people in too limited a perspective. We determined to create a program that would look not only at one or two dimensions of people, but would instead treat them and their careers holistically and honor their complexity.

Out of this research, we created the eight Personal Vision Factors. These offer a way to get at all of the factors that influence the right fit between you and your career. Several things make it completely different from other programs, tests and processes. Over the years, we have refined and expanded our program in response to our readers' comments and the experiences of our ever-growing army of talented practitioners and Affiliates.

Our program is multidimensional. We don't settle for a simple picture of who you are. You are more than your personality, more than your interests, more than your values, even more than your natural talents. If you don't take a whole picture of yourself into account, you run the serious risk of getting into a job or career that will end up feeling as though it doesn't fit you at all. There are eight factors you need to take into account to find the right fit. The eight Personal Vision Factors presented in this book will help you identify and articulate them and will lead to your own Personal Vision.

It is inside out, not outside in. We don't tell you what to do. If you are looking for an expert who knows more about you than you know about yourself, forget it. No matter how many tests the expert gives you or how many degrees the expert has, he or she will not know one thousandth of what you need to know to find the right fit. But you can find the answers yourself. They are all inside you right now. The eight Personal Vision Factors help you reach them, identify them and make them work for you.

It is structured. The value of the structured approach of the eight Personal Vision Factors is that, if you follow the exercises in this book, you will be well on the way to the promised result. The structure is designed to help you avoid leaving anything out.

The Basic Plan of This Book

The first three chapters deal mainly with why it's so difficult to know what your talents are and to figure out the right fit. They deal with The Lemming Conspiracy, the Stress Cycle, and career development over your lifespan.

The next six chapters show you exactly how to use the eight Personal Vision Factors to create your own Personal Vision. A Personal Vision is a holistic plan that maps what you're able to do best by accurately identifying your talents and figuring out how to use them most effectively.

The last three chapters show how to use The Personal Vision Factors at work, how corporations have used them in the workplace and how they can become tools to use throughout your life.

People have used this book in several ways. What you get out of it is a product of your goals in reading it and of the time and energy you put into it. Here are some goals you can achieve in reading this book:

Find out what natural talents are and how to use them. You can do this by reading the text and looking at the exercises. From this, you will get a good idea about what natural talents are and what the eight Personal Vision Factors are.

Gain some personal insight about your career. You can get this from reading the text and doing those exercises that appeal to you. All of the exercises yield highly interesting information, but if you don't want to go through all of them, just pick out one or two that you find interesting or that strike a chord in you. The more exercises you do, the greater the insight into your own strengths and how you can contribute best at work and at home; and the greater the ability to build a Personal and Career Vision Statement to guide you in developing your most effective leadership style.

Discover the right fit between you and your career and you and your work roles. This is a bigger goal, but it's one that will pay off—both in terms of satisfaction and in terms of success. To do this, you have to take the time to read the text and systematically go through the exercises. We would suggest putting a little time into them every day. This is a process that could take a few weeks or a couple of months, depending on how thoroughly you go about it and how much time and energy you can put into it.

Identify and articulate your natural talents and abilities. Whatever your goals are, we strongly recommend that you take The Highlands Ability Battery™, now available online. You can learn all about it on our website: www.highlandsco.com, and you can order it by calling 1-800-373-0083 or by e-mail to info@highlandsco.com. The Battery is the gold standard among human assessment tools. It is a complete and thorough collection of hands-on electronic ability worksamples that will tell you how you work best, as well as how you communicate, problem-solve and learn. The Battery is followed by a two-hour personal consultation with a Certified Highlands Affiliate. See Chapter 4 for a more complete explanation of what natural abilities are and how the Highlands Ability Battery measures them.

We have had numerous clients over the years who have come back to us after going through one of our programs or after reading the material in this book to tell us that the eight Personal Vision Factors changed their lives. Many people have told us that they use the knowledge they gained every single day. Our favorite endorsement, though, came from one of our earliest clients—a young man in his mid-20s who had been searching for a meaningful direction since college. His father, tired of worrying about his son, paid for him to go through The Highlands Program. When he finished the program, he told his father, "Dad, this is the best thing you ever bought for me—including my car."

In our experience, everyone – undergraduates, graduate students, engineers, research scientists, lawyers, teachers, executives of billion dollar companies – finds the Highlands Ability Battery™ and the eight Personal Vision Factors uniformly helpful. Parents who complete them as part of a work program want their children to complete them; individuals who complete them for their own personal development want their spouses to complete them. We know one family in which both parents and their four children have all completed the Highlands program.

Creating a Personal Vision is perhaps the most important work you can do to make your life more fun, more productive and more meaningful. Gandhi had a Personal Vision. So did Churchill. So did Watson and Crick, who discovered DNA, and Benjamin Franklin, who shepherded the thirteen colonies through the Revolution. A Personal Vision can help you overcome almost any obstacle. Once you see your goal, you can attain it.

Some people use their talents; others ignore them. Our philosophy is this: **TAP INTO YOUR TALENTS – DON'T WASTE THEM.** They are your hard-wired key to personal and professional success.

HOW MANY **MIDDLE-AGED** MEN
HAVE AWAKENED IN THE MIDDLE
OF THE NIGHT WITH THE
NIGHTMARISH REALIZATION
THAT THEIR LIVES FEEL
UTTERLY MEANINGLESS
AND THEIR ENERGIES ARE
BEING WASTED?

HOW MANY
MIDDLE-AGED WOMEN
HAVE **SUDDENLY** SEEN THEIR LIVES
LOSE MEANING WHEN
THEIR CHILDREN LEAVE HOME?

OR HOW MANY
HARD-DRIVING
PROFESSIONAL WOMEN
WAKE UP IN THEIR
LATE THIRTIES AND REALIZE THEY
HAVE FORGOTTEN TO BUILD A FAMILY?

THE LEMMING CONSPIRACY
HAS CAPTURED THEM ALL AND
ANESTHETIZED THEM.

Escaping the Lemming Conspiracy

Why do some hugely talented people seem to bomb out of life? Why do the lives of others who seem naturally less gifted seem to be so much more productive and fruitful? Many people go through life with the strong suspicion that there is some valuable part of themselves that never finds expression. Why is this? And more importantly, how can you make sure that you are using all of the talents you were born with?

This book helps you identify your true talents and figure out how to use them. It is based on work we have been doing for more than fifteen years in helping people find the right fit in their lives, their jobs, and their careers. We have built a growing network of Affiliates throughout the world. Together, we have helped thousands of individuals and have enabled companies to develop their leaders and build their teams.

Before we talk about how to find the right fit, though, we need to discuss why this is so difficult and why so many people are pulled off track.

You may have heard about lemmings. These small arctic mammals band together from time to time and, running in vast herds, throw themselves over sea-side cliffs to their deaths in the sea. As a metaphor, it seems to describe how too may of us live our lives—the authors included.

Let us tell you about a conspiracy—we call it the Lemming Conspiracy—widespread and insidious, that controls what you do every day and even how you feel about what you do. It is a conspiracy that controls your perceptions of yourself and the options in your career.

This conspiracy routinely invades almost every aspect of our lives. Born of benign intentions, but almost totally hidden from our awareness, it operates outside of our conscious will and keeps us from understanding our real talents and what we could really do in the world.

Why do many of us settle for lives that are stressful, frenetic and often empty of meaning? Why do we spend our energy and time acquiring possessions that bring us so little happiness in the end? Why do we ignore people who are important to us, and ignore ourselves in the bargain? We behave in these "irrational" ways because the Lemming Conspiracy keeps us from experiencing ourselves as we really are.

We grow up learning to see a limited range of options as if they constituted all our options. Our schools, colleges, corporations, organizations, friends and families actively work—albeit unintentionally for the most part—to encourage this limited view of our lives. Why? Not because they are evil, certainly, but because they are organized into *systems*. Systems create and perpetuate the Lemming Conspiracy.

The concept of *systems* and how they operate to control cultures, corporations, biology, families, animal societies and human societies is very complex. Scientific analyses of systems are often rather densely unintelligible to the layman. If you bear with us for a moment, however, you will begin to get the idea of what systems are and how they work. For us, as people living in society with each other, systems impose the rules by which our various groups – family, work and social – operate.

How Systems Control Our Perceptions of Ourselves

The fundamental fact about all systems is this: Any system of which you are a member will have its own goals and interests, and those goals and interests are not necessarily the same as your goals and interests.

NOTE: In this book, we will often talk about systems as identifiable units having goals, wanting things, or behaving in other ways as though they were alive. A system is a way of describing how people work together in stable groups like families or corporations. Obviously, a system is really an abstraction and has no will or mind of its own. But systems can and do act as though they do have powers of their own. Many systems routinely produce results exactly the opposite of those that people in the system want to produce.

An Office System

At the very simplest level, everyone in a typical corporate office goes to work at about the same time every day, works steadily during the morning, takes off for lunch at about the same time, works steadily during the afternoon, and finishes the day's work at about the same time. All of the workers in the office know that they have choices about what they do all day long. But they act as though their choices are limited. In order to be members of this particular system—this office—they have to go by the rules. Otherwise the system will not function. Suppose, for example, that a new executive with fresh insights were to join this office. He may try at first to introduce new policies and new procedures, but over time – say six months – he will lose his original incentives and eventually merge into the mold.

Other rules are less obvious but can nevertheless operate more powerfully. Here are some examples of the unstated rules you may find in your office:

UNSTATED OFFICE 'RULES'

- You should strive to make more money and gain a higher position in the organization.

- You must give up significant aspects of your personal life in order to be successful.

- If you don't get promoted, you are a failure.

- Work is not something you should think about enjoying; that's why they call it work.

- You should do whatever it takes to succeed, including, if necessary, work 12-hour days and 75-hour weeks

- Work hard, play by the rules, and you will be successful and happy.

- Happiness has something to do with how much you can buy.

These rules, powerful but covert, may vary from system to system, but they **make the system work.**

If everyone *didn't* act as though moving up the corporate hierarchy and being able to buy a better car were important, then the young people in the company wouldn't be scrambling all over each other trying to compete for the top spots. They wouldn't be willing to put up with drudgery and meaningless labor in order to please someone they may not respect. Middle-aged managers who want something more in their lives might begin to look outside the corporation. The collapse of the corporation would follow, with civilization not far behind – at least, this seems to be the driving fear that motivates systems to remain ever the same.

The *system* acts as though its rules are real and relevant. It assumes that you as a member buy fully into the rules and are willing to share them. Systems are conservative; they don't change their rules easily or often. Superficial changes rarely, if ever, change the fundamental rules of a system. As a member of the system, you are under a great deal of pressure to believe, buy into and live out its rules. And most people do.

Either subtly and silently, or overtly and crassly, systems can encourage employees to forget about their real talents, interests and passions, and to think of their life goals in terms of money and promotions. Employees are not encouraged to explore and develop their natural gifts and talents. They are even discouraged from looking closely at their deepest values. At work, people are often discouraged from engaging in any real self-exploration.

> *Systems see each person as a collection of simple skills and functions. They operate most smoothly when you see yourself in this way, too. As a result, you remain distant from yourself, defining yourself firmly in a limited way, when the reality of yourself may be entirely different. This situation creates and perpetuates the Lemming Conspiracy.*

Companies that adhere to systems are increasingly unable to meet the challenges of our modern information and technology-based society. New generations of workers are less and less willing to accept the rules imposed by systems. More and more managers are being forced to rethink the process of motivation – especially when break-through thinking is needed.

How the Lemming Conspiracy Begins— the Family of Origin – a Trip Down Memory Lane

The Lemming Conspiracy begins in the family of origin—the family in which we grow up as children. Our families give us a primary sense of what we are. This happens outside of our awareness, but it is a fundamental fact of our development. Our perceptions of ourselves – smart, stupid, good-looking, capable, incapable, affiliative, distant, and all of the hundreds of other ways we describe and think about ourselves – start forming by about age four. They become solidified by the time we are 18 and ready to move out of our family homes into the wider world.

Children absorb a sense of who they are and what they "ought" to be doing in the world from their parents. The rebellious teen fights this influence: "I don't know who I am, but I know who I am not. I am not like my father." What is hidden from the teenager who mutters this is that his father, when he was 18, probably had exactly the same thought about his own father.

Sometime around age 30 to 35, people often realize, with some horror, "I have become my parent." This recognition frequently occurs after they have children of their own. They have, of course, been like their parents all along without realizing it. Their first conscious memories are of the time they were 5 or 6 and their parents were 30 to 35. When recognition strikes, they are simply recalling their first memories of their parents.

This process of acquiring a fully formed image of ourselves, a picture which includes both parents, is almost completely subconscious, but is one of the most powerful forces in our lives. It is called identification. It is the fully formed picture of who we are – a picture we learn in our families of origin, and then take into adulthood. Without it, people could not grow up. They could not leave their families. They could not form ties and relationships in the adult world. They would not know the "rules" of adult life.

Who We Are and Who We Are Not

This image of ourselves gained through identification makes it possible for us to enter the adult world, and creating this image is the main function of the family system. But this image also has limits. We not only learn who we *are* in families, but we also learn who we *are not*. We learn, clearly, what role we are to play in the adult world, and we learn how to play it. As part of the family system, we start to see a divergence between how the *system* sees us and how we see the potential in ourselves. Later, we will talk about the difference between our System Self, the self that the system sees, and our True Self, the person we are able to become.

The family of origin is a system. It is a closed circle of relationships that has its own history, rules, roles and customs. All of these remain stable over time. If you study a family for many years, you will see that certain roles and types keep reappearing, generation after generation. When we leave home we take our "model" of the family system out into the world and recreate it when we start our own families.

Our family system is also the model for any other system that we become involved in, join or create throughout our lives. We join systems that "fit." We choose our friends, churches, synagogues, clubs, organizations, schools, companies and corporations, and they choose us, because they fit, and we fit. There is a role we can play in the system that we learned in our family of origin. This role may be exactly right for us. It may tap into every one of our natural talents and satisfy our deepest goals in life. It may express perfectly our fundamental values and involve aspects of life that we find intrinsically fascinating.

Or not. We learn roles in our family of origin that may have more or less to do with our personal makeup. As we enter the adult world, we usually discover much more about ourselves than our families see. But our families – and other systems in which we become involved – persist in seeing us in the same interpersonal roles they always have. Their perceptions of us don't change easily.

All systems strongly encourage you to see yourself as they see you. If you fulfill your role in the way the system expects, then the system operates more smoothly, if not more creatively. The problem for you is that you may get lost, and it is difficult to get another view of yourself as long as you continue in the same patterns the system expects.

What follows is a true story about a person who did everything right. She went to the right schools, made wonderful grades, got a great job, and was successful at every turn. While she lived out the life her systems encouraged her to live, she steadily lost a true sense of herself and what she wanted from her life. Although she didn't realize it, she was a victim of the Lemming Conspiracy and stood in danger of wasting her most important talents.

> NOTE: We will tell much of this book through the stories of people's lives. In all cases, the stories are based on real people and on actual events in their lives; however, we have changed their names and deleted any personal information about them, in order to protect their privacy.

Sarah's Story

Sarah grew up in a small town in Minnesota. An excellent student in high school, she had many extracurricular interests, including theater, which she loved. School came so easily that she seldom had to work hard. Theater consumed a far more important share of her time and creative talent than academics.

Sarah's father, a successful computer systems analyst, had gone to graduate school right after college, intending to get a Ph.D. in history. At the time, he dreamed of teaching. After he earned his master's degree, he did teach for a while.

Teaching made him happy, but he realized that he could never earn an adequate salary in this field. He had been married two years and had a little daughter for whom he was responsible. His own father's image, that of a man providing well for his family, forcefully urged him to change.

Sarah's father switched to computers, and soon was doing well financially. When he took a job, he generally liked it at first, but it quickly became routine. There was nothing intrinsically interesting to him about computers or computer systems. When his unhappiness reached the breaking point, he simply found a new job. To him this did not seem unusual. He assumed most people didn't really like their jobs.

Sarah's mother was also a successful computer systems consultant. She didn't find her work rewarding either—just lucrative. She stayed in the same job with the same firm for many years and was considered quite good at her role. She didn't find her work particularly interesting, creative or fun. It was work, and she did it and was happy to have a job.

Sarah's mother had a love, too. She created handmade clothes for children. She had quite a following among her friends and opened a shop to sell her creations. She loved all aspects of this enterprise—from the fabrics and their colors, to the design and creation of the clothes, to helping people find exactly the right garment for a family or a child. But she didn't call it work. It was a hobby. In her lexicon, "work" was what you had to do. Enjoyment at work was completely beside the point.

And so Sarah went off to college. She went to a small, select, liberal arts college in the South and did well—earning a 3.8 average. "I figured out very quickly what I needed to do to get an 'A'. I just took the right courses and paid attention in class and always did just enough to slide under the wire. I took history courses and an English course, but what I really enjoyed was drama. I got involved in a theater group the first semester I was on campus. It held the whole focus of my attention throughout four years of college. I loved the life of the theater; I loved the people in theater; I loved everything about it. It easily absorbed 90 percent of my attention and energy."

Sarah never thought about what she would do after college. Even well into her senior year, she did not have a real idea about what she would do when she graduated. An advisor, looking at her transcript, asked her if she had ever thought about law school. She had not. She had never, as far as she could remember, even known a lawyer. But this seemed like a plan.

Sarah applied to six law schools and was accepted by four, among them Yale. She decided to go there. Why? "It's Yale. You can't turn Yale down." She walked onto the Yale campus the next fall without ever having interviewed a lawyer, or worked in a lawyer's office, or even wondered too much about what a lawyer did. She just thought it would be a way to make money.

"I knew as soon as I started that I hated law. But, once again, I could make A's fairly easily. I did just as much as was necessary, nothing more. I joined a theater group right away, and the great majority of my time and energy went there. The saddest day of my life was the day I graduated from law school. It meant that I would have to stop doing what I really liked to do in life and start working to pay back my law school debts."

Sarah's story was published on the front page of a major metropolitan newspaper, because she had secured a job in a distinguished law firm well before graduation, and because she had produced and directed a video about law students, which was broadcast on PBS. In the video, students talked about law and law school, and their feelings of anger and frustration at being trapped in a profession they didn't like and had no real interest in, but which would pay them well.

We talked to Sarah about a year after she started working for the law firm. As a young associate she had so little time that she couldn't be involved in the theater. She succeeded in the firm, but was already thinking that if she moved to New York City, she could earn more money, save it faster and eventually be able to do what she wanted.

Sarah's Family of Origin

Obviously, Sarah had absorbed a great deal from her mother and father. On the positive side, she had worked hard and had done well at whatever she set out to do. On the negative side, she had absorbed both parents' pattern of being in work they didn't like and had no interest in – work that probably ignored their greatest talents. She would turn to her father's pattern of changing jobs in order to deal with her unhappiness and dissatisfaction. And it would probably work no better for her than it had for her father. Her parents had given her the habits they were driven to use, and she had adopted them without realizing it.

Sarah had left her family of origin and established herself independently. By almost any yardstick she had succeeded, and her family had successfully performed its main role and function.

But no system had ever challenged Sarah's basic assumptions or her decisions. Nor could it. This fundamental limitation of systems is the defining fact of the Lemming Conspiracy.

From the point of view of Sarah's high school, everything was fine. One of their brightest seniors had gone to an excellent liberal arts college. To challenge whether it was the right school, with enough options to explore what she really loved, would be unthinkable. She had done well academically; she had been accepted to a strong academic institution. Perfect.

At college, once again, everything appeared to be fine and on course. How could anyone think there was a problem? Sarah herself didn't think there was a problem. It was only when the end of her senior year loomed that any troubling thoughts came to her. What would she do now? Her advisor saw a bright, articulate student with excellent grades, and one clear answer popped into his head—law school. She could get in, and it would make the college look good. Her acceptance at Yale made it all seem so right.

For the school to challenge these events would be foolish in the extreme.

As a small, very selective and expensive liberal arts institution, the school's survival depended on the success of its graduates in getting into graduate and professional schools. Getting graduates into Yale Law validated the fundamental premise of the school: "We are doing a good job because our graduates go on to high-quality graduate and professional programs."

And Yale certainly never challenged Sarah's decision. It was happy to have such a bright student. It was even happier, as an institution, when one of its brighter and more talented students landed a good job four months before graduation. *That* makes a school look good.

The firm in which she landed saw its future in being able to attract smart, talented young lawyers who would work like demons for five to seven years until they were hooked into its financial rewards. Landing a Yale student near the top of her class, and a *female at that*, was exactly what the firm wanted to do. And did.

Each of these systems – high school, college, professional school, law firm – had its own goals and its own interests. Sarah was helping each of these systems to fulfill these interests and goals. But the interests of the systems were clearly not the same as Sarah's true interest – not even close. And Sarah had never looked at what her own interests and goals might be. Nor was she encouraged to. Instead, she was encouraged to think of herself as part of the system she was in – bright, successful and on the way to the top. When we met her, she was unhappy and feeling trapped by debt. The only escape she could imagine was the same as the one her father had used – one that had left him unhappy and trapped most of his career.

How We Get Out of Balance and How That Leads to Stress

Sarah's story, that of a young person who goes from success to success to success and yet ends up feeling trapped and unhappy, shows in clear relief how many people live out their lives in systems. While energetically jumping through hoop after hoop, they never stop to examine who they really are and what they really want from their lives.

With patterns and roles absorbed from our families of origin, we leap into the world in our early twenties. We find systems to join that fit our sense of ourselves and our sense of what roles we could play in life. This works well for the systems, and it appears to work pretty well for us—for a while.

Throughout our adult lives, we experience regular cycles of stability and change. We launch ourselves into the beginning of our careers, just as Sarah did. At first everything may seem fine. We may feel that we are a good match for a system at the beginning. The system's values appear to match our own. Our lives seem interesting and exciting.

But with each passing year, we grow and change. We become different on the inside. We have new ideas, meet new people, have new goals and new wants. But the systems in which we remain do not change their views of us. To our systems (and this includes our family systems), we are always the same. Our systems assume we have remained on the same path, and that we have the same commitment to the system's values and rules that we always had.

System Self, True Self and Life Balance

The increasing disparity between ourselves as our systems see us and what we are on the inside—the difference between the *System Self* and the *True Self*—leads to our becoming increasingly out of balance. But we have a choice. We can either struggle against our system's definition of us, or we can increasingly allow ourselves to be seen as our system sees us. Very few people end up struggling against systems—at least, not for very long.

Instead, we *become* who our systems think we are. This invariably means that we are not attending to or putting enough energy into one or more critically important elements of our lives. Systems have only a limited view of us. We are whole people, but systems see only limited roles and functions. How many middle-aged men have awakened in the middle of the night with the nightmarish realization that their lives feel utterly meaningless and their energies are being wasted? How many middle-aged women have suddenly seen their lives lose meaning when their children leave home? Or how many hard-driving professional women wake up in their late thirties and realize they have forgotten to build a family? One 45-year old woman we know, a successful marketing director, realized suddenly one day that she was living the life that others expected of her – not the life that would express her own true self. Her family of origin had blinded her to life's alternatives.

The Lemming Conspiracy has captured all these people and anesthetized them. These middle-aged men and women suddenly awaken to discover what has really been going on for a number of years: their System Selves, defined by the roles or functions that the system demands, and their True Selves – the whole person that was and is possible – have grown irreparably apart.

The metaphor of the "boiled frog" has been used to describe what happens to us when we get caught up in systems. Conceived by Richard Boyatzis (2002), the boiled frog metaphor goes something like this: if you place a frog in boiling water it will jump out at once, but if you place the frog in a pot of water and bring the water to a boil slowly, the frog will allow himself to be cooked. In much the same way our personalities – who we are and how we face the world – come upon us slowly, until we ourselves are "cooked." Then, in middle age, we try to figure out how we got the way we are.

The Allegory of the Cave

Of course the grand metaphor for how we build a false idea of ourselves comes to us from our Hellenic relative Plato who gave us the Allegory of the Cave.

Imagine, Plato teaches, that all men live in a deep cave. They know nothing else. The entrance to the cave is miles away and has never been found. Trapped in their dark chamber, they conclude that the shadows created by the fires they light constitute the only reality. Various shapes and shadows pass in front of them. From these images they create their own reality. Now, suppose, Plato continues, that one of the men escapes the cave and ventures forth into the world outside. At first, the light baffles him. Suppose, however, that his eyes gradually got accustomed to the light. What would he think now of his old world of shadows? Would he return and tell the others about his new world of light? Would the others believe him or would they turn against him and reject him as a false prophet?

We are all prisoners in a cave trying to find the light. Each of us has to make sense of his or her time here. At some point, if we're lucky, we come to a point in life when we realize that what we have experienced – our model of the world – is but one of many alternatives, one of many possible stories. Each of us, at different points in our careers, tries to answer the eternal questions posed by life: Who am I? Why am I here? What is my responsibility? To myself? To others? And how can I be of use?

These questions are about purpose. When we know the answers, we know life's meaning.

The result of not knowing? Stress. Also anxiety, anger and often depression. When the stress or anxiety reaches a critical point, it often starts to arouse awareness. It is at these times of greater awareness—times we call Turning Points—that we seek new answers and change.

We can find creative answers and new directions at Turning Points, but too often we do not, because the Lemming Conspiracy still holds us captive.

Turning Points and Life Changes

As we reach a critical point of stress and anxiety, we arrive at a Turning Point. At Turning Points we feel ready for change. We actively seek new answers. One of the best-documented Turning Points arrives at midlife, but we have identified eight of them. With remarkable regularity, they come every seven to ten years throughout our adult lives. These all-important times of crisis can lead to positive creativity and change. But all too often, the opportunity is turned away and they do not lead to change.

At Turning Points, we often become aware of the increasing disparity between who we are and the person our systems see. And we often try to change something. But what? The answers too often come from our family of origin. We will often make the same kind of decision, and for about the same reason, as one or the other of our parents made at the same age. We will talk more about Turning Points and how we make these decisions in Chapter 3.

In Sarah's story, we saw the pattern of decision-making at Sarah's Turning Points—both for Sarah and her parents. At the critical Turning Point at the start of her adulthood, Sarah decided to go into a field that was financially secure but offered little personal reward, just as her father had done. Her sense of what work is and should be was formed by what she had observed in her mother and father. She was well on her way to repeating her father's strategy for dealing with stress. We can predict that she would be no more successful in her decision than her father had been.

We were able to see these same forces at work with a young man named Mitchell, who came upon a Turning Point a little later in life. Mitchell became increasingly aware of the disparity between his System Self and his True Self and was moved to make changes. The first answers he thought of came straight from his family of origin, just as they would for anyone. They could easily have led him to repeat Sarah's mistake. But Mitchell took a new path, and his story ends differently from Sarah's.

Mitchell's Story

Mitchell started working for a large technology firm straight out of college. He pursued his career energetically and achieved success early. He worked predominantly in sales. He came to the attention of his bosses, and they wanted him on the fast track. "By age 30, I liked what I was doing. I liked my co-workers and clients. The company had been good to me, but I just felt this restlessness and uneasiness I couldn't put my finger on."

The firm could not help Mitchell with this problem. All of its answers were in the interest of the firm, not of Mitchell. Obviously, as long as Mitchell was productive, his firm would encourage him to "stay the course." It was in its interest for Mitchell to think that a good job, good pay, and good co-workers were enough. That is exactly what Mitchell thought. Or, more correctly, thought he should think.

Once this subtle misconception takes root — that a company's interests and a person's interest are the same thing — stress and imbalance loom on the horizon. Mitchell made this mistake when he delayed his wish for change by admonishing himself to just grow up, settle down and endure. Mitchell's firm could not help him figure out who he was and what he wanted. Mitchell sensed that he had to do something different, and the fact that he was obviously successful just made his wish for change more stressful. Mitchell's True Self had diverged from his System Self, but he had no way to find and identify his True Self. He had no way to create a vision of his True Self which would help him to stand up to his systems.

Mitchell's family couldn't help. The message from his parents could not have been clearer: "Are you crazy? Stay with your job. It's secure." He felt strongly about his responsibility to his young wife and to his newly-born child. He couldn't do anything that would jeopardize their well-being. And yet he needed to do something.

Here, Mitchell's story departs from Sarah's. Mitchell actively sought different answers by going through a structured process that systematically focused on all of the important factors of his life and career. It was crucial that the process not involve his firm, his family or his circle of friends and colleagues. It had to be independent of all his systems and their vested interest in the outcome of his search. As a result, it would help him come up with his own answers—what we call a Personal Vision. With his own Personal Vision, Mitchell could escape the Lemming Conspiracy and start leading his own life.

What is a Personal Vision? What must it include to be effective in illuminating your True Self and defeating the Lemming Conspiracy? Eight critical factors must contribute to the Vision. Leave one out, and you risk remaining entrapped.

Mitchell discovered the things that fit and the things that did not, and why. Mitchell had some idea of his talents, but he couldn't articulate them with any detail. By learning exactly what his strongest talents were, he was able to focus and position himself more accurately. He knew what he wanted to move away from; more importantly, he knew what tasks and roles he should move toward. He also knew why his systems' answers, although compelling, were not right for him. He was able to create a plan and make a significant move in his career to a position and role that he felt expressed his true talents more exactly. He says of his change: "My clients are happy, and I get to play from my strengths and my love. It is truly a wonderful fit."

In this book, we take you through the structured process Mitchell used to change his life and career. We call it using the Eight Personal Vision Factors. We created this process, and thousands of clients have used it successfully. It leads you to self-discovery. You must find your true natural talents and expose your hopes and dreams to daylight. You must identify your most potent skills and even journey back to your original family system. Finally, you will be able to use this process to create your own Personal Vision—the vision of your True Self in the workplace.

Your Personal Vision should have a definite structure and form to be effective. Chapters 3 through 7 take you through each of the eight critical Personal Vision Factors, explaining what each is and what significance it has for your life. We will go through them in a definite order—from objective to subjective, external to internal.

The Thought Experiments at the end of each chapter will help you translate the ideas in the chapters into a more practical reality. You can use these experiments as springboards for thought, or you can actually do the experiments. They are, at the very least, fascinating. They also hold the possibility of helping you transform your life.

Merely identifying and articulating the eight Personal Vision Factors is not enough. A Personal Vision involves creative integration—a creative insight, if you will. Chapter 8 details the creative process we developed for our workshops and seminars. We call it *left-right-left*.

In the end, a Personal Vision must relate to the real world if it is to help you live a balanced life. In Chapter 9, we describe the process we use to accomplish this integration—Surveying. Surveying has incredible power to kick your Personal Vision into motion, to translate it to the reality of the marketplace.

Through all of our chapters, we tell the stories of five actual people at different Turning Points. All of these people go through the process of the book by completing the Thought Experiments. After each Thought Experiment, we revisit all five people to find out what they learned and how they used what they found out.

Chapter 10 shifts our focus to the workplace and shows how to use your own Personal Vision to transform your experience in the workplace. Chapters 11 discusses how the eight Personal Vision Factors have found a place in corporations. You will see the results of our long-term research in corporations utilizing The Personal Vision Factors, as well as actual case studies from many different companies who have used it for retention, motivation, dealing more effectively with diversity, coaching and enhancement of team productivity.

Chapter 12 talks about the Personal Vision at different Turning Points: how it can help propel you into a new job; or how it can make your present job better for you. We end with a discussion of the power of the Personal Vision to expand and open systems and make them more flexible, adaptable and human.

> NEXT CHAPTER: In the next chapter, we discuss the goal of the eight Personal Vision Factors – gaining a Personal Vision. A Personal Vision helps move you out of the cycle of stress, anger and depression we call the Stress Cycle, and toward the more vital cycle of inner-directedness and balance we call the Balance Cycle.

…THE HALLMARK OF THE
STRESS CYCLE
IS ITS RELENTLESS RUSH …
YOU NEVER STOP…
THERE IS NO TIME FOR SUCH
"UNPRODUCTIVE"
WORK AS THINKING ABOUT
YOUR LIFE…
OR FIGURING OUT
HOW YOU REALLY
WANT TO
SPEND YOUR TIME…
IF YOU ARE IN THE
STRESS CYCLE, IT IS
VIRTUALLY IMPOSSIBLE
TO IDENTIFY YOUR
TRUE TALENTS
OR TO TAKE THE STEPS
THAT ENABLE YOU TO
USE THEM…
YOU JUST **NEVER STOP**...

The Stress Cycle
and the Balance Cycle

"I don't know the key to success, but the key to failure is trying to please everyone." —Bill Cosby

The Lemming Conspiracy leads inevitably to the loss of real talent and to lives lived out of balance. The answers to questions about work and career we learned from our families help us move out into the adult world. But over time, they cease to be adequate because too much information is missing. Our systems prevent us from recognizing and changing this situation. As we let some important talents lie fallow, ignore some important aspect of ourselves, neglect a critical value, or do work for which we feel no intrinsic passion, we develop an increasing disparity between our System Selves and our True Selves. We come to live in the Stress Cycle.

Most of the people you know live in the Stress Cycle, as you probably do yourself. The Lemming Conspiracy produces the Stress Cycle for nearly everyone sooner or later. Over time the Stress Cycle comes to rule our lives.

This chapter shows how the Stress Cycle eventually captures all of us and why it has such a profound impact. But this chapter also tells us about the alternative – the Balance Cycle – and what it means to achieve it. We will describe how to move from the Stress Cycle to the Balance Cycle and how a Personal Vision makes the journey possible. We will explain what a Personal Vision is and how you can create one for yourself. You'll learn how to beat the Lemming Conspiracy.

In the Stress Cycle, we feel as though we are jumping through hoops. We work hard and gain little. Our day-to-day lives have little real meaning for us, even when we are engaged in work we used to enjoy. We have the uneasy feeling that something is missing, but it's difficult to identify what that may be. We have the definite sense that there is no time to think about any of this anyway. We barely have time to do the things that are absolutely necessary.

The hallmark of the Stress Cycle is its relentless rush. You never stop. If you are in the Stress Cycle, you have only enough time to do the next task, or concentrate on the next project. There is no time for such "unproductive" work as thinking about your life or finding out how you really want to spend your time.

More to the point, if you are in the Stress Cycle, it is virtually impossible to identify your true talents or to move yourself into circumstances that allow you to use them.

If we operate in the Stress Cycle, we pass the tension on to our children. They see it as the normal and natural way for adults to live their lives. We can tell them a thousand times that they can choose to live their lives any way they want to, and that they don't have to choose the same answers we did – but none of that helps. We see a great many high school students already caught in the Stress Cycle. Many try desperately to avoid living the way their parents live. The hard fact is, if we are in the Stress Cycle, sooner or later, our children will be in the Stress Cycle, too.

How does the Stress Cycle start? Obviously no one would willingly and knowingly choose to live like this. No parents would want their children to live this way. So why does virtually everyone do it?

The Stress Cycle emerges directly from our systems and the Lemming Conspiracy. As we move into our systems from our families of origin, we feel an incredibly strong pull to take the next step: Select a major. Graduate from college. Get a job. Succeed. Earn more money. Buy more things. Move up in the organization. Complete the next project. Gain the boss's attention and approval. Become a boss. Retire. Die.

We are not talking about intelligence or character. We are talking about the universal pull by which systems trap us in the Stress Cycle. We are talking about how difficult it is to separate ourselves from this pull. Even people who routinely help others to look at their long-term goals never think about whether their own lives are expressing a long-range vision.

So, what are the elements of the Stress Cycle?

ELEMENTS OF THE STRESS CYCLE

1. **Short-term focus. Getting the next task done.** "I'll just get this promotion, and then I'll be able to live my life." Probably not. This focus on the task or project at hand means that you are never able to focus on a larger context. What about your real talents? What about your life? Most people spend far more time and energy focused on how they will spend their annual vacation than they do on how they will spend the next 20 or 40 years of their lives. Your systems want you to focus on the short-term goals. It is in their interest for you to do so. They know and rely on the fact that it's difficult to get beyond short-term goals when you have to meet the demands of work and family.

2. **Status-driven goals.** A new car would feel great. A new house. Maybe a second house. A promotion would mean that I'm getting somewhere in life. I want to dress like my bosses and drive their cars. I want to have the kind of lifestyle that I see in magazines and on television. I want more responsibility, so I can have more say in what happens to me. I want to be in charge, so I can have a life. Your systems want you to feel all of this. They want you to work very hard to achieve something that is basically empty of meaning, so that when you achieve it, you will focus on the next goal.

3. **Outer-directed priorities.** Someone else tells you what is important. New car? Promotion? More money? Getting a college degree, earning a lot of money, gaining a position of responsibility and power—these are all worthy goals, but only if they are a direct expression of your own Personal Vision. But, if they are not connected to anything larger in your life, they become empty, and you find yourself being pulled along from hoop to hoop.

4. **Reactive decision-making.** Focusing only on short-term goals. Responding to everyday events as though to crises. When people concentrate only on short-term results, they become vulnerable to throwing all of their energy and creativity into problems that, in a longer view, may not be that important. Researchers in human behavior found long ago that getting people to concentrate on short-term rewards resulted

in increasingly short-term behavior. This narrowing of focus inflates the importance of what are likely to be trivial events. This inevitably leads to stress. How many people have led successful professional lives and accomplished each of their many goals only to discover, too late, that they never developed a relationship with their children? Or their spouse? Or with themselves, for that matter?

People in the Stress Cycle get caught up in achieving the next goal and accomplishing the next task. They are too busy to think about what their talents are or how to use them. Too busy to examine their lives and figure out what could be personally meaningful. But people do not generally start out in the Stress Cycle. It develops over time. Eventually, they become like the frog who succumbs slowly to ever-hotter water. They don't realize that the time will come when escape is impossible.

How the Stress Cycle Takes Over Our Lives

There are many high school students who are completely caught up in the Stress Cycle. In academically competitive high schools, they are probably the majority. The Stress Cycle grips students even more firmly in college. As young men and women move out into the work world, marry, buy houses, cars, baby strollers and vacations, the Stress Cycle becomes as natural and normal as breathing. But answers that worked reasonably well in the family of origin and even for a while in early adulthood, eventually cease to function well at all. This is when stress develops.

When we live with chronic stress, we lose the ability to come up with creative answers. Our focus becomes short-term—we just want to get this job done, and then we can rest. We tend to focus on the goal directly in front of us. We don't have the energy or focus to think about the significance of what we are doing; we just need to do it. We tend to follow any direction presented to us. Unconsciously, we fall back on patterns learned in the family of origin. It is here that we start to become more and more like one or the other of our parents, as we begin to make decisions in exactly the way our parent made them at that age. What gets lost is you—and your own personal talents.

Inevitably the Stress Cycle results in an ever-escalating spiral of short-term pressures. Cycles of Stress are not limited to individuals and family but extend also to teams and organizations! We worked extensively with one team of scientists. In their work, they saw themselves as reactive and crisis-oriented and skilled at solving Quality problems for their company. In fact, the team was highly regarded for its ability to deal with immediate problems and for savings to the company in both reputation and euros. As time went on and the team went from one daily crisis to the next, however, they all began to experience considerable stress. It dawned on them that virtually all of them had the same abilities and talents. These made them excel at short-term problem-solving. What they lacked was the longer-range focus of people with divergent abilities. The decision was made to bring in members who would have a longer term view of problems. This would counter-balance the team's focus on the day-to-day and relieve the team's stress.

Here are the stories of Carol and Jane, two accomplished, successful professionals, who had "succeeded" in the world through intelligence, planning, drive and character. You will see that both were trapped in the Stress Cycle. Their families of origin could not help them overcome the Lemming Conspiracy. But later in this chapter you will see how they figured out their Personal Visions, came to a better understanding of their real talents and started living more balanced lives.

Carol's story shows how answers that start off working well can eventually lead to the Stress Cycle.

Carol's Story

At 38, Carol was near burnout. She had been a hard-driving sales executive for 10 years, but she didn't think she would last two more years at her company. She didn't understand her stress and anxiety. She was still young; her job, if anything, was better than ever. But it just didn't feel exciting enough any more.

Carol's father had been a successful sales executive with a large company and had traveled throughout her childhood. A few years after she moved out of her family home, her parents divorced.

In the same way as her father, Carol had always felt that her first responsibility was to be successful, but she had never challenged or even clearly articulated that perception.

Carol had never married or had a serious relationship lasting longer than six months. She traveled three and four days a week. Almost anyone outside of Carol's family or network of busy professional friends across the country could have told her that she would feel much better if she would create a life for herself outside of work. But her family and friends never challenged her assumptions—they couldn't, because they were all living the same life. Her lifestyle prevented her from coming up with any creative answers herself.

Her bosses certainly didn't challenge her assumptions; from their point of view, Carol was perfect. She was a high performer on the fast track and probably had executive potential. The company had no way of knowing that Carol was considering quitting and that she was operating with markedly reduced efficiency and commitment. Indeed, the company would never know her stress until she walked out the door.

Carol had succeeded in forming an independent life for herself. She had succeeded in a competitive business and could go all the way to the top. But she was caught in the Stress Cycle. Taking on the next project, accomplishing the next goal, pushing ahead with her career plan, she had left herself out of the formula. Now she was experiencing the stress, anxiety and sense of crisis that normally develop when no long-term goal or vision exists.

It would be impossible for the company to help her with this. The company's interests were different from Carol's; it could not help her figure out who she was and what was important to her. Carol's response was absolutely typical; she redoubled her efforts, doing more of what she had always done She used the same answers that had worked before

These answers came from her family of origin; but they could not help her. Carol's life mirrored her father's in many important ways. She had given over all her energy and focus to work, in the same way as her father, treating herself and her personal relationships as secondary to her work. Also like him, she had not been able to develop a rewarding, fulfilling marriage or family relationship.

Systems generally offer only two answers at these crisis points: Do more of the same – or quit. As we have seen, Carol tried to do the first, and was considering the second as a real possibility.

The next story is about Jane. It gives another view of the answers supplied by systems at Turning Points. Business, social and family systems all nurture the forces leading to the Stress Cycle. Jane's story illustrates how the Stress Cycle can develop outside of the business system — but, then, always within some other system.

Jane's Story

Jane raised two children; both went on to college. She had always seen her role as supporting her husband's law career, a role she performed very well. He had started a successful firm, and her talents in connecting with people had been crucial to that success. She believed it was her responsibility to be available for her children and her husband.

At age 50, Jane's carefully nurtured life began coming apart at the seams. Her younger son came home in the middle of his junior year in college. He took a job waiting on tables. He spent most days watching MTV and soap operas and stayed out very late at night with his friends. Her husband, a busy trial lawyer, was seldom home. He sometimes worked seven days a week. Jane had no interests, plans or ideas what to do with herself. She didn't have a clue what she might be good at, other than take care of a household and raise children. She frequently had lunch with other lawyers' wives; their conversation was pointless and boring. She started having migraine headaches that were stunningly debilitating.

Jane's mother had raised a large family in a small Southern town. Her father had been a minor public official. At about age 50, her mother had developed a hip problem that prevented her from getting around. When her father died a few years later, it fell to Jane to take care of her mother full time. She did this until her mother died.

Jane was repeating her mother's life. A physical disability would take all choice away from her. Although the answers supplied by her family had worked well for years, they no longer helped her. Her husband couldn't help her; the Stress Cycle had ensnared him may years ago. Even her son was so trapped in the family's stress that he could not form an independent life. It was interesting, and inevitable, that she would unconsciously choose her mother's solution to the problem – becoming incapacitated by her headaches – at about the same age as her mother had.

Anyone can be a victim of the Stress Cycle, and in truth, almost everyone is at some point. But what is the alternative? We all live in systems. We all have to live in a stressful world. All of us get some answers from our families of origin and then take them out into the world when we start our own lives. The answers we get will not be dispositive and will eventually lead us to another crisis and a new Turning Point.

But these "crises" in our adult lives don't have to be negative. At these times, we can become more receptive to change. We can look for new answers. Instead of adopting the system's answers or our family's answers, we can use this opportunity to find our own answers. Over time, we can move from the Stress Cycle to the Balance Cycle. We can learn to recognize and use our most powerful talents every day.

Just as in the Stress Cycle, the elements of the Balance Cycle relate strongly to each other. One element leads to the next, and then to the next. Once you get into the Balance Cycle, it perpetuates itself. And, you can pass the Balance Cycle along to your children—but only if you're living in it yourself.

So how does the Balance Cycle work? What are the elements?

ELEMENTS OF THE BALANCE CYCLE

1. **Long-term focus.** Ultimately, everything you do should connect clearly to a fundamental value or goal. In the Balance Cycle, intermediate and short-term goals are steps toward a larger goal. When concentrating on a current project, it is important not to lose sight of why you undertook it in the first place and how it relates to the next project.

2. **Meaning-driven goals.** What you do every day should contribute to giving your life meaning. If it doesn't, why are you doing it? The old saying runs: "No one ever got to the end of his life wishing he had spent more time at the office." Time at the office doesn't provide the answers all by itself. Unless it is connected to something larger, it is just work. The meaning in work, if it comes at all, comes from its connection to all you want and need in your life.

3. **Inner-directed priorities.** People in the Balance Cycle move toward goals they have chosen for themselves, not the goals imposed by their systems.

As we have seen, it is often difficult to separate what we want from what our systems want us to want. This is why building your goals on a structure that is outside your systems is so necessary and helpful.

4. **Vision-based decision-making.** One executive explained how he used his Personal Vision: "It is a template. Whenever an opportunity comes up, I match it up to my Personal Vision. If it will move me toward my Vision, I take it. If not, I politely decline. People often ask me how I can be so decisive and sure about important decisions. The reason is that I know where I'm trying to go, I know why, and I know it with a great deal of clarity and specificity." Another executive in a global company was recently caught up in the downsizing of his company. His original dismay at the unexpected turn of events was relieved when he received his generous separation package and he turned to the Vision Statement we had helped him to create many years earlier.

People who operate in the Balance Cycle have a positive Personal Vision of their future. They feel that what they do will lead them to ultimate happiness and satisfaction. They see satisfaction in a larger context than as immediate gain. They actively seek and find meaning in whatever they do.

When you're in the Balance Cycle, you can create a life in which you can use your talents. Not only in the context of your immediate job, but in the larger context of your entire life. Your talents are more or less constant throughout your working life, but there are many other critical factors that change throughout your life and threaten to pull you away from your real talents. These factors put you in danger of wasting your true strengths.

People in the Balance Cycle are not surprised by change. In the Stress Cycle, stress, anxiety and depression build to the point of crisis, and the crisis precipitates a change which may or may not be salutary. People in the Balance Cycle have already considered what may be next and why. Change becomes part of the whole Personal Vision or plan. People in the Balance Cycle approach Turning Points with a blueprint for making decisions. Above all, they approach Turning Points with the idea of adding significantly to their lives, not merely getting rid of things that are causing them stress.

The Balance Cycle is an obvious and worthwhile alternative to the Stress Cycle, but how do we get there?

Personal Vision

The vehicle for moving you from the Stress Cycle to the Balance Cycle is a Personal Vision of your life and career. A Personal Vision is an image of yourself in a future in which you are using your most powerful talents, doing work that is meaningful and fulfilling. It connects you to your own future. It can help you at each Turning Point when you make decisions about your life and career. It can help you every day to make those small decisions that lead either to the Stress Cycle or to the Balance Cycle.

Though it helps you to see and steer into the future, a Personal Vision must be firmly grounded in the present—in you. It must include every significant aspect of who you are, what you're hard-wired to do and what you want from your life.

The Structure of a Personal Vision

I. To be effective, a Personal Vision must comprise all important elements of your life and career. It should take into consideration:

A. Your natural talents and abilities. This is how you're hardwired. Theses are the you naturally do well—your inborn gifts. If you work against them, work becomes labor. If you work with them, everything is easier and more fun.

B. Your skills and life experience. What you have learned in life creates a collection of hugely valuable assets to use in the next stage of your career. Your Personal Vision will help you to identify and use these assets as you grow older and your life changes. The skills you develop add to your strengths and compensate for your weaknesses.

C. Your Interests and fascinations. What draws your attention, what pulls you. This often-neglected factor acts as the source of your most important creative energy. Follow your passions.

D. Your interpersonal style. Accurately identifying and working through your personal style means that you can work more productively, expend less energy, and experience less stress. We're talking about analyzing your personality – how do you relate and respond to ideas and people.

E. Your values. The things you feel are worth doing in life. Your values give your life an overall sense of direction and purpose. More and more, we are associating values with character. Do you live your values?

F. Your goals. What you want to do in life. What you want to accomplish. Many people find out with a shock that they have been pursuing someone else's goals—too late. Defining your goals will give you the steps to follow, the way stations on your path.

G. Your family of origin. As we have seen, some of the most fundamental concepts you take into adult life develop in the family in which you grow up. Including this knowledge in your Personal Vision gives the Vision integrity, depth and meaning, often in profound ways. Don't think about the problems within your family, but how each person looked at the world. What role did each play? How were decisions made? How was stress managed? Go back three generations. For many of you, this will be the most helpful and insightful part of the process of building your vision statement.

H. Your stage of adult development. The Personal Vision of a high school student setting off to college will be different from that of a 42-year-old woman who would like to do something different with her life, or a 65-year-old executive planning retirement.

II. Your Personal Vision needs to involve both objective and subjective elements. The place to start is with a completely objective look at your natural talents – your basic hard-wiring. The only way you can really assess your talents is through objective measurements involving action-based worksamples. Once you have defined and understood your natural talents – information you can put to use with increasing objectivity, the direction and scope of your Personal Vision will be modified by more subjective factors such as interests, personality, values and goals. The Highlands Ability Battery of objective worksamples is the best tool for understanding your natural abilities.

III. Your Personal Vision should be based on a structure that is outside of your current work and your social and family systems. Advice from your family, friends or business associates, however wise and well-meant, can only have meaning when it's viewed from the perspective of your own Personal Vision. To gain a more objective and complete view of yourself, you need to step outside your personal systems for a time. This is the only way you can know for sure that your Personal Vision is not just another manifestation of your family's messages, or of answers from your other current systems.

We recently conducted an intense three-day retreat among 23 executives in three different teams of the same company. The company was being merged into a larger company and many jobs were on the line. Beginning with the Highlands Ability Battery, each participant did a serious amount of work in preparation for the retreat, which lasted from 8 AM to 6 PM every day. The results exceeded everyone's expectations. Everyone was now prepared to face the interviews leading to new jobs and prospects. The participants had accomplished three things: they had gotten out of their systems and worked within a new structure; they had explored all the eight Personal Vision factors; and they had made a commitment to monitor their Vision Statements throughout the forthcoming transitional period.

IV. Your Personal Vision should provide a blueprint for important life and career decisions. People who have a Personal Vision are sure of themselves. At important times, they can act and decide independently of their work and family systems because they have thought through all of the important factors that they want to influence their lives.

Now that we have seen what a Personal Vision is, let's go back to Carol and Jane to see how they each developed a Personal Vision and moved from the Stress Cycle to the Balance Cycle

Carol's Story, continued

As you may remember, Carol had reached a point near burnout in her career. She felt her only answer was to quit, and definitely thought she would quit within the next two years. But as she constructed her Personal Vision, she realized that she was, in many ways, ideally suited for her job. Her talents and abilities were a positive asset, and she loved both the technology involved and the people she dealt with every day. In looking at her natural talents, however, she understood that, in addition to sales, her talents were ideal for teaching. She had thought she might like teaching and had thought at one time that she could go back to school, and eventually teach; now, her new objective knowledge of her talents gave her the courage to think she could actually do something different.

When Carol did her family-of-origin analysis, she realized that the powerful messages she had absorbed from her family were still controlling her life. She realized that her company had no interest in changing these patterns because the changes required a long-term focus that systems rarely possess. The only way Carol could change her outlook would be to take charge of and manage her own life and career.

As Carol constructed her Personal Vision, she realized that even though her present company was a great fit for her, significant aspects of her job needed to change. As she got a clearer picture of what she wanted to do, she begin to create a position for herself that would meet her needs and the company's needs, too. She knew that her natural talents would help her as a teacher and trainer. Combining these with her desire for a helping role and a schedule that would allow her a personal life, she formed a plan.

She began working with the training department on a consulting basis. She found she was in fact a gifted trainer, and was able to shift more of her responsibilities there. Eighteen months later, she is much more satisfied and has no plans to quit. She feels she is a more valuable asset to the company because she now trains many others to see as effectively as she once did.

By getting outside her corporate system, her family system and her system of friends and colleagues, Carol was able to come up with a new answer. She could continue to work in the company, but in a new capacity that would give her more time for a personal life.

Jane's Story, continued

Jane's natural talents aimed her at management. In completing several exercises on values, Jane realized she had a strong wish to do something positive for children in her community. She joined a public-service organization that was devoted to helping young girls at risk to stay in school, find jobs and discover new opportunities. She eventually became a board member, and finally ended up being executive director of the board. Her managerial talent was obvious to everyone.

Jane's headaches disappeared following one occasion when she insisted on attending an important board meeting over her husband's objections. Realizing that if his mother could stand up to his father, she would probably take him on next, her son got off the couch shortly after this, and eventually graduated from college. Her husband doesn't work on Saturday or Sunday any more. The entire family system was transformed by Jane's Personal Vision.

Creating a Personal Vision

The process of creating a Personal Vision and moving from Stress to Balance is vital. It's easy to understand the theories behind the Stress Cycle and the Balance Cycle, and how a Personal Vision can help you move from one to the other. But it's not enough merely to understand the ideas and grasp the concepts – something more is needed to accomplish results as real and profound as the changes in the lives of Carol and Jane. That something is the creation of a Personal Vision vivid enough to guide your life. Here's how to get there:

1. **You must stop.** The Stress Cycle will keep you in constant flux. It will keep your mind constantly focused on events in the here and now. You must stop and give yourself a period of concentrated, uninterrupted time in order to do the work of getting to a Personal Vision. Not 15 minutes when you don't have any other appointments or commitments, but significant blocks of time over several weeks or months that are scheduled and inviolable. Chapter 3 deals with those natural times of crisis and change in which we are emotionally ready to stop and look for alternative answers. Even in the most compelling life crisis, however, nothing will change unless you decide to stop.

2. **You must get outside of your systems.** Next to stopping, this is the most difficult step. You need answers different from those your family, friends or corporate systems can provide. Not because there is anything wrong with them, but because their stock of answers is virtually identical to your own initial stock of answers. What you need at a Turning Point is the ability

to take a fresh look at your answers and preconceptions. This book guides you through a process we developed to help you do this. It takes time and energy, but the payoff can be significant, in terms of both success and satisfaction. At the end of this chapter and each of the following seven chapters, we have included a series of Thought Experiments. These Thought Experiments provide an action framework to help you create your own Personal Vision.

3. **You must engage in a structured exploration of all eight Personal Vision Factors:** abilities, skills, interests, personal style, values, goals, family of origin and stage of development. If you leave one out, you risk creating a blind spot in your Personal Vision that will force you to stumble back into stress and crisis at the next Turning Point. Chapters 3 through 7 explain how to explore all of the eight Personal Vision factors involved in a Personal Vision.

4. **You need to integrate creatively all eight of the Personal Vision Factors.** This task is too complicated and intuitive to perform logically. How do your values interact with your goals? How do both relate to your natural talents? These are not linear questions and they don't lead to linear answers. In order to arrive at a Personal Vision, you must use the more creative elements of your mind. Chapter 8 explains the principles of creative integration, and the Thought Experiment in that Chapter will teach you how to use the right and left portions of your brain to create a Personal Vision.

5. **You need to apply it to the real world.** A Personal Vision that is just an idea or a dream is not complete. You need to bring in information from the real world in order to make it a useful tool for your life. In Chapter 9, we talk about Surveying, an extremely powerful process for translating your Personal Vision to real life.

Thought Experiment A:

A Personal Vision Notebook

The Thought Experiments included at the end of this and the next seven chapters are meant to guide you to your own Personal Vision.

Personal Vision Notebook. Buy a spiral-bound notebook of 50 pages or more. You will use this notebook to record and summarize everything you discover in the other Thought Experiments. If you think this sounds as though it may involve a lot of writing, you're right. Forcing yourself to write down your discoveries about yourself makes your thoughts, feelings and ideas more usable. Each time you record your findings from Thought Experiments in your notebook, you set the stage for creative and integrative insights. Feel free to sketch or doodle in your notebook, or staple pictures, headlines, advertisements or articles in it. Use it any way that seems helpful to you. But also use it to record your findings about yourself in words.

For anyone for whom writing is a particular labor and who feels it would be an unproductive stumbling block, we suggest recording your responses into a tape recorder.

FOUR STORIES OF PEOPLE AT TURNING POINTS

After each Thought Experiment, we will tell continuing stories of four actual people as they proceeded step by step through the program outlined in this book. They will tell you—mostly in their own words—what they discovered from completing the Thought Experiments.

Tracy—23 years old

Tracy graduated from college nine months ago. Since graduating, she has lived at home and worked as a secretary in the law firm of her father's friend. In college, she majored in psychology, intending to earn a Ph.D. and become a psychologist. In her junior year in college she realized that, due to changes in managed care, it was becoming increasingly difficult for psychologists to have satisfying careers or even to earn a living. She gradually gave up her idea of going to graduate school in psychology, but had no alternative plan. When she graduated, she didn't know what to do next. She took the job in the law firm thinking that she could just earn a little money until she could figure out her next step, but nine months later she was no further along than when she started. "Since I graduated, I've been miserable. My parents are supportive, but I know they hate it that I don't seem to be able to bring myself out of this funk. I always did well in school, but this is something I haven't been able to figure out." How is the feeling at this point? "Depressed. Discouraged. No self-confidence. Cynical about the work world."

Brian and Janet—both 30 years old

Brian works for a major telecommunications company in marketing. He started working there while in college, and was offered a job immediately after graduating. He typically puts in 10- to 11-hour days and works most weekends. He has been married two years to Janet, whom he met at work. "At the end of the day, we are both so exhausted we don't want to cook dinner. We just fix a bowl of cereal and sit and read the paper. Janet wants to have children," but I'm thinking, "We can't have children yet. I need to get another promotion under my belt." Brian looks at the people above him in the hierarchy, and most are just a little older than he is. One or two are younger. He feels that if he doesn't make his mark soon, he will lose his chance and be shuffled aside, or even out.

Brian's feeling now: "I want to get ahead."

Janet has been working in the same company for three years in customer relations. She has never been promoted. "I feel completely unfulfilled at work. I want to be successful there, but I don't like what I'm doing, and I don't really know how to get out of there. What else would I do? What department would I go to? It's confusing. I think if we had a baby, I would just quit and be a mother."

Janet's feeling now: "Tired. Discouraged."

Elizabeth—43 years old

Elizabeth is an executive in a large technology firm. "I work 75-hour weeks. I travel, I never see my child. My husband and I are strangers. There has to be another answer."

Her feeling? "I have to do something. Maybe this will help."

Carl—51 years old

Carl has been vice president in human resources in a major entertainment company for nine years. Six months ago he was laid off as the result of a merger. This has not been as difficult for him as he thought it might be. "I was ready for a change anyway. This just meant that I have to change now, which, of course, isn't too comfortable. I have no idea whether I should go back into a large company or whether I should try to get a job in a smaller firm. Or maybe start my own consulting business."

His feeling now: "Interested. Hopeful."

NEXT CHAPTER: In the next chapter we begin to move toward a Personal Vision. We start with the adult development cycle — the predictable Turning Points of adult life.

AT
TURNING POINTS
IN THEIR LIVES, PEOPLE SUDDENLY
BECOME **OPEN TO**
NEW IDEAS…
THEY MAY BECOME
INTERESTED IN
DIFFERENT CAREERS, OR
WANT DESPERATELY TO MOVE ON.

A WOMAN
MAY SUDDENLY DECIDE
TO **START A BUSINESS** OR
HAVE CHILDREN
FOR THE FIRST TIME.

PEOPLE SEEK WAYS TO EXPAND THEIR
AREAS OF COMPETENCE
AND **EXPRESS THEIR TALENTS**
MORE COMPLETELY.

Crisis & Change

Beware of the tyranny of making small changes to small things.
Rather, make big changes to big things.

— *Roger Enrico, former Chairman, PepsiCo*

Both Sarah, the law student in Chapter 1, and Mitchell, the young man in technology sales whose Personal Vision helped him use his talent more effectively, had reached normal adult Turning Points when they felt something had to change. We saw Sarah move from high school to college, the first adult Turning Point, and then from college to the work world, the second. At the second Turning Point, she wondered if her earlier decisions had been good ones, but she saw nothing she could have done differently. Mitchell, at the Age-30 Turning Point, felt that his career, although a good fit in many ways, still lacked something that he had difficulty articulating. He used the structured process in this book to help him assess and create real change.

We all face Turning Points during our working lives, about one every seven to ten years. They continue to occur even in retirement. We have Turning Points every seven to ten years throughout the 60s, 70s, 80s and beyond.

Each Turning Point in adult development is initiated by a crisis. "Crisis" can have a theatrical meaning: i.e., the many plots in a person's life come together at a decisive moment in time. Or "crisis" can mean simply "catastrophe." Turning Points can have elements of both.

At Turning Points, the strands of our lives unravel slightly, and we must decide how to weave them back together. Sometimes at Turning Points, however, we feel as though the entire cable has severed, separating our lives into before and after. In any case, at all Turning Points, we make decisions that affect the course of the next seven to ten years of our lives for better or worse. In early adulthood (age 18-25), the search contains three elements: accepting responsibility for one's decisions and actions; making independent decisions; and learning to become financially responsible. At this Turning Point, people ask: what kind of work will I find most satisfying in the long term? And what kind of work will best fit the person that I am?

What Are Turning Points and How Do They Affect Us?

Despite the name, Turning Points are not solated points in time, or even short periods of time; they usually spread over one to three years. They signal periods of heightened awareness and introspection. At Turning Points, people unexpectedly become open to new ideas. They may check out the self-help books in bookstores, or the section on Eastern philosophy. At mid-life, men may become interested in political magazines, or social issues, or want desperately to connect. A woman may suddenly decide to start a business or have children for the first time. People seek ways to expand their areas of competence and express their talents more completely.

Turning Points and crises develop out of the Stress Cycle. As we get further and further into the Stress Cycle, we increasingly feel that significant talents and passions are not being expressed. Our System Self becomes increasingly different from our True Self. The life we lead no longer expresses who we are, and we become aware of this fact. We recognize problems in our current lives, and consider alternative solutions. At all Turning Points, we start looking for new answers and try to find something new.

Unfortunately, at Turning Points most of us don't succeed in escaping from the Lemming Conspiracy without effort. What does a 42-year-old man do when he wakes up one morning to find that he doesn't want to go to work? He can't stand the thought of doing again what he has done all day every day. This is not an unnatural feeling, nor is it uncommon. A person in this condition may find himself unexpectedly grasping for new answers and seeking new points of view.

A flurry of activity and change may follow. New clothes, new hair-style or color, new car, new city, new wife, new family. These changes are all external to the True Self. Our 42-year-old in the midst of this flurry may feel that each new change expresses the "new me," but unless he has done some serious work in defining his True Self, most of these changes will not lead to any new or creative answers. They will simply end up throwing him into another round of the Stress Cycle.

Most divorces happen at Turning Points. People also tend to quit jobs or make sudden career moves. This is no accident. People want answers, and they mostly look for these answers in the externals of their lives. No creative solution emerges from this approach. A simple change in externals will rarely bring people closer to their True Selves.

To discover the answers that will really change your life, you must first look inside yourself. You have to find out who you really are. Not your System Self, not the "you" your family knows, but your True Self—the self that cries out for expression at times of crisis and Turning Points. After you have a clear sense of your True inner Self, you can look productively and externally for ways to express that sense.

In Chapter 2, we described how crises develop from the increasing disparity between our System Self and our True Self and how this leads to the Stress Cycle. Let us see how the different crises and Turning Points develop over the adult life span.

The Eight Turning Points of Adult Life

At all Turning Points throughout our adult lives, we must solve the problem of achieving a personal balance between connectedness and productivity. Between being and doing. Between love and work. Sigmund Freud taught that our solutions to love and work go to the heart of our mental health and happiness.

At the earlier Turning Points, we tend to choose one of these over the other without any sense of the need to create balance. Our commitments and energy go into our family and marriage, or into work and "making it." Traditionally, in our society, men have gone one way, and women another. This traditional separation in the roles of men and women is no longer predictable. When people speak of "having it all," they are usually referring to the traditional split between work and family; they want both work and family. They may not intend to make a black-and-white choice, but they often choose one over the other in spite of themselves. The wish for both frequently leads to frantic exhaustion in the pursuit of everything.

Balance implies a choice between options. We each have a limited stock of time and energy— a difficult concept for anyone 30 years old— and we must choose where to invest them. The more fully and completely we know our True Selves, the easier these choices become. At 30, at least for some people, choosing less of this and more of that causes indecisiveness and immobility. At 40 or 50, these choices seem more reasonable.

After midlife, lives become less of an either/or proposition. Having made it (or not), men may want more intimacy. Some women, especially those who have been intensely involved in family for years, may want to see what they can do in the wider world. Other women, having invested their energies in the business world, may suddenly find that they want more intense involvement with their families. In any case, the either/or decision is a blind alley. It doesn't lead to a satisfying long-term resolution. We find that as people mature, as they encounter the Turning Points after midlife, they are increasingly capable of creating solutions that express both balance and careful choice rather than simply striving for everything. People who achieve this balance seem to have a calm and wisdom from which we can all learn.

Each Turning Point represents a window of time during which we have the energy and drive to examine our former solutions and try again to discover more satisfying ones.

High school to college (17-18 years old): Think back for a moment to how you decided to go to the college you attended. We know of a young man who went to Princeton. Why? Because it was Princeton. No other reason seemed necessary. Looking back on this important decision, he views it now as embarrassingly ill-considered. Princeton was the perfect choice, or the very worst choice. Without any serious thought to what he wanted to do with his life, or what he wanted to get out of college, how could he possibly have known?

Where to go to college is the first career decision most of us make. It begins the difficult but critical process of breaking away from our families of origin. We often can't see its importance until we are older and look back, wishing we had explored a different opportunity, or not spent so much time on a dead end. High school seniors and their families typically make this decision with almost no real information about the ideal course. Most decisions about college are made through some combination of high school grades, SAT scores, teacher recommendations and the reputation of the college. All of these are external, impersonal factors; someone else has passed judgment on the individual or the school. None of these factors tell students anything about the internal Self—about such crucial factors as their true talents, their interests, their goals in life, or how their personalities work. Indeed, most students at this age have never considered these internal factors in any detailed way, and have never been encouraged to. Yet their success in college, their success in the adult world, and how much they enjoy their lives depend far more on these factors than on grades and SAT scores.

The most important information high school and college students need is an assessment of their natural talents and abilities. This tells them how they are hardwired—what's going to be easy for them, and what difficult. We talk about this and about the Highlands Ability Battery more fully in Chapter 4.

Students should also start addressing the "softer" issues (and college is an ideal time to do this)—interests, personality, family, values and even life goals. These all become increasingly important as we mature. If students get the idea that these factors are worth paying attention to, they will be helped immensely in college and later.

We have talked to some adults who report themselves to have been extremely happy with their careers over extended periods of time. They are markedly different from the driven young men and women in their 20s and 30s who work constantly, have no personal lives but tell you, "everything's just fine!" Those adults who have been so satisfied with their work lives always report the same thing: as teenagers, they were positively encouraged by their families to pay attention to and actively follow what they enjoyed. Their parents followed this advice themselves. In these families, the family value was clear: what you experienced internally was paramount – more important than the bottom line. We cannot stress enough that children absorb the values their parents live by. If these values correspond to what the parents say, then children get a congruent message. If, however, parents live one message and proclaim another, the children inevitably absorb the message their parents actually live out. They also learn that what you say does not necessarily need to reflect reality.

High School to College: Two Stories

Ben went to a college-preparatory high school and did well. His grade point average, SAT scores and teacher recommendations allowed him to enter Cornell University. He was excited about going to his father's alma mater. At Cornell, he enjoyed his classes, but he failed to find a peer group with whom he felt compatible. He became increasingly depressed, and when he came home for Christmas break, he decided not to go back.

Ben waited on tables for several months after dropping out of college, but he also became interested in producing and showing his art. A talented artist, he started an artists' cooperative with two acquaintances.

Ben had never thought about his art in relation to college or to his career. He was academically talented, but obviously there was another part of him that needed expression. He had never considered exactly what he wanted to accomplish in college; it was enough just to be there. He had put off thinking about a career altogether.

Patricia, on the other hand, went to college with several ideas in mind. She thought she might like to explore journalism. She was definitely interested in law and also politics. Patricia deliberately chose a college that offered her the ability to explore all three of her interests.

Patricia worked for the college newspaper for two years. She rose to campus editor before deciding that her personality was wrong for newspaper work; she was forcing herself to capture interviews or statements in a pushy way that she didn't like very much.

Patricia also worked in her state representative's office for almost a year as part of an internship. She wrote replies to letters from constituents. She enjoyed the feeling of doing something important, and remained interested in politics. But it was her law courses that really enlivened her. She became intensely involved in capital punishment and public-interest law.

Patricia graduated from college four years after entering. This put her in a minority. Of her group of seven high school friends, she was the only one to graduate in four years. She went to law school and is now a practicing lawyer. She remains interested in politics, and thinks of becoming a judge someday.

Ben had ignored a hugely significant aspect of his natural talent when choosing a college. He was never encouraged to think about himself and what he wanted to do with his life. He was never encouraged to think about college as a springboard to his career or to think about how what he did in college would connect to him personally.

Patricia had been encouraged to figure out what she was looking for—in some detail. The college she chose was not the most prestigious one to which she was accepted. But it was the one that offered her the clearest opportunity to experience personally the three career fields in which she knew she had an interest.

It is important to understand that Patricia did not pull her thoughts about possible career fields out of the air. She went through a structured process like the one in this book while she was still in high school. She knew where she could use her natural talents (journalism, politics and law all rely heavily on the natural talents that Patricia has), and she knew where her interests led her. When she chose a college, it was with the help of insights resulting from a great deal of information about herself.

College to the work world (22 to 25 years old): This is, for many, the final step out of the family home. If successful, a young man or woman finally leaps into the adult world. If not, he or she falls agonizingly back into the family fold and can become dangerously stuck. A recent article in the New York Times indicated that one in seven males between the ages of 22 and 29 lives at home with parents.

Many factors conspire to make the transition to the work world more bewildering now than in the past. Although this has always been a difficult step, today there is no clear path. No one joins a large corporation out of college expecting to work there until retirement. Corporations expect young people to be free agents, hired for a tentative period to do a particular job. For corporations, the premium rests on people who can clearly articulate their long-term value to the company. Unfortunately, this is difficult for anyone who has never examined in any detail just what he or she has to offer an employer and doesn't know how he or she is hardwired in the first place.

College students and recent graduates can easily get caught up in externals. The imperatives are simple: Get into the work world. Start being a productive adult.

But what are the right questions to be asking? What pays the greatest return? What industry offers the most security or the largest stock options or the most growth potential? What career fields will capture headlines in the next century? What company provides the best benefits? Is there a secure career track? As important as all of these considerations are, they ignore the central questions: Who am I, what do I want from my career, and how can I put myself in a position to do what I do best?

It's no wonder that college students don't usually ask what they will do after college until they are within months of graduating. Job? The work world? It's easy for college students to feel that these don't have anything to do with life when they haven't made any effort to figure out how they can use their talents in the adult world.

We talked to hundreds of college students as we researched the ideas in this book. Since the first edition of the book, we have helped thousands of students to discover and develop their talents. The almost universal feeling among them has been that when they leave college and enter into adult life, they will have to give up most of what they really enjoy. They will have to settle down and work hard at jobs that are essentially meaningless so they can earn enough money to buy the kinds of things that don't bring their parents much happiness. Many go to graduate school or professional school just so they can put off making a commitment for a few more years.

College students need to pay close attention to their natural talents. After their natural talents, they should look at their skills. What have they learned in life? How can they use that knowledge? Again, their interests, personalities, values and goals should play an important part in gaining a sense of direction. Ideally, the first job would build upon experiences in college, internships and summer jobs, and be a positive step in a career direction that makes internal sense to the student. Simply joining the firm that sends recruiters to campus can lead to much unhappiness—and yet that is the predominant way in which college students choose their first jobs.

But it doesn't have to be that way. Highlands has developed several programs that help high school and college students to find the right first job. These programs focus on the process by which students see themselves for what they are. The process begins with the Highlands Ability Battery, gold standard among assessment tests.

College to Work: Emily's Story

Emily majored in marketing at a good college. Her first job was copy editing for a publishing company. She moved from there to a music company and worked in marketing for them, but soon left. While looking for something more to her liking, she took a job as a receptionist at a real estate company. One day she woke up to realize she had been a receptionist at the same company for almost four years. She had never actively pursued anything else. This realization devastated her.

Emily, age 28, went through the program we describe in this book. She discovered that her natural talents, personality, interests and values all pushed her in the direction of counseling. At her Age 30 Turning Point, she started back to graduate school to earn a degree and eventually a license to practice counseling. The point is, Emily could have known this about herself much earlier—before college, during college or after college. If she had expended concentrated effort and attention to figure this out, she could have made better use of her time in college. She would have worked in jobs that expanded her horizons and helped her career ambitions, and she would have focused her energy on graduate school earlier, instead of trying desperately to make it in jobs that weren't rewarding to her. She didn't need to waste so much of her time and talent—and feel so misdirected for so long.

Age 30 Assessment (28 to 33 years old): Regardless of the direction in which we launch ourselves in our early 20s, we do some reassessment around age 30. If we jumped right out of college into a job and started working like crazy, by this time we begin asking some predictable questions. Is this getting me what I want? Can I see myself doing this for another 10 years? How far can I go with this company? What else should I be doing? Should I make a move to get myself on the fast track? If our jobs seem to be getting us what we want, we start asking about lifestyles. Shouldn't I get a new car? Maybe it's time to get married. Maybe it's time to have a baby.

People always make some decision at this age. Just as with earlier Turning Points, most people look to the outside for their answers. The answer to the discomfort of the Stress Cycle is usually a new car, or marriage, or a child, or a new job or a promotion. They almost never start by asking themselves who they are and what they would really like to be doing in the first place. The significant questions at this age are more like these: Am I really using my most important talents? Are there some talents I have that I don't know about yet? Is this what I want to be doing? What doesn't fit? Is my career where I want it to be? Why? What do I want to add to my life to make it fuller?

At this Turning Point, after the question of how to use your most powerful talents, the main issues revolve around goals. What do I really want in life? Is what I am doing going to get me that? If not, I need to do something different. If so, what else should I be shooting for? People who have been paying attention all along to the softer, interior issues like interests and values are in a much better position to use the creative energy of this Turning Point to position themselves in a career they will actively enjoy over the next 10 years or so. At this Turning Point, people begin to question the structure on which they have built their lives.

The majority have not been paying attention. A great many young people in their early 20s get started in jobs that will not take them anywhere. How many young college graduates or dropouts do you know who are waiting tables or working at some other dead-end job? They are (perhaps) able to support themselves in an apartment, pay for gas, and pay for their entertainment. At the Age 30 Assessment, it suddenly dawns on them that these jobs cannot help them fulfill significant life goals. They can't get married, can't have a family, can't have anything like the life of their parents. Often young people at this age start over. They may go to school or become serious about finding a job with a future. We saw this pattern in Emily's story above.

Another main group consists of the young people who have started in a career or a profession and at this Turning Point start to get serious about it. It's not a lark any more. If they are going to get to the top, they have to do it now. The top, of course, is one of the fundamentally subversive myths of the Lemming Conspiracy. The top is understood without question or comment to be a positive goal and unquestionably worth achieving. Like all myths, it imparts a message about values and the way one should live. But it is a dangerous myth because it never addresses the interior of the person. Our experience in conducted personal development programs is that many participants question the very basis for their earlier decisions and are prepared to accept new and different answers.

Regardless of how well or poorly people make decisions at the Age 30 Assessment, they move into their 30s and a period of stability. They may be miserable and hate their jobs, but they don't change course during these years. Even if the 30s are productive and satisfying, people inevitably come to view midlife as a time of change, transition and starting over.

Age 30 Assessment and Beyond: Paul and Melinda's Story

Paul and Melinda both worked in large corporations: Paul as a manager in a technology company, Melinda as an accountant in a large international accounting firm. Married at 25, they were now in their early 30s. Both Paul and Melinda sensed that time was running out. Melinda felt that if she was going to have children, it must be now. Paul felt that he had to get on the fast track in his company in the next two years or he would never make it as far as he wanted to go.

They decided to have children, and their first was born when they were both 32. Another child followed a year later. Paul enrolled in an executive M.B.A. program; in addition, he asked for, and got, extra projects from his boss. Melinda was offered a promotion, but she would have had to move overseas, so she decided not to take it. They had money for the first time in their marriage; they moved into a new house and bought nice cars. They hired a nanny. Melinda was offered another promotion that required moving to another city. She felt she would have to take this promotion or see her career evaporate. Paul put in for a transfer to a city near the one where Melinda and the two children would be, but he felt this would definitely be a backwards career move for him. His boss was now actively interested in him and promoted his cause in the company. The new city would not have the kind of visibility that he now enjoyed. Paul already felt some resentment about being asked to make this choice.

The last thing either Paul or Melinda wanted to hear was that they should take a few weeks to sort through their lives and figure out what they really wanted. The Stress Cycle gripped both like an iron vise. Although each had goals, and they expended a great deal of energy toward attaining them, neither felt in balance. They tried to pursue everything society and their families had laid out for them to do, thinking all the while they were fulfilling their own lives. The trouble is that they had never stopped to take a close and objective look at their lives and so they were being hammered by forces over which they could exert no control-- and they weren't even aware of it.

Both Paul and Melinda made significant career moves and decisions during this Turning Point. Neither, however, dealt with limits. They wanted marriage and children and expensive things and career advancement and success and recognition. (How far? How much? "As far as possible" and "Everything" were their only answers.) They didn't want to choose between these goals.

By age 34, they were trying to maintain a marriage at a distance. Paul decided not to move so that he could continue working with his boss. His ambition settled on moving into the executive ranks. Melinda was being offered steady advancement in her firm, but this entailed a great deal of travel. They earned enough to have a full-time nanny who took care of the children. By their mid-thirties, Paul and Melinda had grown far apart. They seemed to be waiting for a signal that it was time to divorce.

Eventually they will be brought up short. Paul may get downsized. Melinda may have an affair. One of their children may develop problems at school. They might get divorced. Any or all of these life events tell us one thing: "You have to stop." It sometimes happens at the Midlife Transition.

The Midlife Transition (38 to 45 years old): The Midlife Transition can be one of the most important and significant events in people's lives. Or it can be an unmitigated disaster. It is no coincidence, certainly, that people in their early 40s and in the midst of mid-life turmoil often have teenage children who are in the midst of the turmoil of leaving home. The parents and the teenagers are trying to solve the same problem. They both seek to create or recreate themselves so that they can function in the adult world. Midlife transitions are often complicated and distorted by personal pressures such as the loss of a parent or the need to provide for the care of an aging parent.

Our society is used to thinking of midlife as a crisis. Midlife is really no more important than any of the other Turning Points. It may be just the first time many people become aware of any change in their lives. It is a catastrophe for many because they have ignored their True Selves for many years, accepting systems' answers for who they are and what they should be doing. Eventually, most people become aware of the disparity between the person they feel themselves to be and the person through whom they function—their System Selves. When the disparity is large and the effort to keep it hidden from awareness is overwhelming, the realization can be sudden and intense. It can lead people to seek sudden and catastrophic answers.

Stories are legion. People at midlife have affairs. They get divorced. They suddenly derail from the fast track. Problems like drinking, drugs or gambling that have been lurking around for years suddenly become destructive addictions. They get depressed; they take Prozac. They want to buy sports cars or have surgery, or both. They may want to start their own businesses, change jobs or change careers. It's exciting. It's crazy.

It's scary. One of the worst outcomes of midlife is doing nothing. Many people, confronted with feelings of stress, anxiety and depression, choose to ignore them. It's too frightening. To open the door to change is to release demons and lose control over them forever. Better to simply endure.

In the short term, this strategy of perseverance may appear successful. The upsetting feelings of midlife go away. People settle down to the life they were living before. But the feelings don't really go away; they just go underground. The True Self still needs expression. People who just endure have only given themselves a short reprieve. They often find that when the feelings of upset come back at the next Turning Point, they are much more intense and overwhelming. And solutions are correspondingly more catastrophic.

Besides figuring out how to use our talents, the main issues at midlife revolve around values. Usually, we know how far we can go in our careers by the end of our 30s. We know whether or not we can get to the top. We have a sense of how much income we can expect to bring in. We have a sense of what we can accomplish. We also turn an invisible corner sometime around age 40; half our lives are over. So a question begins to impose itself: Does what I am doing seem worth doing?

This is life's great question; wrestling with it makes us grow and figure out what we want. Too many people confront it, though, and then try to forget about it. There doesn't seem to be any ready answer. Change feels unthinkable.

And how do you figure out what's worth doing anyway?

It becomes increasingly important as you get older to feel that what you are doing is meaningful. What makes work meaningful is different for each person, but too many people don't consider this question important. They feel that being an adult means holding down a job and providing for a family— and that's it. Often at midlife they are surprised by feelings that their lives aren't enough. What's missing is the interior—the True Self.

Midlife Transition: Steven's Story

Steven, age 44, was married with three children. The oldest was 15. He had been married 20 years. He had worked in banking since he graduated from college. He had been with the same bank for 13 year and was the manager of a department in the home office. One morning he read in the paper that his bank had been acquired by a larger bank in a complicated merger.

Within six months he was laid off because of the merger and restructuring of the two organizations. He had six months of severance pay and a good outplacement package. In the outplacement counseling, he was told that anger and depression were common reactions to his situation, but that the best answer was to dust himself off and get right back out there. Clearly the best way to jump back "out there" would be to land another job in banking.

Steven was suddenly acutely aware of his life and that now he must choose. He could return to banking, a world he knew, or he could strike out in a different direction.

Steven chose to go through a program like the one presented in this book. He sorted through what made his life valuable and meaningful to him, and what seemed beside the point. In a practical sense, he knew he needed to capitalize on his banking knowledge, contacts and background. But in an emotional sense, he realized he would rather sell hot dogs than work for another banking conglomerate. In our program, he discovered natural talents in sales and strategic marketing that had never been evident to him. He had long held that his family came first, and he determined that anything he did would not compromise that value.

Steven ended up making a proposal to a smaller firm that outsources human resource services to large firms, such as banks. His contacts and experience in the banking world make him quite knowledgeable when talking to potential customers. He does not get paid as much as he made before, but he feels much more control of his life. Learning a new job and a new field has been very exciting. "I feel that I have gotten to try a whole new life—and I like it. I like the entrepreneurial feel of the company, and I like it that some days I go to work and I just make it up, because no one has tried what I'm doing before. I love that feeling!"

Age 50 Assessment (50 to 55 years old): You may notice that throughout the adult developmental cycle, the questions become increasingly complex and subjective, although love and work are always at the heart of the issues. The Age 50 Assessment, just like the Age 30 Assessment, is a Turning Point in which we reassess the answers of the previous Turning Points. If those answers were grossly inappropriate, such as quitting basically productive jobs and rewarding marriages, we may start over at this Turning Point. If we did nothing at midlife, if we just had the feelings and simply endured, then the anxiety and depression of midlife come back in spades. If our solutions at midlife really brought the way we live closer to an expression of our True Selves, we may make small course corrections at this Turning Point.

By the Age 50 Assessment, it is impossible to pin down a single issue that is more important than the others, although attending to one's spiritual life seems to assume greater and greater prominence. Living a life that feels meaningful is the only real way to come to terms with the end of life. The alternative to meaning is despair.

Just as the Midlife Transition is particularly powerful for men, the Age 50 Assessment appears to have particular relevance and meaning for women. In fact, some evidence indicates that, for women, the true Midlife Transition may not be at 40, but instead at 50. Whereas men who have been trying to make it in the world suddenly feel their isolation at age 40 and begin grasping for connection, women who have connected all along, by age 50 are seeing many of those relationships change and disappear. Children leave home and start lives of their own. Parents die. Marriages break up. It is at this age that women's bodies say clearly, "Childbearing is over."

Many women whose focus has always been toward family and connection find that they move outward at this age, in the opposite direction from men. Now they want to see what they can do in the world. They want to make an impact. Women who have had successful careers may find themselves, like men at this age, wanting to make some changes to bring more balance to their lives.

Both men and women must find a different way to communicate inside their families. If they don't, and many do not, they run the significant risk of isolation. Children, now adults, no longer need their parents' constant time, energy and attention. Husbands and wives must find a new basis for their relationship. Many men, in an effort to create the intimacy they missed in their first families, start new families. Many women look for a new "baby" to nurture—a business, a cause or a lover.

Both men and women need fuller lives at this age. Both need to achieve a balance between being and doing, relating and producing. Change is inevitable here, and just as at midlife, often catastrophic "solutions" like divorce are nothing more than attempts to deny and ignore change. Ideally, couples at this Turning Point can discover a partnership between equals. Once they have gotten over the fact that things are different, they can go on to figure out how and why they are different, and they have many more options to create different relationships.

By this age, our lives are the accumulation of all of our choices and decisions. It is difficult to take back earlier choices that limited us or kept us from expression of our True Selves, or from even knowing who our True Selves were. But any choice we make at this Turning Point to help us know who we really are can open doors to express our True Selves.

Age 50 Assessment: Wade

When Wade was 52, his company asked him to take over a division in New York. It would mean a higher profile, being closer to the decision-makers at the home office. He refused. He did not want to move to the Northeast. He did not want to uproot his family. He did not want a more pressurized life. He knew his position in the company was secure, but that this decision not to move would take him off the fast track he had been on for much of his career.

Wade realized that he and his wife were virtual strangers after years of raising children and maintaining two careers. He also realized that, unless he did something, they would stay that way. He took some vacation time. He and his wife spent almost a month on a walking tour of England and Wales. It was the best time he and his wife had had together since they dated in their 20s.

Age 50 Assessment: Marjorie

Marjorie, 53, was a successful counselor. She had been single for years and her children were now grown and out of the house. She enjoyed her counseling practice, perhaps more now than she had in years. She no longer felt so stressed by her clients. She liked them more and felt more warmth toward them. She had cut back her hours a little the previous year, and now cut them back again. She felt financially secure, although she was not wealthy.

At age 50, Marjorie had started art lessons. As a child and young adult, she painted a great deal, but marriage, children, a career and divorce had drained her energy for art. Now she threw herself into art with great enthusiasm. She tried different media and experimented with different styles. She put her art in her office and home. She loves having her art around her. She has a network of friends who are artists also, some younger, some older. She finds this association with a different set of people from her academic and counseling friends very rewarding.

Marjorie does not think she will ever retire completely from counseling; however, she plans to cut back her hours even more, spend more time with art and perhaps travel a little with friends

Pre-Retirement Transition (60 to 65 years old): Just as in the transition from the family to the adult world in our 20s and the midlife transition of our 40s, at this transition, we again create a new life. Once again, the biggest mistake is ignoring the issue, assuming that retirement means the absence of work. Or assuming that if you have planned financially for retirement, that's all the planning you need to do.

Far from being a time of idyllic rest, retirement for many is a time of aimlessness and emptiness. People die from lack of meaning. If you don't believe that, look at statistics for death by suicide among senior citizens. But suicide isn't the only reason people die. When people feel no purpose to their lives, they tend to get sick and die within just a year or two in any case.

By this age, a fact of all lives is loss. We lose parents, spouses, friends, relatives, school chums, even children. We may stop working, and that is a loss. Our bodies may change; we become visibly older. We lose the strength, health and potency of middle age. We creep into the region inhabited by old people.

The most productive answers at all Turning Points add to life. They supply some important element we have missed until now. This general rule becomes even more critical as we grow older, when it is often so tempting to give into loss.

The Pre-Retirement Transition sets the stage for one of the major movements of life. According to demographic statistics, people who live healthily to this age will probably live past 80. This means that at this Turning Point you make preparations for a period of over 20 years. This significant span of years can be mainly marked by emptiness, loss and meaninglessness, or defined by connection, meaning and productivity. The difference between one and the other relates directly to the quality of one's Personal Vision.

Ideally, the Pre-Retirement Transition, like all of the other Turning Points, should build on everything that has gone before. It should be an expression of all a person has learned, believed in, wanted to accomplish and is. But it should also be new. People looking at retirement should be thinking about what they want to continue doing in retirement, what they want to drop and what they want to add. They should be creating a Personal Vision for how their lives in retirement will be and what will be meaningful for them.

Generally, this is not something that a person should tackle after he or she has already retired. We feel that the process of thinking and planning for a life of retirement should begin at least five years before. (Clearly, this is true of the other Turning Points, too. As people become more aware of the regularity of change at midlife, we may find that they become more proactive about planning changes in their careers to make them less catastrophic and more productive.) The questions that are important have to do with summing up a life. What do I want to leave the world? What will be my legacy to the world for having been here? How will the next 20 years contribute to that legacy?

Having a Personal Vision at this age that answers these kinds of questions undoubtedly helps people live longer. But it also helps them live better, more fully, with more satisfaction. If you see those rare senior citizens who are vital, active and alert into their 90s, they have a Personal Vision. They have a reason to live and a purpose for pushing ahead. A Personal Vision can save your life.

Pre-Retirement Transition: Tom's Story

At age 60, Tom's company asked him to take a retirement package. He had a comfortable income from investments, a home that was paid for, and a wife of ten years who was 12 years younger than he. She was a physician with a successful practice.

Tom had always known he would retire, but had never thought about what he would do. He was happy to be away from his company, but was angry about being shoved out. About a month after retiring, he decided to take up woodworking. He bought several expensive power tools and had some workmen come in to transform some unused basement space into a shop. He hovered over them as they worked, constantly criticizing their work. Several carpenters quit before the job was done. When the shop was finished and the tools installed, Tom had no idea what to make. He thought he would make some toys for his grandchildren, but became frustrated with several elaborate projects before they were done.

Tom became increasingly morose and isolated. Calling a former business associate to have lunch with him was intensely humiliating. The former business associate could not figure out why Tom was calling him, and he didn't have a free lunch date open for weeks. "But let's stay in touch. Say, Tom, sorry, I have another call coming in. Let's talk soon." Tom started watching soap operas during the day. At night he talked about their plots with his wife.

Six months into retirement, Tom's wife knew he was clinically depressed. She was actually the catalyst for change: "If you don't figure out what to do with your life, I'm going to divorce you. Period." He went through the structured program we describe in this book. It was clear he was not ready to retire, and that he would be much happier working for a while longer. He took some consulting work in his old industry—enough to feel creative and productive. He and his wife plan to retire together in 10 years or so.

Age 70 Assessment (70 to 75 years old): The most important career questions at this age have to do with what you can give back to the world. By this age, you have a huge stock of knowledge and experience, but what can you do with it? All of us need to feel connected with others. In the same way, we also need to feel we are productive. This doesn't mean holding down a high-powered job, or earning mountains of money. We can feel productive if we are able to pass on our experience to a younger generation and help that generation grow and thrive.

Having a Personal Vision for these years can make the difference between living and dying, both emotionally and physically. We all need a purpose—a reason to get up in the morning and keep breathing. We all have this purpose inside, if we can identify and articulate it.

This Turning Point gives us a chance to assess and correct decisions we made earlier. Change comes rapidly during this period of our lives. Our bodies change, our friends' bodies change. People close to us die. If we have not accepted retirement, it is often forced upon us. People tend to separate into three groups by this age:

• The majority who settle down, become less active physically and mentally, and create familiar lives close to friends and family.

• A large minority who become increasingly isolated by distance, illness, poverty, death of significant others, and/or gradual personality change.

• A small minority who shift their activities into new arenas, but who remain physically and mentally vital. They do not release their holds on life, but seem intent on returning gifts from long and productive lives to the community as a whole. Jimmy and Rosalynn Carter, as well as Paul Newman and Joanne Woodward and many other people, both well-known and not, exemplify this kind of choice.

Age 70 Assessment: Robert's Story

For 35 years, Robert was the principal of a high school. He retired at 60. At this time, his wife became ill with bone cancer, and he cared for her full time for the next eight years until she died. Robert maintained a wide circle of friends in the small town where he lived. Many people there had been his students in high school; others had been friends since they and Robert were in school together.

Three years after his wife died, Robert met a woman slightly older than he who had been married to a well-known physician for many years. He had died of a heart attack the previous year. Robert and this woman began seeing each other regularly, having dinner together almost every night. They started dance lessons, and went dancing most weekends. They then started a dance group among their friends. Every few months they traveled—sometimes with a group to Europe or Asia, sometimes to see their children and grandchildren. Robert maintained a large garden and became an accomplished grower of roses. He volunteered his time with a neighborhood youth program and at the senior citizen center. He feels healthy and alive; he feels his life is busy and that what he does means something to others who are important to him.

Senior Transition (80 to 85 years old): Change continues. Here change involves the gradual shift from independence to increased dependence. Now your Personal Vision must help you make the creative leap toward connection and productivity while dealing with appropriate dependence. Above all, one must achieve a working balance—remember, this means choosing the proper adjustment between dependence and remaining a vital actor in one's own life.

The factors that go into a Personal Vision are the same as those in earlier Turning Points. It is just as important here as at other Turning Points to seek a good balance between your personal growth and health on the one hand, and feeling productive and of benefit to others on the other. Figuring out how to remain physically active within one's physical limitations—through yoga, tai chi, walking, running or even weight lifting—becomes increasingly crucial to your health. Figuring out how to remain mobile—through walking, bicycling, public transport or hiring young people to drive you—again, within your limitations, can add immeasurably to your mental well-being. Figuring out how to add to the world by passing along your experience to younger people can help you feel that your life has a larger meaning than just the life and death of your physical body. In all of these areas, a Personal Vision that incorporates your talents, interests, personality, goals, values, skills and family of origin can make it far more easy for you to find what your passion is and create a life in which to express it.

It may be easy to ignore the fact that this transition is just as important and may shape just as much of your life as the other major transitions of your life. People who reach this transition and are healthy may be making decisions about the next 10 or 20 years of their lives. This is why it is so important to make plans and be proactive about keeping alive mentally and physically.

It is too easy to make King Lear's mistake. Lear decided he had graduated in life to the point that he should be taken care of, rather than take care of himself. He had accomplished much, given his children much and now he wanted to reap his reward of rest and passivity. The result was disaster, of course. Lear wanted to abdicate the role of actor in his own life. He felt he deserved to be cared for as he wished, without participating in that care.

This time in life can be an opportunity to be positive, to accept oneself and one's life as it is. We often see people of this age who are able to use their lives' balance and stability to give—not necessarily money, but a sense of reinforcement and reward to a younger generation.

Why Real Change Rarely Happens

As we have seen, each of the adult Turning Points is brought on by the Stress Cycle, the disparity between our System Selves and our True Selves, and the sense of crisis this engenders. We want change; our old answers cease to work well; we feel stressed. At these times we seek a better expression of our True Selves.

But rarely is anyone able to get outside of systems during these periods of openness and change. As we have seen, corporate and school systems cannot help anyone discover anything about True Selves. The System Self is all any system can deal with. Most of our "spontaneous" answers at Turning Points actually come out of our families of origin. As we have seen with Mitchell's story and Sarah's story, we will invariably use the same kinds of solutions for about the same reasons as one or the other of our parents used at the same Turning Point.

There are three common outcomes at Turning Points:

Stay the course. Ignore your feelings of stress and anxiety, tell yourself to grow up, and keep on doing what you are doing. As we have seen above, this effectively puts off the issue of change for five to seven years, but sets up an even more catastrophic change at the next Turning Point.

Appear to change (re-arranging deck chairs on the Titanic). Many people, when confronted with the wish for change, do not know what to do with it. Systems urge us to pay attention to the outside, not to our interiors. A new car can be wonderful, but it won't make your life meaningful. Neither will a new job, unless it is connected to a Personal Vision. Even with a drastic change such as divorce, people usually find that the same issues of stress, anger, anxiety and depression come back. These external changes can't bring your True Self and your System Self any closer together.

Make a real change (systems re-calibration). This is a rare outcome. It is always the result of getting outside your systems and doing structured work on who you are and what you really want from your life. You have to sort out the messages from your family of origin that may be perfect for you from those that may not fit anymore.

Real change usually involves adding to your life. It is almost never a product of simply removing something.

With real change, your first goal is to figure out how your System Self and True Self have diverged, but ultimately the goal is to find the best expression of your True Self. This may involve giving up some aspects of your job or personal life that do not fit anymore. But this is never enough. You must add something to your life that is missing.

Real change is virtually impossible to accomplish alone. Any answer you discover on your own will probably be one derived from your systems: your spouse, your friends, your company, your church, your lover. They know you too well. They are all part of your systems. The answers we get from systems may feel real and obvious, but they don't lead to any real change at Turning Points. And the truth is – you know this, but you're willing to accept the comfort of hearing a familiar refrain from a friend who knows you well or from a family member.

Richard's Story

Richard, age 41, was a veteran 20-year insurance executive. He had worked for the same large international company since he graduated from college. On the fast track, he was definitely heading toward the top. He was well-liked by his boss and known to the management of the company.

"I sat at my desk with the door closed one day, going over my options. The only thing I could think to do was to quit. It seemed like the only option that made sense. My boss and my friends at the company would have been very surprised if they had known where my thinking led me that day. None of them had any idea about these feelings, but they had become increasingly apparent and important to me."

Richard was at the Midlife Turning Point. His feelings were normal and made sense in a larger context. But they didn't make sense to him at the time. He could not articulate exactly what made continued work for his company impossible. He knew he was just as productive as ever, but it wasn't fun anymore. He loved his wife and kids, and his job allowed him time and energy to be with them. But he didn't feel any challenge to life.

Instead of quitting, Richard "embarked on a quest." He read everything he could about change at mid-career and talked to all of his friends about what they were feeling. He found out that some level of discontent at his age is the overwhelming norm—for both men and women.

The Steps to Change

What is real change, and how does it happen? Richard, in the story above, didn't need a simple answer or new motivational talk. He also didn't need the answers coming from his systems: "Don't be a fool. Just keep doing what you're doing, and you'll be set for life." "You've got a good job with a good paycheck, a family to raise, and good prospects for the future. Don't rock the boat." These, or their variants, are the system's answer to Richard's dilemma.

In order for Richard to discover his own answers, he must first get outside the system. He must escape the Lemming Conspiracy. In the course of his research, Richard found a structured process with which to look systematically at each factor of his career. This process was independent of his systems, and its goals were fundamentally different from those of his company, his family or even his friends.

Systems kept Richard from really looking at himself and what he wanted. They asked him to focus on results, on the outside, his position, his possessions, his responsibilities. They did not, nor could they, ask him to focus on Richard. In order to beat the Lemming Conspiracy, Richard would need new information. He would need information that was not in his systems and that he didn't yet know about himself.

It turned out that one of the most crucial pieces of information Richard needed was about his natural talents and abilities—that inborn hard-wiring that makes it easy to do some kinds of tasks and difficult to do others. Richard found out that he had a natural problem-solving ability we call Classification. (We will talk about Classification in detail in Chapter 4.) He knew how he liked to tackle new problems, but he had not known what a powerful impact Classification had on his work life. As he looked forward to a comfortable life in the insurance industry, he saw no outlet for this ability to solve new problems and deal with rapid change. He understood that this could be the source of his unhappiness and lack of fulfillment.

In the next chapter, we will talk about abilities in detail, specifically about the powerful Driving Abilities that shape so much of what roles we are particularly suited for, and what ones we are not.

Richard had known he wasn't happy. But he thought he should just grow up, buckle down and do his job. The new information he now had was that, objectively, his job would not make use of his most powerful and insistent ability. He could make a completely effective case to this boss, and his wife, because he had acquired information from outside the systems and had used this information to create a Personal Vision. We will see more of what happened with Richard in Chapter 5.

A Structured Process to Escape Systems

One of the most difficult aspects of gaining your own Personal Vision is sidestepping the Lemming Conspiracy—getting outside your own systems. We have found that the most effective strategy for defeating the Lemming Conspiracy is to follow a structured process. The process we developed includes all of the factors a person needs to consider at life's Turning Points. Following a structure insures that you systematically take into account not only factors that are comfortable to you, but also ones that you might not think about otherwise. If you only include factors in your Personal Vision that feel "right" to you, or that you would find for yourself, you will only follow your own system. On the other hand, if you follow an external structure for creating your Personal Vision, the structure itself will force you to pay attention to what is important, whether it feels "right" in your system or not. This chapter and the next five chapters detail the structure we researched, developed and tested, and have used with our clients.

GETTING OUTSIDE OF SYSTEMS—
HARDER THAN IT MAY APPEAR

Your friends, your family, you colleagues, your boss, your relatives, your fellow church, synagogue or club members—they are all part of the Lemming Conspiracy. In spite of their most loving intentions, they are connected to you in a way that makes it impossible for them to help you gain a new perspective on your life. They are part of the very fabric of your life and share your patterns of thinking, feeling and doing. Basically, all they can do is help you keep doing what you have always been doing. Even if you change jobs, change cities or change marriage partners, you always eventually wind up stuck in the same place you have always been unless you escape your systems.

ESCAPING YOUR SYSTEMS: A PRIMER

We have discovered several factors that help people escape the boundaries of their systems in order to see a wider picture.

One of the most difficult aspects of gaining a Personal Vision is stopping—setting aside a significant amount of time and energy to do the work. As we have seen, the Stress Cycle makes stopping seem impossible. The Stress Cycle makes it appear that everything is urgent and nothing can be put aside for a time so that you can figure out how you want to live your life.

The structured process we developed and describe in this book will help you get to all of the important factors you need to consider at the Turning Points of your adult life. It is thorough and effective. We did not create it to be a Band-Aid or motivational trick to excite you for a while, but lead nowhere. It is a process to use now, and at any future Turning Point, to help you envision the next stage of your life.

Doing the work of articulating each of the eight critical Personal Vision factors and then integrating them into a Personal Vision is not something you can do in a day, or even a weekend. You need to give your creative mind and logical mind a chance to work on the problem of getting to a Vision over a period of several weeks or months. As you tackle this work, you will find that you may labor over a problem—how to integrate values and goals, for instance - only to be frustrated by coming up empty-handed. A week later, you may be be surprised to find you have an answer waiting for you. Your unconscious mind worked on the problem while you had been thinking consciously about something else. Our Process makes deliberate use of your creative unconscious. For the kind of complex problems we deal with—how to live your life fully and with enthusiasm—it is the most powerful part of your brain, by far. You will find that the Thought Experiments used your logical mind and your creative mind. You'll need both to create a transforming Personal Vision.

Thought Experiment B:

A Personal Vision Notebook

In your Personal Vision notebook, make a page for each Turning Point of your life from the first one, High School to College, through the Senior Transition.

1. High School to College (age 17-18)
2. College to Work (age 22-25)
3. Age 30 Assessment (age 28-33)
4. Midlife Transition (age 38-45)
5. Age 50 Assessment (age 50-55)
6. Pre-Retirement Transition (age 60-65)
7. Age 70 Assessment (age 70-75)
8. Senior Transition (age 80-85)

Write answers to the questions below in your notebook. But don't write about them in the past tense as though you are looking back; write in the present tense as though you are looking forward. For instance, for you high school to college transition section, you might write, "I plan to be a doctor, but I am not sure, because I'm afraid it could turn out to be fairly boring. I just don't know what else to look at."

Proceed to each Turning Point, writing in each as though you were at that age. Do your present (or next) Turning Point. Go forward to all future Training Points. Use the questions to get started, but write about anything that seems significant in how you are assessing your life at the time (or imagine yourself assessing it in the future) and in making plans for the next section of your life.

HIGH SCHOOL TO COLLEGE (AGE 17-18)

Answer these questions as though you are 18. What are the main issues on my mind? What are the main decisions I face now? What relationships are about to change (e.g., between me and my parents, or me and my high school friends)? In looking to the future, what are the most important factors I now think about? What are my plans for the future? Why? What plans do I have for a career? Why? How did I choose that direction among all the possible directions I could have chosen? What are my main talents? What dreams do I have about the kind of life I want? Why?

COLLEGE TO WORK (AGE 22-25)

What skills have I developed? What experiences do I have? What kind of work am I most interested in? In choosing a career path, what is the most important deciding factor? What kind of lifestyle do I want? Is what I am doing leading me to that kind of lifestyle? What are my feelings about the adult work world? How do I think I will fit in?

AGE 30 ASSESSMENT (AGE 28-33)

What has been working about the course I chose? What hasn't been working? What do I want to achieve in the next 10 years? How will I do that? What would I need to change to put myself in a better position? What do I want my life to be like 10 years from now? What values do I need to pay attention to? What interests? What are my family goals? How am I balancing work and family? What would be most meaningful to me at this point in my career? What could I add to my life to make it more interesting and meaningful?

MIDLIFE TRANSITION (AGE 38-45)

How do I feel about my family? How do I feel about work? What changes would I like to make in the balance of work and family? How connected do I feel to others? What excites me about work? What has become old and stale? What else besides work would I find exciting? Or, what new direction in my life would feel interesting and fascinating to me? What could I pursue that would be interesting and meaningful? What values do I need to pay attention to? How can I carry them out? What goals do I have for the next 20 years of my career? What needs to happen to accomplish them? What experience and what skills from the first 20 years of my career do I want to be sure to take with me into the next?

AGE 50 ASSESSMENT (AGE 50-55)

Note for women: Many of the questions of the previous section on midlife may apply to you at this Turning Point.

What has been working about the course I chose? What hasn't been working? What do I want to achieve in the next 10 years? How will I do that? What would I need to change to put myself in better position? What do I want my life to be like 10 years from now? What values do I need to pay attention to? What interests? What are my family goals? How am I balancing work and family? Is what I am doing meaningful? If not, why not? How can I make my career more meaningful? What can I add to my life to make it more interesting and meaningful?

PRE-RETIREMENT TRANSITION (AGE 60-65)

How do I feel about my family? How do I feel about work? What changes would I like to make in the balance of work and family? How connected do I feel to others? What excites me about work? What has become old and stale? What else besides work would I find exciting? Or, what new direction in my life would feel interesting and fascinating to me? What can I pursue that would be interesting and meaningful? What values do I need to pay attention to? How can I carry them out? What goals do I have for the next 20 years of my career? What needs to happen to accomplish them? What experience and what skills of the first 40 years of my career do I want to be sure to take with me into the next phase? What can I give back to the world? How can I do that? Who could benefit from my knowledge and experience

AGE 70 ASSESSMENT (AGE 70-75)

What losses am I contending with? What losses can I expect in the next 10 years? How can I provide enough reinforcement in life to keep me healthy and happy? What has been working about the course I chose? What hasn't been working? What do I want to achieve in the next 10 years? How will I do that? What would I need to change to put myself in better position? What do I want my life to be like 10 years from now? What values do I need to pay attention to? What interests? What are my family goals? How am I balancing work and family? Is what I am doing meaningful? If not, why not? How can I make my career more meaningful? What can I add to my life to make it more interesting and meaningful?

SENIOR TRANSITION (AGE 80-85)

What losses am I contending with? What losses can I expect in the next 10 years? How can I provide enough reinforcement in life to keep me healthy and happy? How do I feel about my family? How do I feel about my day-to-day life? What changes would I like to make in the balance of activity and family? How connected do I feel to others? What excites me about my daily life? What has become old and stale? What other kind of activity would I find exciting? Or, what new direction in my life would feel interesting and fascinating to me? What could I pursue that would be interesting and meaningful? What values do I need to pay attention to? How can I carry that out? What goals do I have for the next 10 years of my life? What needs to happen to accomplish them? What experience and what skills of my working life do I want to be sure to take with me into the next phase? What can I give back to the world? How can I do that? Who could benefit from my knowledge and experience? What forum or group could use my experience?

Wait for a few days, and then read over everything you have written about Turning Points. Do you see any recurring themes? What issues keep coming up? What new issues come up, and at what age? What were the key decisions you made in your life? How did you make them? Were you always aware of what the impact of key decisions would be, or not? What key decisions can you see in the future?

FOUR STORIES: TURNING POINTS

Tracy

"At 18, I didn't know what I wanted to do; I just picked the best college I could get into. I guess I had always assumed I would be a doctor, but I didn't want to be as driven as my father, who is a doctor. The only kind of life I could imagine would be some kind of professional. I'm at a Turning Point now, and I still want to be some kind of professional; I'm just confused about how to do it. I imagine the future being just about like the lives of my father and mother. I'm a doctor or lawyer or something; I work all the time. I pull in a good income. I help people."

Feelings now: "I'm surprised at how hard this was. I'm also surprised at how the only thing I can really picture is my parents' lives. My main feeling is, 'How dull.' "

Brian and Janet

Brian: "When I was 18, I knew I wanted to go into business. I chose a college that had a good business school with a strong marketing department. My vision at the time was of going all the way to the top. I could see myself wheeling and dealing in a large company as a vice president or something. When I graduated from college, I already had a job, so I felt like I was right on track. I still feel on track at the Age 30 Turning point, but now I have the sense of 'now or never.'

"As for the future, I play out two scenarios in my mind. In one, I keep going for the top, get promoted and end up in an executive office. I have plenty of money, but maybe I'm not married to Janet anymore. I know I want to have major responsibilities, but it's hard to picture myself in charge. It's also hard to picture the life I would be leading—except that I would just be working all the time. The second scenario is more troubling. I picture myself flopping. Not getting promoted. Maybe getting laid off and having to take another job I don't like as well. I picture myself anxious and getting more frightened as I get older and my options diminish. It's actually that scenario that drives me. It's a lot clearer to me than the other one. I can imagine how it would feel and what I would be doing. I work like a demon because I can't let that happen."

Feelings now: "Impressed with how powerful that negative image is. And how much I work to keep it from happening?"

Janet: "When I went to college, I didn't know what I would study or what I would do after college. I don't even have any real clear memories of high school. I think I felt down or depressed most of that time. I think my parents probably were, too. When I went to college, my only goal was to make good grades.

"I interviewed with my company on campus in the spring of my senior year, and they offered me the job I'm in now. The main thing that happened in my life at this Turning Point was that I met Brian. We're such opposites, but it's like we had known each other for our whole lives.

There was never a question but that we could get married.

"At future Turning Points, I see our marriage playing out. We have children; we stay married. The children grow up, and then they have children and live close to us, and as we get older we stay together and have close relationships to our children and grandchildren. I don't really see the future too much in terms of my career. If I could quit, I would, so I feel that when Brian is successful enough, I won't be working, but just taking care of the family."

"Feelings now: "I found myself irritated by the questions at different Turning Points. I just see the future as being the same, not changing all the time."

Elizabeth

"When I was 18, I did not have a clue about what I would do. I figured I still had plenty of time in college to think about it, and I was having too good a time to worry. I figured, whatever I do, I'll succeed. Actually, the thought that I might not succeed never even once occurred to me. The winter of my senior year in college, some companies interviewed on campus, and that's how I got my start. I skyrocketed. It was then that I realized I was just like my dad. In fact, his image is in my mind a lot when I make decisions and go through my day. I feel I have this compass inside my head. I always seem to know exactly what the right move will be. It never fails me. At 29, I was put into the executive pool. One of the youngest. Everything has always seemed right on track—until now, that is. At this Turning Point, nothing seems clear. As I look to the future, I don't think I can keep on this course. I picture wanting more quiet and balance and fulfillment. I don't want my children to grow up without my ever knowing them. I would like to think at age 50 or 60 that I will have a close relationship with my husband."

Feeling now: "I realize that I have been doing everything pretty much as I planned it, but that I'm not very happy with the result. I want my life to be different in the future. But how?"

Carl

"I never planned too much. I just concentrated on taking advantage of the opportunities that present themselves. I was not a sterling student in either high school or college. My first job after college was in a new business a friend was starting. I ended up running that business for about 18 years. I got married when I was 29—that was the 30s Turning Point. Then I got recruited when I was 40 for the job I just got fired from. The future? I guess I'll just do what I've always done. The questions about retirement and later transitions made me think. I don't have any sense about what retirement looks like. Playing golf? Working? Living in a retirement village? None of it seems to fit me very well."

Feelings now: "Wondering where this is all going."

> NEXT CHAPTER: In the next chapter we discuss the basic groundwork of your Personal Vision, your natural talents and abilities. Your natural talents tell you what kinds of tasks and roles you are naturally suited for, and which you aren't. This is the basic starting information you will need at each of your career Turning Points as you start to construct answers to what you will do with your life.

OUR **NATURAL TALENTS**
UNDERLIE EVERY JOB,
ROLE OR
CAREER WE UNDERTAKE
THROUGHOUT OUR LIVES.

YET THE
OBJECTIVE INFORMATION
ABOUT WHAT WE
NATURALLY DO **EASILY** AND WHAT IS
**INTRINSICALLY
DIFFICULT**
IS ALMOST **UNKNOWN** TO THE
VAST MAJORITY
OF US
AS WE MAKE
CRITICAL DECISIONS
AT **CAREER TURNING POINTS.**

Our Hardwired
Talents & Abilities

Jack Palance: It all comes down to one thing.
Billy Crystal: What's that?
Jack Palance: That's for you to figure out.

—*City Slickers, 1991*

Figuring out a Personal Vision may be the most complicated problem anyone of us ever has to solve in life. But the rewards of working through to it are immense, whether calculated in terms of success or of satisfaction. As we described in Chapter 2, to have the most positive impact, a Personal Vision must include eight critical factors: stage of development, abilities, skills, interests, personality, values, goals and family of origin—these are the Eight Personal Vision Factors. In the last chapter we discussed how your age and life development stage influence your Personal Vision. The present chapter deals with the most fundamental aspect of what you bring to your career: your natural talents and abilities—how you're hardwired to do some things with sublime ease and why other things will always be more difficult.

Before launching into natural talents, however, we want to be clear why it's so important to look at all eight factors, not just one. As powerful and rich in guidance as your natural talents and hardwiring are, they don't tell you everything. We integrated the Eights Personal Vision Factors because it was completely evident to us that people are too complex to be defined by just one or two factors. Generally, we find that the more objective factors, such as talent and skills, help you make such basic decisions as how you go about work or how you position yourself in your job. Career direction, and, even more importantly, passion for what you do, comes from the more subjective factors like interests, values, family and goals.

The Eight Personal Vision Factors and Personal Vision

Many writers, test contractors, corporate program creators and motivational speakers feel that any one of the Eight Personal Vision Factors is a sufficient basis upon which to frame your life and career. The Lemming Conspiracy, the power of systems to control how you think about your life and career, teaches us that these simple, unitary views are too confining. As powerful as each of these factors is individually, *none* is powerful enough alone to help you escape the power of systems and help you figure out a career direction that makes sense for you. We designed the Eight Personal Vision Factors to bring together all of the factors necessary to give you a Personal Vision that is a complete picture of yourself.

When we study the research in the field of human behavior over the past 50 years, the Eight Factors that form the basis of our model have time and again been identified as instrumental in achieving career satisfaction, clarifying choices, promoting development, and enhancing personal effectiveness. While our focus on these Eight Factors is not new, what is new is bringing all the factors together into one program that systematically examines each factor and its relationship to the others, and then facilitates a creative synthesis of the data into a meaningful and unique Personal and Career Vision.

Most experts in the field of career and job counseling see their roles in terms of gathering information about their clients and then telling them what to do. One of the first experts to break with this model was not a counselor or trained expert at all; he was just a businessman trying to solve a problem. He felt that the ideal job for any one individual should be so unique to that individual that no one else could help to define it. Everyone should discover his or her ideal fit by a process of self-exploration. The central insight was that direction should come from the inside of a person, not from the tests or insights of some expert.

The philosophy that informs this book is that you have the answer for your life's work inside yourself. The process we describe is a structure to help you identify it, describe it and put it into action.

Our natural talents underlie any job, role or career we undertake throughout our lives. Yet this objective information about what we naturally do easily and what is intrinsically difficult is almost unknown to the vast majority of us as we make critical decisions at career Turning Points.

Your Natural Talents:
What Are They, and How You Know Them?

Many years ago, an engineer at General Electric named Johnson O'Connor was given the task of figuring out what people should do when they applied for work at G.E. It seemed to O'Connor that if the different occupations at GE could be measured scientifically, the results would show what abilities were best suited to each occupation. Each occupation could be reduced to functions that could in turn be measured by objective hands-on worksamples. Should a prospective employee be a line worker? A supervisor? An engineer? A manager? What training would be most beneficial for a new employee? What kinds of jobs would a new employee definitely not be suited for? This was before the era of universal college education, and so a person's educational background did not necessarily tell G.E. much about what a person could do.

With no preconceptions about the problem, the engineer started assembling tests that would measure what he called "aptitudes," or natural talents and abilities. He was not interested in what a person could learn through experience. Rather, he wanted to find out the unique abilities and talents that each person is born with.

Thus began the long and difficult task of devising worksamples for each ability needed for the work at GE. Nearly 3,000 GE workers volunteered to participate in the research. One of the first worksamples measured finger dexterity in meter assembly. In a few months, the test identified eight new workers faster in finger dexterity than any trained operator. Next came a worksample for observation as a test for choosing inspectors. This was important, because inspectors do nothing except look at work in progress, and no one else can tell objectively what they are looking for. By selecting persons who scored high in observation for inspector jobs, quality control was improved and complaints from customers fell off significantly

A strong aptitude for a particular task makes that task easier to do. A weak ability makes it relatively difficult to do that same task. We are not talking about intelligence or motivation. Intelligent, highly motivated individuals can accomplish many things for which they have little or no talent. But they may not be happy or satisfied doing those things if they really have little or no talent for them.

O'Connor discovered that certain patterns of talent make it easy for a person to work with tools and understand machinery. Other patterns allow people to understand processes and systems, or to work as salespeople. Some ability patterns mean that logical, step-by-step explanation of difficult problems is a piece of cake. Still others make managing people in organization feel like second nature. These patterns remain relatively stable over the many years of a person's working life. A person can't learn a pattern of abilities; he or she is either born with that pattern or not.

As the work by O'Connor progressed, a group of O'Connor researchers conceived of the idea of translating the O'Connor laboratory tests onto paper and pencil. They worked over many years to devise tasks on paper, which would measure the same essential abilities and produce the same essential results as in the O'Connor laboratory. Their work finally resulted in a battery of tests, which ultimately required the performance of twenty-one different worksamples

In completing their paper and pencil battery, these researchers contributed a new and exciting perception — that a valid assessment of innate abilities did not require attendance at a designated laboratory but could be done anywhere that a paper and pencil test could be administered by trained personnel. Further, the tests could be scored empirically and without intervening interpretation by the person administering the test. Over time, norms were calculated and applied to assure reliability.

In 1992, the rights to use the paper and pencil test developed by the O'Connor researchers were acquired by the Highlands Company. Over the intervening years, the Company has trained scores of affiliates to administer the test, to interpret the results, and to deliver an analytical and instructive feedback to each client.

Beginning in 1997, the Company devoted its energies and resources to development of a computerized version of the test. The Company's efforts have resulted in a Battery of nineteen worksamples which can be completed on a CD or online. It is called the Highlands Ability Battery.

As a result of O'Connor's work, it has become stunningly clear why some organizations function as inefficiently as they do. In *The Peter*

Principle, Laurence Peter forcefully draws a Monty Python-esque picture of organizations in which people who perform excellent work are promoted rapidly and continuously until they occupy positions for which they are totally incompetent. There they stay until they retire.

Who has not heard the story about the legendary salesman, a killer who would chew through doors to make a sale? His customers like and respect him, and his numbers break all records. As a reward for work well done, management promotes him. He now manages twenty salespeople—only to fall flat on his face. Sales plummet; his salespeople hate him and quit; his former customers go elsewhere: a disaster. The Peter Principle? Yes. But of infinitely greater importance, misplaced abilities – and the Lemming Conspiracy.

The pattern of talents that makes selling easy is well-known. So is the pattern that makes managing easy. But they are completely different patterns. To ignore that is as though we identified a player on a basketball team as a particularly effective rebounder and then said, "I've got a great idea, let's make him our ball-handler and play-maker!" Our salesman, so effective at closing a sale with a client, was totally at sea when asked to manage other people who were supposed to close sales. Not because he lacked motivation or intelligence, but because it ran exactly counter to his natural talent.

There is another current in the story of the salesman. It has to do with systems, and The Peter Principle describes accurately what happens. The goal in systems is always to get to the next level. To stay in the same position is to stagnate. To move sideways is to fail. Up or out, that's the rule.

The goal of moving up in systems is dictated externally; it is part of the Stress Cycle. Most often, it has nothing to do with the individual. The salesman would have been much wiser and happier had he remained a killer salesman. But he didn't know that, and his system never recognized the issue. From the perspective of the system, a bright, ambitious young man must move up to get ahead in the organization.

Another typical dilemma faces the manager of a small plant. He knows that if he's going to move up in his company, he has to move over to the executive suite. Should he do that? He won't really know unless he examines carefully into the Eight Personal Vision Factors. They will show whether he will be happier in the intangible world of ideas and communication or in the "real" world of machines and people. In the case of one manager we know, it took the Highlands Ability Battery to confirm that he had the talents to manage but would not be happy and successful as a junior exective.

Let us tell you about another man, Joseph, who faced a similar dilemma.

Joseph's Story

Joseph, 41, was a senior partner in a large corporate law firm. He worked most weekends and many nights during the week. For several years he had been managing partner of the law firm. He was generally considered an excellent manager of the firm. He thought of himself as financially comfortable and successful.

But Joseph also felt great stress. He did not enjoy his work. It took him away from his young family, but he didn't know what he could do about it. He felt his firm needed him as a manager. He felt his family depended on him to work hard and provide for them. Joseph had enjoyed law for many years after joining his firm, but for the last few years he had not enjoyed his work at all. It felt more like a burden. He worked longer hours now than when he started as a young associate.

Joseph was only vaguely aware of these problems. He probably would not even have described them as problems. From his point of view, what he experienced in his work life was just what everyone experienced. That's just the way things are. His firm was happy with him. His wife accepted the situation as a given and dedicated her time to their children. None of Joseph's systems challenged his decisions.

Joseph went through a corporate program that used the Eight Personal Vision Factors to create a Personal Vision—the same process we describe in this book. For him, one of the most interesting pieces of objective information was that he had an extremely poor pattern of natural talents for management. His pattern of talent superbly fitted him for law and legal work, but management duties went completely against his grain. (We should note that natural talent cannot alone determine whether a person can or cannot perform a role. Because he was intelligent and highly motivated, Joseph performed the role of manager in his firm exceedingly well. The problem was that it missed his pattern of talents so completely, that he was forced to work twice as hard to achieve a result much less satisfying to him emotionally.)

Even though his role was dissatisfying and made him work against himself, it was easier for Joseph simply to keep doing what he was already doing than to seek new ground. His firm benefited from it and expected him to continue. But he was not happy. He quit his role as managing partner— over the protests of the other senior partners. His wife worried over his decision; she was afraid Joseph would have less prestige and pull in the firm.

Joseph's systems tried to get him to stay in the Stress Cycle. They wanted him to have a short-term focus: He should not make a change because the firm would be upset by having to change managing partners. They wanted him to focus on wealth, power and status; what about the prestige of being managing partner? They wanted him to take his direction from the system, not from himself. They wanted his decisions to be reactive, not self-driven.

Joseph insisted on a change, because he knew objectively he was right. He also set his priorities for his work time. He was not going to work on weekends or evenings anymore. He would accomplish this by concentrating on the kind of work he loved, and for which he was particularly well suited.

Joseph's partners were not wild about this change—at first. But after several months, Joseph's team was more productive, and he brought more business into the firm than ever. Besides that, he was happier. His team was happier. And they found another manager.

Astute readers might be asking themselves right now: "Well, how did he manage to go up against all of his systems and make them listen to him?" Resigning as managing partner was not something any of his systems were prepared to accept.

Of course, Joseph's decisions were more complex and involved more issues than those defined by his abilities. Personality, interests and family of origin all strongly influenced his actions. We will take up Joseph's story again in Chapter 7 when we talk about the family of origin and its influence.

But just what are natural talents? And how do you discover yours? In the next section, we discuss the most powerful and influential talents, the Driving Abilities.

The Driving Abilities:
What They Are and How They Affect Your Life

Driving Abilities are so important because they drive or influence everything you do, whether they are high or low. If you ignore them, you run the significant risk of getting into a role that doesn't use your strongest talents or that demands a talent you don't have. Our experience has been that a great deal of dissatisfaction at work can be traced to having strong talents that are never used. We saw this in Joseph's story. His strong abilities for law were not being used well in his role as a manager. He always felt dissatisfied, unfulfilled.

We will describe four Driving Abilities to give you some idea of what they are and how they relate to each other. The Thought Experiment at the end of the chapter includes a self-report measure to help you assess your own Driving Abilities.

CLASSIFICATION

Classification uses your right brain to solve problems. This part of the brain takes information from everywhere—something you heard on the news, something you might have noticed without being aware of it, something somebody said—and pulls it all together into a rapid, virtually spontaneous, solution. In Classification, your right brain takes a plethora of related and unrelated observations and arrives at a way to explain them. Another name for this is inductive reasoning.

Classification involves quick responses. People who have high Classification love to use it. It's fun. But the very quickness and sureness of their problem-solving also makes it difficult for people with high Classification to get along easily with people who have other equally valid ways of solving problems.

Let's drop in on the hectic world of Allison, a person with strong Classification ability. We can see how she solves problems, what kinds of tasks are easy for her, and what drives her crazy.

Allison—A Person with Strong Classification. Co-workers describe Allison as quick and self-assured. Given a problem to solve, she knows the answer before anyone even has a chance to explain the problem to her. She sometimes starts responding to what people say before they can finish their sentences. She has an irritating habit of being right and knowing she is right. She has little patience with people who are slower than she is at seeing the answers. She often feels she is metaphorically tapping her foot, impatiently waiting for her boss to see something that is completely obvious to her.

Allison is happiest when she is fully engaged by problems that come at her fast and furiously, with scarcely time to breathe. She is most miserable when she has nothing new to sink her teeth into.

Allison has high Classification. She doesn't solve problems logically or in a linear fashion; she solves them with her powerful right hemisphere, the one that doesn't speak. Pulling answers together from many different sources simultaneously, people with strong Classification don't necessarily know how they get to an answer; they just know what the right answer is. Quickness of problem-solving is one of its defining characteristics.

When you hand a report to a boss, a report that you have worked on for weeks in order to make it perfect, and he scans it briefly, remarking only that "I would change the order of the chapter titles," he is probably using Classification. People with strong Classification are able to spot a problem with amazing speed—to the general irritation of those around them.

Classification demands to be used—more than any other strong ability. A person with high Classification who is stuck in a menial job that requires doing the same thing over and over will be very unhappy, perhaps even dangerous. One theory holds that many young people who become delinquents as teenagers have high Classification, but low educational and cultural attainment—i.e., no prospects. The most they can hope for is menial labor, which will not use their high Classification ability at all.

People with high Classification who cannot use this ability at work often create problems themselves, seemingly just to have the opportunity to make use of this powerful ability. On the other hand, when they do have the opportunity to use it, they are like children in a room full of toys. An engineer we know was asked by his company to build and set up a new manufacturing plant in Mexico. He did not speak Spanish and had never built a plant before. But he built the plant in record time. And then he built another; and another. Years later, when he was asked to look back and describe his happiest days, he picked the days in Mexico. "Every day there were a million new challenges I had to overcome. I was working on all cylinders and I made it all happen. What other job could use so much creative energy?" Perhaps he didn't realize it, but he was drawing on his strong Classification ability.

To test Classification objectively, you must give the person a problem to solve—not just any problem, but preferably a visual one that involves many separate elements with some possible common association. The problem must be designed so that it leans almost exclusively on the right hemisphere of the brain. People with strong Classification jump to the correct solution at once. People with other problem-solving abilities must go through a much more elaborate process to get to the answer. We cannot, of course, recreate an objective test for Classification in this book. However, you can get a sense of your Classification ability in the Thought Experiment at the end of the chapter.

CONCEPT ORGANIZATION

Concept Organization is at the opposite end of the problem-solving pendulum from Classification. Concept Organization uses the left hemisphere to solve problems logically and linearly. While Classification pulls information from anywhere and everywhere at once, Concept Organization deals with information one step at a time. It lines up parcels of fact and observation in logical order. It enables you to start with a theory and proceed to a logical conclusion. The name for this process is deductive reasoning.

The ability to line up facts logically is generally not as much fun as Classification, but it can help you do things that Classification cannot. People with high Concept Organization are able to see into the future in a way, because they can start with an idea about what they might want to happen and then logically construct a chain of events that can bring it off.

People with high Concept Organization are also able to communicate easily in words. Words are linear. Words are small parcels of information that must be lined up in a logical sequence for communication to happen. You may have had the interesting experience of trying to relate a particularly vivid dream to someone. Dreams are holistic images created in the right hemisphere. They contain complex symbols, images and feelings. As you start to tell someone your dream, you may feel the vividness and richness of the dream evaporate as you attempt to put it into words. Words are simply unable to carry the enormously complex images and symbols that the right brain loves. What is left, except occasionally in poetry, is the rather thin and meager content of the dream. But without words, we could not even communicate the content of a message. Without the logical and linear left hemisphere, we could not really communicate complex ideas at all.

Let us look at Jill, who has strong Concept Organization. What kinds of things can she do easily? What kinds of things are difficult for her? How does she feel about her talents?

Jill—A Person with Strong Concept Organization. Papers, files and folders spill everywhere around Jill's desk and office. A stranger would wonder how she can ever find anything. But if you were to ask her for a particular piece of paper out of all the piles in her office, she would go to it immediately. It is as if there is a filing system in her head. She knows where everything is according to a logical system that she created, but never thinks about. As a result, she feels no real need for an external system or external order to help her keep track of things.

When Jill's boss told her that she would need to prepare an annual report, she replied that it would take two weeks. She had immediately assessed everything else she was working on, re-prioritized all of it, figured out the tasks she would need to accomplish, and allowed some extra time for unknowns. All of this was completely obvious to her, but she had worked with her boss long enough to know that he didn't think in the same way as she did. He had worked with her long enough to know that if she said two weeks, this was probably the best estimate he could get, even if he didn't immediately see why it would take so long.

Jill is able to organize the thousands of details of her life and family without strain or noticeable effort. Sometimes, inevitably, things happen too fast at the office, or there are too may projects competing for her attention. At these times, she shows some strain and anxiety. She can't figure out what she ought to do first or, even worse for her, what she just ought to leave undone.

Jill can write more clearly and logically than her boss. But she likes it better when he gives her the direction he wants her to take in a letter. She knows that sometimes he has an idea that seems as though it's from outer space, but that ends up being effective anyway. Jill doesn't like doing anything by the seat of her pants. When someone asks her what her gut reaction is to something, she will respond with a logical conclusion. She knows she works most effectively when she's given time to figure everything out logically. She knows she is least effective when she is overwhelmed by multiple tasks that need to be handled all at once.

Jill's ability to solve problems logically feels almost invisible to her. Often she is not aware of using the ability, nor is she aware of how powerful a tool it is for her. She assumes that everyone thinks in the same way she does.

Objective measures of Concept Organization give participants a logical, linear, verbal task to perform. The left brain can do this task quickly and with ease, but it is almost impossible for the right brain to tackle it. You can get a sense of your Concept Organization ability with the self-report quiz in the Thought Experiment.

TWO FREQUENT ABILITY PATTERNS

Steve—A Consultant's Pattern of Abilities. Steve is a corporate consultant who sees executives all day long in one-to-one mentoring relationships. He thinks on his feet. His clients ask him about business concerns, personal problems, tricky staff questions, tactical issues and long-term strategies. He never really knows what a session will be like before it starts. Steve is good at this, and he likes it. He has both high Classification and high Concept Organization.

When a client asks him about a problem, Steve usually knows how to tackle it before he or she finishes talking. He describes this as having a picture of the answer. This is his strong Classification ability at work. But when Steve responds, it is not with a picture or in any kind of impressionistic way. Rather, he gives a closely reasoned, carefully thought-out summary of his point of view with his thoughts and arguments compellingly marshaled. When Steve first solves the problem—when he gets a picture of the solution—he uses Classification. When he presents his point of view, he uses Concept Organization.

Steve works by using both Classification and Concept Organization. This is most efficient and productive for him. With training and practice, he could do his job using many other talent patterns, but he would have to go about his job differently to be equally satisfied and productive.

John—An Executive's Pattern of Abilities. One of Steve's clients is John. He is older than Steve, and has been an executive in his company for many years. He started as a young trainee right out of college and worked his way up through the layers of the organization. He says of himself that he has made every mistake in the book—some more than once. But he has developed an instinct over the years that now makes it easy for him to provide clear and accurate direction for the people he manages.

When someone asks John his gut feeling about something, he responds immediately with his gut feeling. He has an unerring sense of what people should be in what jobs, and he has a sure ability to provide the kind of work environment in which people can do their most productive work. John is an experiential problem-solver—he scores low on both Classification and Concept Organization.

There has been a great deal of interest among psychologists about these experiential problem-solvers. They arrive at an answer to a problem by checking with their experience of similar problems in the past. What psychologists have found, often to their surprise, is that this is often a much more direct and efficient route to a solution than trying to solve it through logic in the way someone with high Concept Organization might do, or by coming up with a new solution to every problem, in the same way as a person with high Classification.

People with high Classification and/or high Concept Organization are often one step removed from their experiences. They often feel and act as though their thoughts and conclusions were more real than reality. People who are low in both of these abilities are able to access their experiences more easily than others.

Steve was often struck by John's ability to say, "This is what is important here. I won't worry if we never get to the rest." But when John first started with the company as a young man, he was sometimes overawed by others his age who seemed quicker or more able to handle complex projects. He tried a lot of different roles, failed a lot when he first started, but rose steadily because he was able to manage people so effectively. To him, this talent was like breathing. "What's the big deal?" But his ability to lead a team, give it a goal and vision, and create the conditions in which each worker could function most effectively made him able to rise much higher than many of the bright stars he started with.

John discovered how he worked best, and it was different from how others work. John's talent pattern makes it supremely easy for him to manage, motivate and direct the work of other people. An important part of that overall pattern is that John is such a strong experiential problem-solver. This pattern made it slower, perhaps, for John in the beginning—experiential problem-solving requires experience—but he eventually discovered that by working through others, he could make his best and highest contribution. And be a lot happier.

IDEA PRODUCTIVITY

When high, Idea Productivity is second only to Classification in its impact on a person's life. Idea Productivity describes the rate of flow of ideas. If asked to think of solutions to a problem, a person with high Idea Productivity might come up with 25 different answers in the space of five minutes. A person with low Idea Productivity contributes quality and detail in his or her ideas. It may be that two or three of the ideas generated by a person with low Idea Productivity will end up being useful, while only one of the many ideas of a person with high Idea Productivity will be helpful. High Idea Productivity alone does not predict how good or creative a person's ideas are. People with high Idea Productivity find that ideas and thoughts come to them constantly, even when they wish they wouldn't.

Andrew—A Person with Strong Idea Productivity. Andrew loves selling. He can sell anything to anyone. He loves finding just the right "hook" to get people interested. He loves hearing their objections so that he can deftly steer them around the obstacles. He never knows what he's going to say; he always flies by the seat of his pants when he's making a sale. He picks up on nuances of meaning and speech and uses them to direct his pitch to his customer. He is overjoyed when a potential customer has a new objection because it gives him a challenge. The challenge is to develop, instantaneously, exactly the message that this potential customer wants to hear. Andrew is a master at this.

What he does not do well is keep records. This involves too much detail. He may get started on lists for his customers, only to drop them and start on something else in less than 60 seconds. A few minutes later, he will drop that, too. Andrew has a hard time paying attention to details for long periods at a time, but not because he is distracted by outside noises. He is distracted from the inside, by his own thoughts. As soon as he starts working on something, a completely unrelated thought strikes him and takes his attention. No sooner does he start thinking about that, than another thought interrupts.

Andrew's friends sometimes get irritated because he is always interrupting them. Andrew's boss has noticed that he is a wonderful salesperson, but that he has his limits when asked to think about strategy. Andrew will generate ten alternatives, none of which seem particularly creative or useful. But Andrew can persuade anyone to come around to his point of view. That's what makes him such a powerful and effective salesperson.

Idea Productivity is such a powerful ability because it demands to be used almost constantly. A person with high Idea Productivity who is asked to concentrate on the same task all day long will be miserable and unproductive. A person like this may wonder why his or her concentration is so bad, but actually it's only that his talents are not being used properly.

In the work world, we need people with high idea productivity and people with low idea productivity. The people with high idea productivity gravitate to work in marketing and public relations. The people with low idea productivity are happiest in jobs that require concentration and precision, such as brain surgeons and accountants.

To measure Idea Productivity objectively, you simply count the number of ideas that occur to a person when given a standard problem to solve in a given span of time. You can get a rough sense of your own Idea Productivity from the Thought Experiment quiz at the end of the chapter.

SPATIAL RELATIONS

Spatial Relations ability is the best understood and most researched of all the abilities. It is the ability to manipulate and envision three-dimensional objects and three-dimensional space in your mind. When we measure Spatial Relations, we give participants a task in which they are required to "see" a three-dimensional object in space and then mentally rotate it to "see" how it would look another perspective.

In all studies in the literature, men score higher on Spatial Relations as a group than women do. This is deceptive, however, because many individual women score extremely high in Spatial Relations, and many individual men score low. Without actually measuring this ability objectively, you can't tell exactly how high or low in Spatial Relations any one person is.

In general, high school courses and most college courses do not use Spatial Relations ability. Many people score high in Spatial Relations on objective measures who had absolutely no knowledge or sense of this ability. It was invisible to them because they had never had an opportunity to use it.

People who are high in Spatial Relations have a particular affinity and feel for things and objects. They like to work with tools. They enjoy making things. They are interested in how things work. They like to figure out how things are constructed. They are interested in the structure of things. They often become engineers, physicians and scientists. For a person with high Spatial Relations ability, abstract concepts never seem real. A chair feels real. But dealing with abstractions like feelings and relationships, as a counselor might do all day long, would eventually feel empty and frustrating to a person high in this ability.

Some experts feel that if you are strong in Spatial Relations ability, you need to use it in your work. If you don't, you run the risk of never feeling fully engaged in what you do all day long.

Elaine—A Person with Strong Spatial Relations Ability. Elaine is a successful architect. She went all the way through high school and most of the way through college taking liberal arts courses, never realizing that she had strong Spatial Relations abilities. She could never identify what she wanted to do in life, and when she was junior in college, she decided to take a year off. She spent this year teaching skiing in Aspen. During this year off, she met an architect, and talked to him at length about what he did and how he got to do what he did.

Elaine was fascinated by their discussions. She began reading books and inquiring about architectural schools. She found a program that would admit her, but she had to spend an extra year in college. She then got a master's degree in architecture.

Elaine now designs and builds visitors' centers for several Native American tribal councils. This job challenges her to help people of European, African, or Asian cultural backgrounds to understand something about the alien Native American culture through the architecture of the centers. This task requires all of her abilities and background. She must envision the structure and the space that people will occupy. She must be able to see it from the point of view of someone looking at the building from the outside and from the point of view of someone inside, looking at the exhibits.

It is interesting that even Elaine's background in liberal arts has been helpful to her. She has had to spend a great deal of time with Native American tribal councils listening and learning what is important to them and figuring out how to extract all that and interpret it for people with cultural backgrounds that are unrelated to Native American cultures.

As Elaine moves from the design to the actual building of the projects, she becomes more engaged with materials and structure. She is able to envision how each of the materials contributes to the overall look, stability and strength of the buildings. She also deals with the scheduling and timing of the projects, and in how to get the buildings to come together in a rational, orderly way.

Her Spatial Relations ability makes it possible for Elaine to do all of these tasks easily and well. In fact, the only difficult part for her is communicating her vision of the space and structures to people who do not "see" in three dimensions as easily as she does.

People like Elaine are called Structural thinkers, while people who score low in Spatial Relations are called Abstract thinkers. Abstract thinkers are comfortable and happy in work dealing with abstractions and ideas. They are the lawyers, accountants and teachers in our society. Most CEO's of large companies are abstract thinkers.

A fit in one's career as precise and creative as Elaine's is seldom really an accident, nor is it simple. It weaves together many strands of the person's life into a whole fabric. Your natural talents are the place to begin your Personal Vision, but they are never enough to make accurate and creative decisions about your career. All Eight Personal Vision Factors are vitally important, and weaving them together may require a series of creative leaps. This is why it is so important to follow all the factors together when creating your Personal Vision. You can be sure this way that you are getting to all the pieces.

Thought Experiment C:

Driving Abilities

I below can give you some indicators of your Driving Abilities, but the objective, carefully validated measures of The Highlands Ability Battery™ can give you much more information, more objectively. In addition, you can find out about many other, more specialized abilities. You will receive a detailed written report on your results. You will also arrange to have an individual two-hour feedback session with one of our specially trained Affiliates. If you are contemplating any significant career decisions, this can be critically valuable information, and it will give you a complete and objective view of your natural talents—how you are hard-wired. It is the ideal foundation upon which to build your Personal Vision.

You can arrange to take the Battery by contacting the Highlands Company. Contact information appears on the last page of this book.

SELF-REPORT MEASURES OF DRIVING ABILITIES

You can get an idea of your Driving Abilities by answering the following questions about yourself.

The Highlands Driving Ability Quiz

In your Personal Vision Notebook, using the scale below, write down the number indicating how well or how poorly each of the following statements describes you:

Not at all like me		Mostly not like me		Sometimes yes, Sometimes no		Somewhat like me		Exactly describes me	
1	2	3	4	5	6	7	8	9	10

1. I *like* problem-solving and arrive at solutions very quickly.
2. I sometimes feel restless waiting for others to 'get it.'
3. I usually know exactly how to solve a problem.
4. Mostly I know what someone will say before they finish talking.
5. My solutions are usually the best ones.

6. I can organize and explain information easily.

7. I can plan quickly and well.

8. I appreciate a logical order to things.

9. It's easy for me to see the logical steps for future plans. I can easily see how to get there from here.

10. I feel more comfortable thinking through things step by step than just leaping to a solution.

11. When trying to solve a problem, I know I'll think of many ideas.

12. I am good in brainstorming sessions.

13. Ideas come so quickly to me that sometimes I interrupt others who are talking.

14. Ideas frequently crowd my mind.

15. Sometimes I am distracted by my own thoughts.

16. I am often interested in how machines work.

17. I have an intuitive understanding of machines and structures.

18. I like to work with tools.

19. I enjoy working with things I can touch and see.

20. I like to have real product or "thing" to see and touch when I finish something.

ADD UP YOUR SCORES AS FOLLOWS:

Questions 1-5 _____ Classification

Total score, questions 1-5:	Low	5-30
	Medium	31-40
	High	41-50

Questions 6-10 _____ Concept Organization

Total score, questions 6-10:	Low	5-30
	Medium	31-40
	High	41-50

Questions 11-15 _____ Idea Productivity

Total score, questions 11-15:	Low	5-30
	Medium	31-40
	High	41-50

Questions 16-20 _____ Spatial Relations

Total score, questions 16-20:   Low   5-30

                                        Medium   31-40

                                          High   41-50

You should be aware that no self-report quiz can provide the same kind of validated, precise and accurate measurement of abilities as measurements using objective worksamples.

HIGH CLASSIFICATION

If your self-report in Classification is in the high range, this can mean that Classification is a powerful ability for you, and may influence almost every aspect of your working life.

This is an ability that demands to be used if your score is in the high range. Almost anyone who has this ability strongly gets positive enjoyment from using it. The flip side of that statement is important to remember, however. If you find yourself in a position that does not use this ability, you may be unhappy with your work.

The high Classification person loves to solve problems and to figure things out. This person enjoys change and challenge. There is nothing he or she likes better than taking on a new task, because learning something new uses this ability.

MEDIUM CLASSIFICATION

This section applies if your self-report score is in the mid-range in this ability. Classification is a powerful ability and your score in the mid-range indicates that you should take it into account when thinking about your work role. In a sense, you have more choice about using your Classification ability than if it were either high or low. You should be able to work in fast-paced environments or more stable, less chaotic environments. It may be that you will choose one type of work environment over another for reasons unrelated to Classification. Being in the mid-range on this ability gives you that option.

LOW CLASSIFICATION

A low self-report score would indicate that you may find any work situation stressful that is chronically chaotic and that requires rapid-fire problem-solving with very little information. You will be happier and more productive in a work environment that is more stable and more structured.

The strength of your score is that it shows the ability to persevere long enough to become proficient. You can become expert by acquiring increasing levels of knowledge and experience.

HIGH CONCEPT ORGANIZATION

A high score in Concept Organization suggests an aptitude for any planning activity. In being able to see the logical sequences of events, you can predict, order and plan schedules for things that are going to happen. Even more important, this is the primary ability needed to communicate ideas to other people. Since you may be able to arrange ideas easily into a logical sequence, creating written materials and presentations of ideas that make sense to others may be easy for you. You may be able to see how all of the pieces of a project fit together to make a coherent whole. You will be able to use this ability effectively in any work in which there is a recurring need to organize materials or information.

People who are high in Concept Organization find that they want to use this ability often. Most people have ample opportunity to use it in their everyday lives, both at home and at work, and so we don't see people who are tremendously unhappy if the ability is not used in their jobs.

MEDIUM CONCEPT ORGANIZATION

In the workplace, Concept Organization is a fundamental ability. A medium self-report score indicates that you should be able to perform essential work and office tasks—planning, predicting, scheduling and communicating—with relative ease.

LOW CONCEPT ORGANIZATION

A low self-report score on Concept Organization can be an advantage in an environment that places a premium on action. If a person must act quickly and decisively, the kind of logical planning that is the hallmark of Concept Organization is actually counter-productive. It delays action.

A low score in Concept Organization means that it is relatively laborious for you to plan, organize and prioritize internally. It is much easier for you to use various external means of organization. These can include schedules, lists of priorities or lists of tasks to accomplish. People who are in the low range in Concept Organization like an external world that is fairly neat and orderly. This helps them stay focused on what they feel is important.

HIGH IDEA PRODUCTIVITY

A high self-report score in Idea Productivity indicates that you may have many ideas flowing through your thoughts during any given period of time. It is important to remember that Idea Productivity is not an ability that you can turn off at will. Ideas will occur to you whether you want them to or not. You will be much happier and more productive when you can use your Idea Productivity in rapid idea production, in problem solving and in adjusting to new ideas, instead of trying to struggle against it.

Conversely, you will feel very confined by a task that requires long attention to meticulous detail, or highly detailed follow-through on someone else's plans and ideas. You may be capable of such concentration, but you will be struggling against your instinct for Idea Productivity to achieve it. You will feel much more involved and fulfilled in your work if you have a real outlet for your flow of ideas during most of your working day.

MEDIUM IDEA PRODUCTIVITY

A score in the medium range in Idea Productivity indicates that you will have some of the advantages of a high score, as well as some of the advantages of a low score. You are able to come up with ideas at a sufficient rate to be useful to you in solving problems and overcoming objections. You will enjoy being able to use this ability at times. Your rate of idea production is such that you probably feel somewhat confined by a task that requires long attention to meticulous detail, or highly detailed follow-through on someone else's plans and ideas. You are capable of such concentration, but you will not enjoy it if it consumes all your work day. You will feel much more involved and fulfilled in your work if you have some outlet for your flow of ideas during some portion of your working day.

Some uses for your rate or flow of new ideas can be in dreaming up solutions for problems, or in "selling" your point of view to others. You are in an ideal position to have enough concentration to work out a solution to a problem and dream up alternatives, and then adroitly overcome others' objections.

LOW IDEA PRODUCTIVITY

Idea Productivity confers an advantage whether you are high or low, provided you choose the appropriate work environment. A self-report score in the low range in Idea Productivity may indicate that you are able to focus well, and work without undue distraction on a given project for a considerable length of time. You will probably work most effectively in a stable, rather than a volatile, work situation, where an ability to maintain undistracted focus is a positive strength. You will probably want to avoid being in situations in which you have to persuade or sell to others in an impromptu manner.

In work areas requiring a high degree of concentration, a low score in Idea Productivity is a distinct advantage. A low score in Idea Productivity will be helpful in any task that requires you to pay attention to details and follow through to a conclusion.

HIGH SPATIAL RELATIONS

This is an extremely valuable ability in many areas of business. It is, of course, a fundamental ability for someone interested in science, design, construction, manufacture and technology. This ability allows a person to experiment mentally with different options or arrangements of elements or objects without actually having to see them.

An important consideration to keep in mind, however, is that eventually someone who is high in Spatial Relations will want to see the physical result of what he or she is doing. People who score high in this ability need to have their hands on something or produce something. They are most at home with provable facts, products, machinery and tools. Many roles at work do not deal in such tangibles. Roles and tasks that deal mainly in ideas, relationships, information or influence can end up feeling quite unreal to a person who is high in Spatial Relations. Some experts in the field of abilities consider this one of the most important factors to take into account when planning a work role.

There is a compelling quality to Spatial Relations in the sense that people who are high in it eventually feel pulled to use it. Often this pull does not make itself felt until a person is middle-aged. It is most often experienced as a wish to do something real—to have a tangible result of one's efforts at the end of the day.

MEDIUM SPATIAL RELATIONS

A score in the mid-range on this ability is sometimes difficult to interpret. Typically, people either have this ability or they don't. People who are high in Spatial Relations usually want to see the results of their actions in a concrete and immediate way. If they manage a business, they are more satisfied if the business produces a concrete product such as a chair, rather than an abstract product such as information. A score in the mid-range on this ability indicates that you may have the ability to visualize the concrete results of what you are doing in your work. If so, you may want to consider being sure to use this ability on a daily basis.

LOW SPATIAL RELATIONS

A self-report score on this measure in the low, or abstract, range has several important implications. People in the abstract range are typically quite comfortable in work that deals with people, relationships, information or influence. They do not usually experience a strong wish to be involved in the concrete world of physical objects in their work. Training, managing, counseling, law and accounting are all examples of typically abstract work roles.

FOUR STORIES: ABILITIES

Tracy

"I have strong scores in all of the Driving Abilities. This means I can do anything, basically. It's called a multi-ability pattern. The good side of it is that I have a lot of strong abilities. The bad side of it is that it makes it hard for me to choose anything that will use all of those abilities. Over all, I don't feel it's been hard for me to figure out a direction.

"Finding out about my abilities was interesting, because I never thought of myself as a scientist or anything. But I can do science or medicine. It might be that law or even psychology would not use all of my abilities. I guess I don't really know that much more than when I started, but at least I know I can do something else. I realize now why I

hate my job so much. It doesn't use any of my abilities. I guess I had lost a lot of confidence. After I graduated, I suddenly realized, "I don't have a clue here."

Feeling at this point: "Better, More hopeful."

Brian and Janet

Brian: "Well, my abilities were right on target. High Classification, High Idea Productivity. It's no wonder I thrive on the pace at work. I feel like I have ideas and energy running out my fingertips. Whatever I do, I need to be in a work setting like the one I'm in. It seems perfect for me."

Feeling at this point: "I feel good about my job. Maybe why I feel so stressed is because of other things besides the job itself."

Janet: "The main thing I found out was that I like to take my time and solve problems logically. I have very high Concept Organization. I get frustrated with customers because they are so unreasonable. I can show them exactly why something happened, but it doesn't make any difference to them. It drives me crazy. I think my ability pattern is a hindrance rather than a help in my job."

Feelings at this point: "Interested. More confident."

Elizabeth

"I'm at the mid-point in both Classification and Concept Organization. My Idea Productivity and Spatial Relations are both low. I like to have problems to sink my teeth into. But not too many at the same time. I can see why I like my job—when it's not totally overwhelming. I can also see why it's so easy for me to deal with problems."

Feelings now: "This means a lot to me. I know how to position myself better at work. I feel encouraged."

Carl

"I have low scores on all Driving Abilities: This means I am an experiential problem-solver. I don't stop and figure out a logical solution. I usually solve problems at work by thinking of some past experience that this reminds of. Then I have a good idea about what to do. I know I have

a strong innate understanding of what makes people tick. If you put me in a group of people, they always seem to elect me as the leader. People listen to me. At least they have ever since I turned 35 or so."

Feelings now: "Still hopeful. Still wondering where all of this is going. Getting a little impatient to find an answer."

NEXT CHAPTER: In the next chapter we continue the construction of your Personal Vision with more pieces of The Eight Personal Vision Factors, your skills, interests and personality. As you continue to add pieces, your Personal Vision will increasingly become a useful, working tool.

FOR MANY PEOPLE
"INTERESTS"
AND
"WORK"
ARE LIKE TWO SEPARATE BOXES.
THEY RARELY SEE
ANY CONNECTION
BETWEEN THEM.

BY TAKING A CAREFUL LOOK AT
WHAT YOU ARE **DRAWN TO** AND
FASCINATED BY,
YOU CAN DISCOVER YOUR REAL
SOURCE OF **CREATIVITY**
AND **ENERGY.**

Skills, Interests & Personality

Just knowing what your talents are is not enough. You have to make sure that you can use them every day in the work you do and in the life you lead. We developed the concepts of The Eight Personal Vision Factors and of a Personal Vision to make sure you would be able to take information about your talents and translate it into your life.

A Personal Vision should have a definite structure and internal coherence. It should embrace and comprehend your whole life, not just the hours you spend making a living. It's often easy to "forget" part of your life—you just leave it out of your plans. If you leave a piece out, you run the risk of being subtly trapped by your systems into the Lemming Conspiracy—and possibly ending up wasting your most important talents. This is why The Eight Personal Vision Factors are so important.

As we saw in the last chapter, your natural, inborn talents and gifts form the base, or foundation, of your Personal Vision. In this chapter, we build on this base of talent. We start with the more objective factors of your Personal Vision: your skills and experience, your interests and fascinations, and your personality—how you habitually interact with others.

Skills and Experience: What Have You Learned in Life?

When Dan was 42, he had a sudden insight: He hated his job, and he would rather do anything than go to work every day. Everyone may have this feeling from time to time, but for him, the feeling didn't go away. In fact, it got worse. Eventually, he was sure that the only way to save his sanity was to quit his job altogether, move to the beach, and, using his retirement money, open a shop for tourists. He went so far as to check real estate listings at his favorite beach resort and to call his pension manager to find out how much money he could withdraw when he quit.

Fortunately, Dan didn't do any of that. He had been a corporate lawyer for 16 years, had never sold anything to the public, had never run a business, and didn't really know the first thing about retail trade. It was a fantasy of a more relaxed, easier life, without the stress and greed that he encountered every day in his clients and their adversaries.

Dan faced a number of problems with this dream of a beach-front surf shop. But the main one was that it didn't take into account the enormous wealth of education and experience that he had so carefully built over the 42 years of his life.

Most people are unaware of the richness of their own skills. Many simply overlook their most powerful and effective skills, because they have always used them so effortlessly. Their most significant skills don't seem like important assets, because they're so easy. When asked to name their best skills, most people will name something that was particularly difficult for them to learn. Dan would have said, for instance, that the only thing he had learned in 16 years of lawyering was how to plug the loopholes in most contracts.

In one of our seminars, Dan told a story about some events from his childhood that had meant something to him. He had nearly flunked math in the eighth grade, but by dint of labor and will had managed to press on in math through high school with mostly B's and C's—the only subject in which he had been unable to earn virtually effortless A's. At the time, he felt tremendously frustrated, because he believed that school was really the only thing he could do, and now that wasn't going particularly well. Eventually, he decided that maybe he should try something unrelated to school. And he did. He learned to play the guitar, started a rock band, crafted music and lyrics, wrote humorous pieces for a school magazine and ended up as editor-in-chief of the school newspaper during his senior year.

Dan didn't see what was special about this story. It was just what he had done in high school. It remained mildly embarrassing to him that math was almost totally beyond his ability to understand. But other people, people outside Dan's systems, saw much more in this story than the picture of a high schooler struggling through a difficult school subject. You, the reader, can undoubtedly see much more, too. It was just invisible to Dan.

Dan's story is actually quite rich. The other participants in the seminar identified dozens of skills and talents Dan had clearly shown in responding to his frustration with math. For starters, he had transformed this frustration into positive, meaningful events in his life. By accepting a limit, he had been able to branch out into other, nonacademic pursuits. He loved music and enjoyed playing in a band with others. But his real talent was writing. He wrote most of the band's songs. He wrote for the school newspaper, and made people laugh at themselves in very funny columns. Later, as editor-in-chief, he was able to get other writers to meet deadlines and to organize all of the hundreds of tasks that go into a finished newspaper. He assumed the responsibility of directing stories and editing writers' copy. He got them to work within limits, instead of fighting them.

As the other seminar participants told Dan what they saw in his story, it occurred to him that he had helped his law clients to find alternatives where they saw none, and to accept realistic limits when they didn't want any limits at all.

Dan had never ascribed any importance to the fact that he had formed and led a band of high school boys. Nor had he thought much about his role as editor of the school newspaper. What both of these roles had in common was the ability to hold people with strong personalities and strong agendas together and steer them toward a common goal—a goal he had first articulated and set out to accomplish. This, of course, was exactly what he so deftly managed when he negotiated agreements between clients. Dan now had an entirely new perspective on his skills. His skills had made him a great corporate lawyer, but he could also use them in many other fields. As he reviewed his experience and skills, attempting to figure out how to use instead of discard them, the fantasy of a beach-front shell shop made less and less sense.

Dan realized that the beach shop was an expression of a goal: a less hectic and stressful life. He knew he would be throwing away some of his most important assets if he were to throw out corporate deal-making altogether. He pondered how he could reach his goal but also stay with his firm and the job that fit him so well. By working with his partners, setting clear limits and sticking to them, he was able to cut back his stress significantly. He now spends more time at the beach. He recently published a story in a literary monthly.

Once he figured out how important his skills were, a crucial part of Dan's story became naming and ordering his life goals. In Chapter 6, we talk more about articulating and prioritizing goals. Another crucial part of this story has to do with setting boundaries on your life—even when your systems definitely don't want you to. We will talk about setting boundaries in Chapter 10.

In the Thought Experiment at the end of this chapter, you will find a variation of the exercise Dan used to discover his real skills. It will help you understand your skills and experiences and how they contribute to what you do well. Remember, Dan's most important skills remained invisible to him until he did a specific exercise. This is true of virtually everyone. We designed the exercise in the Thought Experiment to help you see the most important things you have learned in your lifetime.

In the next section, you'll learn about one of the most overlooked factors of all: interests. In reality, your interests sometimes are the most direct path to your creativity and enthusiasm.

Interests: Direct Line to Where You Really Live

"Follow your bliss." Joseph Campbell's oft-quoted line could not represent a better or truer piece of advice. When we talk to people who have led particularly full and satisfying lives and ask them how they managed to find just the career that suited them best, they all say some version of the same thing: "I always did exactly what interested me." What appears to be extraordinary luck or the product of unusual confluence of talents is actually neither.

When you pay attention to what you find personally interesting and fascinating, you get to include this magical pull in your own career. You can be more creative, happier and more enthusiastic. Work doesn't have to seem like work. The fact that somebody pays you to work can seem like the most extraordinary luck of all.

For many people, "interests" and "work" are like two separate boxes. They rarely see any connection between them. By taking a careful look at what you are drawn to and fascinated by, you can discover your real sources of creativity and energy.

When people assign their passions to a box labeled "not work" and relegate it to those times when they are not utterly exhausted by the routine of their days, it often takes some focused attention to bring interests to the forefront and make them important. Sometimes, successful executives in the middle of one of our workshops have looked up suddenly in surprise and said, "I never realized that my interests could have anything to do with work."

Many leading commentators and researchers have studied the fundamental relationship between interests and work and have confirmed that when a person's work is built on his or her interests, the work is more productive and more enjoyable. Often, people in the stress cycle lose sight of this fundamental fact. But we have found in our programs and seminars that when people look around and redefine and rediscover their interests, they reawaken to what is really important to them. Strangely, they rediscover what originally attracted them to the work they're doing and what may have gone wrong.

One group of researchers has commented on the intricate relationship among interests, abilities and skills. They have suggested that a person's abilities may direct his or her activities to specific interest-related areas. In other words, interests may direct where one's "ability capital" is invested. They great importance of interests is that they drive effort and practice, and practice drives the acquisition of skills.

Richard's Story, continued

You may remember the story of Richard, in Chapter 3 — the 41-year-old veteran insurance executive who had thought his only alternative was to quit. It turned out that his interests became the key to discovering satisfaction in his job. He had many passions in life but felt he would never get to them if he kept working as he had been. We have seen how discovering his Classification ability made him understand his discontent. But what should he do?

Richard completed a long-term exercise on his interests very much like the one you will find in the Thought Experiment at the end of this chapter. He realized that the hundreds of ideas, images and people that came his way every day fascinated him. From long habit, as soon as some idea grabbed his attention, he just as quickly let it go. He couldn't deal with it. He didn't have the energy to pursue it. He had a responsible job, a family, a life. He had no time to pursue anything beyond work. He became just a little more resigned inside.

In the exercise, Richard began to "catch" the many images, thoughts, ideas, words, stories, pictures, articles, people and events that momentarily grabbed his interest. He began to cut them out, write them down, and make brief notes about them. He became adept at holding onto a spark of interest long enough to identify it and make a record of it. He saved all of his records.

After a few weeks, he sorted the records into groups. Almost all of his interests lumped together into three broad categories: music and dance, art and photography, and one that he labeled loosely "adventure." These categories had remained stable for years. He had always been interested in them.

It dawned on Richard that his interests and fascinations, so long ignored and pushed down in the name of adulthood, could give his life more texture and substance. He decided to take them more seriously. He wanted to build a life in which they could play a role.

Once that goal was clear, things changed rapidly. As so often happens, when Richard knew what he wanted clearly enough, a way opened for him to obtain it. Actually, a way had always been there; he had just never noticed it until he realized he needed it.

Richard's insurance company had instituted a policy of flex time for employees several years before. He was aware of this policy, but as an executive he assumed the policy had nothing to do with him. It was for tellers and bookkeepers, mostly women who had to deal with child care.

As Richard ruminated on the question of how to pursue his passions in life, a memo came across his desk about the flex time program. Inspiration struck. He could use flex time just as well as the administrative staff. He put in a request to his boss to work four days and take Wednesdays off. He would work the same number of hours, but not on Wednesdays. He would then be able to pursue other ideas and interests outside of work.

The reaction was volcanic. His boss explained carefully, as if to someone slightly dim, that the policy was not for employees like Richard. Richard knew he would win out, though, because, as it happened, his boss had written the policy. It had been a political move to make the company seem more forward-thinking. Of the company's 30,000 employees, fewer than 30 had put in requests.

This is an example of the Lemming Conspiracy at work. The insurance company had a limited number of answers and actively resisted *any new ones. No one behaved malevolently. But the system did not care what Richard wanted from his life. Had Richard quit his job, his boss and friends would have been surprised, and his co-workers would have been momentarily disturbed. But there would be a new person in his spot within days, and the system would proceed, having learned nothing.*

Before his quest into his interests, Richard's boss, his friends and co-workers, and Richard himself, for that matter, defined Richard's options as the options defined by the system. It was only when Richard got outside the system and went through our process for gaining a Personal Vision that he was able to see himself more clearly and see that many more options existed than those the system offered.

Richard did win. He now takes Wednesday off, and has for two years. He plans to pick something each year from one of his major groupings of interests to pursue and explore. This year, music takes center stage. He is learning to play the violin and he and his wife are learning to dance. He doesn't know where this will lead, and he doesn't care. It adds joy to his life; he feels more productive at work.

Richard feels his life is completely different now than it was two years ago. His heightened sense of creativity is a perfectly normal by-product of actively pursuing his fascinations. He is just as productive, but a lot happier. The insurance company benefited because it kept one of its most valuable employees. Richard benefited because he feels he is living his life for the first time in years.

But there is more to Richard's story. In defining his Personal Vision, that is, getting a complete picture of what he wanted his life to look like over time, Richard became very clear about the kinds of jobs he liked to do at work and also the kinds of projects that made best use of his particular set of talents and abilities. Now, if a project comes his way for which he knows he is not suited and would not enjoy, he turns it down. On the other hand, when someone proposes a project that Richard knows will be perfect for him, he jumps at once. Co-workers often express surprise at Richard's self-confidence. Sometimes he is more enthusiastic about a project than the person who tentatively proposed it in the first place. He has become something of a guru among his contemporaries in the company. Often, someone will pull him aside in whispered tones and ask him how he did it. The most difficult part of explaining his story is trying to convince people that the key is not in how he put it to his boss or in the structure of his proposal, but rather in learning about himself.

When we learn about our interior selves to create a Personal Vision, it is important to understand how we relate to others. This is the next building block of Personal Vision – personality.

Personality: The Interpersonal Environment

Many people have become excited and enthusiastic about the idea of understanding personality, only to draw a blank when faced with putting their enthusiasm to work in a day-to-day setting. A personality inventory workshop becomes the talk of the office for a few days. But a month later everyone has forgotten about it, and not much has really changed. Experiences like these may lead to cynicism about the usefulness of personality measures; however, in the context of the whole person, personality is an important piece of the puzzle.

One of the most limiting aspects of personality, as it has been used in business and corporate settings, is that it is so often used in isolation. Zealots proclaim, "Hi, I'm an ENTJ," or "Hi, I'm a Proactive-Idealist," as though this were the sum of it all. Some feel that this kind of shorthand explains all there is to know about themselves. Nothing could be further from the truth. This is using one of the building blocks of Personal Vision to stand for the whole structure. But it's not enough.

Personality testing carries at least two other burdens. First, almost all traditional personality testing is self-reported. You tell the test about yourself, and then the results of the test tell you what you've just said. Obviously, no one knows you as well as you do yourself. On the other hand, you can't very well have an objective view of yourself, either. Furthermore, consultants and others have often used personality testing to predict patterns of behavior and predict how well a person will perform in a given job. But many other factors than personality affect job performance. Unless all of these factors are taken into account, any prediction will be subject to some error. This said, when personality testing is used by individuals as one aspect of judgment about their own lives and careers, it can be powerful and informative.

The idea that certain patterns describe how we habitually interact with our fellow humans is an extremely old one. From the Greeks on, philosophers and pundits have described types of people who engage in more or less consistent patterns of interaction with each other.

Some people love to talk to others; some prefer to be by themselves. But even the most garrulous extrovert likes to be alone sometimes. And even the most intense introvert reaches out to others sometimes. We are not talking about something that can be measured with 100 percent accuracy. Personality traits are usually described by referring to two ends of a continuum. Extroversion, for instance, is at one end of the continuum, introversion at the other. People are located somewhere between the two extremes.

We will describe two personality dimensions we have found to be particularly helpful in thinking about what you want to do with your life: extroversion vs. introversion, and generalist vs. specialist. In the Thought Experiment we included a brief self-report quiz you can use to form an estimate of where you are on each of these dimensions, and a short summary of how your score describes your pattern of interacting with others.

INTROVERSION-EXTROVERSION

You can think of Introversion and Extroversion in terms of energy. Where do you get your energy? When an extrovert is tired after a busy day and wants to recharge, he or she will talk to someone. The extrovert gets energy back from the interaction with others. For very strong extroverts, nothing seems very real unless they have discussed it with someone. Often, strong extroverts think through their ideas as they talk them over with a friend. Talking about an idea is an important part of the whole process of thinking for the extrovert. Extroverts like being around other people, being in groups and being in the know. At parties, extroverts get around the room and talk to everyone.

Not so the introvert. For the introvert who is tired after a day at the office, nothing is as restful and recharging as to go home, go through the mail, pet the dog, read the paper and not talk to anyone. No matter how skillful and comfortable in interacting with others the introvert learns to be, it is always work. There is always energy going out. Introverts like to think ideas through before they share them. When they share ideas, especially personal ones, introverts feel more comfortable when they have a long history of trust with the other person. Introverts don't enjoy groups. When they're at parties, they often find an old friend and spend the evening talking to that one person.

No personality dimension is absolute. But we have found that understanding your own tendency can be important when figuring out a compatible and productive work environment. If an extrovert is asked to sit alone in an office, working on projects all day long, day after day, he or she will feel profound stress. The source of the stress may not be apparent, but forcing extroverts to be non-interactive cuts them off from their most productive work style and causes everything to feel somewhat incomplete and unreal. In the same way, forcing introverts to interact all day long also leads to stress.

Margaret— an Extrovert. Margaret is a sales representative for a large private hospital. She had originally wanted to be a psychologist but, after earning her master's degree, she realized that being a therapist did not involve interacting freely with people. It involved keeping most of your thoughts to yourself. To be effective, you had to lead the patient to see for himself. Frankly, this drove Margaret crazy. She was never sure what she should say and what she should hold back. She felt she was spending the whole day sitting on her hands.

As a sales representative for a psychiatric hospital, however, she was in her element. Her training and degree gave her credibility; she obviously knew what she was talking about. Her job now asked her to call on companies and insurance providers who were important sources of potential business for the services of the hospital. As Margaret saw it, her job was to form relationships with key people in these companies—people who would know her, remember her and call her when they were thinking about something the hospital could do for them.

Margaret loves this job. She likes talking to people all day long, she likes knowing them and they like her. When she has a meeting with someone important, getting to know this person, getting to like him, and getting him to like her, occupies her primary attention. She can spend an hour and a half at lunch with an important client and never mention the hospital. Because of her ability to connect, Margaret has been successful at her job—and happy.

Mark—An Introvert. Mark is a corporate consultant. He has a Ph.D. in industrial psychology and has been in practice for 15 years. He has two partners, both of whom are Ph.D.s. He likes to start his day by drinking coffee and reading the paper with his office door closed and his phone blocked. After about a half-hour, he emerges and begins his workday. He typically works with one or two corporate clients each day, talking to their executives, working with system problems, writing reports, talking to staff. After lunch, Mark likes to close his door and shut off his phone for another half-hour or so to recharge for the afternoon. Mark interacts with people all day, except when he is analyzing data or writing reports, but all of his interactions are structured. He is an expert; his clients seek his help, and he provides it. When he has lunch with a client, they discuss the company, its problems and its future goals. The only time Mark really talks about his personal life is with his wife and with one or two old friends. Mark likes his job. He feels he is very good at it, and it suits him perfectly.

Mark and Margaret are at the two ends of the continuum between introversion and extroversion. They have both found positions in which their personalities are a positive force in their work. Margaret's ability and drive to connect at a personal level make her an exceptionally effective representative. Her sales contacts sense her desire to connect personally. They trust her because she's not trying to sell the hospital all the time. She wants to know who they are and what their problems are.

Mark's introversion makes him able to assume the rather lonely role of expert. It also has the subtle effect of making him seem more trustworthy to his clients. They feel he will not say anything merely for effect. He means exactly what he says. He never becomes a part of any organization he helps. And that's just fine with Mark. He enters an organization, provides his expertise and leaves.

Introversion and extroversion, like other personality styles, do not in general determine what kind of work a person should do. Rather, they determine how a person goes about doing what he or she does. Margaret and Mark could trade jobs and undoubtedly be effective, but only by going about their jobs in a totally different way from each other.

The next personality dimension, generalist-specialist, is equally important, but not nearly as well known as introversion and extroversion

GENERALIST-SPECIALIST

If you were to ask 1,000 people in the United States what is the first word they think of when you say "table," about 280 of them would respond "chair." Other responses, like "lamp," "cloth," or "floor" follow in terms of frequency.

Some people, given this same stimulus word, adopt a fundamentally different kind of response: "Dalmatian," or "clock," or some equally idiosyncratic response. When asked the connection, they reply with something highly personal. "When I sit at my dining room table, my dog, a Dalmatian, always comes over and lies down at my feet."

This observation forms the core of the difference between specialists and generalists. Generalists comprise about 75 percent of the population. They are the ones who answer "chair." The defining characteristic of generalists is their gut-level understanding of how other people respond to things around them. They understand because they respond to things the same way. When generalists are in meetings, they don't need to worry about whether participants have arrived at consensus. They know. All they have to do is check their gut reactions. Generalists have a clear sense of what is going on with other people. This makes the generalist brilliant at understanding, motivating and leading other people in organizations. The generalist functions supremely well in groups, teams and systems.

The specialist is a different breed. The highly personal and idiosyncratic response noted above is the way the specialist goes about life. It's important for specialists to love what they do—almost completely. The name specialist refers to their long-observed tendency to find a particular area of knowledge and pursue that one area for an entire career. In organizations, specialists do not generally fair well. In fact, a true specialist is like an interplanetary alien who has somehow stumbled into the organization's world. If specialists do make it in an organizational structure, it is because they have found some particular area of expertise that is necessary to the system's functioning and have somehow managed to stick with that one particular specialty. They concentrate on that one area until they know more about it than anyone else. They rise in organizations because their special area of knowledge is crucial to the organization. What generally happens, of course, is that a specialist who is really performing well and who loves what he is doing, will get promoted to a more general job. At this point, he loses that vital personal connection to his job that makes him want to get up in the morning. When this happens, he frequently becomes depressed and dispirited, often without knowing why.

Specialists and generalists have two fundamentally different views about work. When you ask a generalist what she does at work, she is likely to describe the big picture: the company produces this; the team is working on that product; the department is moving in a new direction. Generalists function well in organizations because they can relate what they are doing to an overall result that is the product of many people working together toward a common end. They don't fundamentally care whether they are doing this piece of the work or that piece of it; they care that the team or organization is doing what it set out to do, and that they are rising comfortably in the organizational hierarchy.

Specialists are concerned with what they, personally, are doing. When you ask specialists what they do, they tell you about the particular project that they are personally working on. It's the only thing that makes any real difference to them. Specialists often have a real passion for what they do; that's what makes them so competent in the areas they have chosen.

Joseph, the lawyer we talked about in Chapter 4 who was managing partner of his law firm, but unhappy with it, was unsuited by his abilities to be a manager. He was unsuited also, because, like many lawyers, he was a specialist. He didn't really care about the overall organization of the firm or the direction it was taking; he just knew he could manage deals with his clients better than anyone else, and that's what he wanted to do.

Specialists tend to populate professions like medicine, accounting, law and dentistry. These professions have defined areas of expertise, and practitioners function within these areas throughout their careers. They tend not to be parts of large business organizations. If they do form professional groups out of financial necessity, these groups are best described as collections of independent practitioners. Artists, writers, actors, teachers and performers are mostly specialists. Again, these are people who get ahead because they completely own what they do.

David—A Generalist. David is a manager in an international technology company. He has been on the sales side for many years. He sees his job as motivating his people. He is a master at this. He supports them, pushes them, moves them, finds the right roles for them or helps them move on to a better fit if they can't find a good role under him. He has been a top producer for years, but is somewhat bemused by this. "I love to get the right person in the right job. I seem to know just how to get people moving and involved in what they are doing, but it's not something anyone taught me. It's as though I've always known it. As far as what I know, I know a little about a lot of things. People who work for me know a lot more about their areas than I do. That's fine with me. They love this stuff, but I leave it as soon as I walk out the door."

David is an extrovert with a manager's ability profile. He is the quintessential manager. Recently he was transferred to production. This is fine with David; what he does won't change. Like most generalists, he sees progress in his career in terms of the organization's structure. Production will be a useful springboard upward in the company. This is quite unlike the specialists who often work for David; thy see progress in terms of exercising more control over the one job they want to do.

Specialist-generalist is an extremely important dimension in envisioning a career. Asking a specialist to be a manager is an organizational bad joke. Lacking that gut instinct about others that is the defining characteristic of generalists, specialists often do not have a clue about how to motivate anyone. Basically, they have never seen motivation as much of a problem. They are motivated. Isn't everyone? Specialists' leadership style, when effective, could be called charismatic. The specialist believes totally in his or her mission and gathers people around who believe, too. These "believers" are usually generalists.

Specialists' defining characteristic of owning what they do makes them generally less effective as managers. "Do it my way. This is my project, so don't screw it up. Here, let me show you how to do it. Just do it as I tell you to. I'll do it." These are all the utterances of specialists, utterances that would probably never even occur to a strong generalist. A team of specialists working on the same project (or more likely, on their personal pieces of the same project) can be a beautiful study of accomplishment and efficiency—as long as a manger is in charge. Could the atomic bomb have been built by scientists alone? No – not without General Groves.

Interestingly, the reverse problem of generalists landing in "specialists" jobs does not come up very often. Given any choice in the matter, most true generalists aren't that interested in specialists' jobs. They would feel pigeonholed and limited – leave that for the experts. If, by some happenstance, a generalist does land in a specialist job, he or she will almost always go about it differently. Generalists in the professions, for instance, tend to become involved in the organization of the profession—in the professional societies or the state regulatory boards. That's fine with the specialists, because they aren't interested in that stuff anyway.

In the Thought Experiment, you will find a short self-report questionnaire designed to give you a sense of where you fall on the two dimensions of personality we've discussed here: introvert-extrovert and generalist-specialist. Taking both of these dimensions into account will give you a picture of the kind of work environment in which you will feel most at home. There is also a short interpretive section so that you can see what the results of the questionnaire mean for you.

A Note about Anxiety

At this point in the process of creating a Personal Vision, when they are studying all the pieces and trying to put a picture together of what they want their careers to look like, most people become anxious. At the beginning of this process, people make fascinating discoveries about themselves. They discover new talents they didn't know they had before, or didn't know the meaning of. They see themselves in new and unexpected ways. They reexamine assumptions that they didn't even realize they were making.

So where does the anxiety come in? You have all sorts of new information, but it's hard to tell yet where it's all going. There's no picture yet. You can't know yet what it all really means. "I keep adding new bits of information and new insights, but where is it all leading?" Intellectually, you may realize that this is a big job that will take a while to figure out, but you may still feel anxious as you go through the process.

We know that this anxiety is an important part of the creative process inherent in building a Personal Vision. When you start feeling this anxiety, you know that both parts of your mind, the left and right hemispheres, are engaging fully in the problem of how to put all of the information together. It is as though your unconscious, creative mind is worrying the problem, turning it over, pushing it this way and that, trying to figure it out. Your logical, linear, problem-solving left brain wants an answer. And it knows that it can't provide one.

Researchers who study creative people with the idea of delineating the process of creativity often comment on this anxiety. The first stage of the creative process involves information gathering and logical attempts at solutions. As the problem takes shape, as the scope and extent of it become clearer, the creative person starts to feel anxiety. It is perhaps the mind's way of prodding itself to make a creative leap. This is the beginning of the second stage of the creative process.

The best thing to do is trust yourself. And keep plugging away at the problem. Before you get to the answer, you will need to add three more pieces to your Personal Vision—values, goals, and family of origin. Then you will be ready to integrate all the components into your Personal Vision.

Thought Experiment D:

Skills, Interests and Personality

1. UNCOVERING YOUR SKILLS

The objective is to get you to take a fresh look at your skills. You will need a tape recorder so that you can record one or two stories about yourself.

Think of an event in your life when you were younger, one that you feel positive about in retrospect. Think about what happened right before and right afterwards. Think about what you felt, what you did, and what happened. This can be a small event that would be meaningful only to you, or it can be a bigger event that anyone would recognize as positive.

Now tell the whole story into the tape recorder. Be sure to include details of what led up to it, what you thought, what you felt, what happened next, how other people responded and how they felt.

Now record a different story, again one from when you were younger. This time, make it a story about an event which you found frustrating or disappointing. Be sure to include the same amount of detail as in the first story.

Now leave your stories on the tape for at least two weeks. Don't listen to them or even think about them if you can help it. When the two weeks are up, listen to the stories again. If it helps, pretend they are about someone else. In your notebook, as you listen, write down every positive skill you hear in the stories. Many people write down 15 to 20 different skills in even a simple story. Even in the negative story, be sure to find and write positive skills. You may find that you see the same positive skills in both stories.

If you get stuck trying to find positive skills in your stories, give them to someone else to listen to and find skills in them.

What skills appear in both stories?

Can you see some recurring themes? Do your skills fall into natural groups? How would you name or describe these groups?

2. FINDING YOUR INTERESTS

Start an Interest File: Get a file folder or a box and put it someplace where you'll see it. Use your box or file to collect notes about anything that gets your attention: articles, pictures, or even random thoughts about what really interests you in life. You don't have to be choosy here. You're not wedded to anything you put in this file; the more you can play with it, the better. What looks like fun? What would you like to find out more about? What has always fascinated you? Make a note; put it in the file.

Keep Your File at Least a Month: Longer is better. Don't look in it. Just keep putting stuff in it. If you are surprised by anything, particularly delighted by something, or if something doesn't turn out the way you were expecting— these are all clues to what you might find interesting both now and later. Put a note in your file. Some of the best items are pictures that catch your eye. You don't have to know why it's interesting; just add it to the file.

Don't Try to Make Sense of It Right Away: Give yourself time. This is one of the most important secrets of creativity. Just add to your interest files; you don't have to explain or justify any item, or even make sense of it for now. You want to get as wide a sampling as possible of everything that gets your attention during the day. The items you select will represent the directions in which you are actively drawn, not the things that you are forced to do.

After a Few Weeks. Go Through Your Interest File. This is where it starts to be fun. Pull everything out that you have been collecting and spread it out on the floor. Arrange the items in piles. Sort all the items into groups. What interested you about that story? What was fascinating about this picture? Are they related? If you don't see any real groupings or patterns, put it all back and keep collecting for a few more weeks. Try again.

Give Names to Your Groupings: Begin to give some names to the interests you've assembled (examples: politics, nature, animals, religion, people, education, movies). You need a name for them, because it will help you focus on what your interests are. Make a list. Put it in order of things that interest you most, if you want to.

Compare Your Interest Groupings with Your Skill Groupings: Any similarities? Any differences? What important skills would you definitely include in your Personal Vision? What Interests?

3. SELF-REPORT OF TWO PERSONALITY DIMENSIONS

Read each item and then use the scale below to indicate how accurately the statement describes you. Write your answer in your Personal Vision notebook.

Not at all like me		Mostly not like me		Sometimes yes, Sometimes no		Somewhat like me		Exactly describes me	
1	2	3	4	5	6	7	8	9	10

1. At parties or in social groups, I like to seek out one person and talk to him or her.
2. People have a hard time knowing what I feel about things.
3. I would prefer reading a good book to going to a party.
4. I give a good deal of thought to things before I say them.
5. I have one or two very close friends, as opposed to a great many acquaintances.
6. I often initiate conversations with strangers when we are thrown together.
7. Sometimes I don't really know what I think about something until I talk it over with someone.
8. I find parties and social gatherings relaxing most of the time.
9. I like to work with others all day.
10. People usually know what I'm feeling.
11. I like working on my own particular projects.
12. It makes me nervous to delegate anything.
13. I don't like working on teams as well as I like working on my own project.
14. I have some specific areas of interest and expertise.
15. I have my own particular way of going about things.
16. When assigned a task, I try to figure out who can do it best.
17. I like working on a project with others. I'm a good team player.
18. It usually doesn't matter to me what part of a project I take, as long as I contribute to the overall goal.
19. It wouldn't matter too much to me to be transferred to another set of responsibilities.
20. I enjoy the thought of working with other people on a project.

To develop a score for yourself:

I.   Add your scores together for items 1-5, 6-10, 11-15 and 16-20 (four separate scores in all).

II.   Subtract each of the totals for items 1-5 and 11-15 from 50. Example: if your total for items 1-5 was 10, you would subtract this from 50, yielding a score of 40.

III.   Add the result (total for 1-5 subtracted from 50) to the score for 6-10. Add the other result (total for 11-15 (subtracted from 50) to your score for 16-20.

IV.   Your result for items 1-10 is for the introvert-extrovert dimension.

V.   Your result for items 11-20 is for the specialist-generalist dimension.

VI.   On the introvert-extrovert dimension, rate yourself as follows:

A. Score: 10-44, Introvert (Paragraph A below)

B. Score 45-65, Combination introvert-extrovert (Paragraph B below)

C. Score 66-100, Extrovert (Paragraph C below)

VII.   On the specialist-generalist dimension, rate yourself as follows:

A. Score 10-44, Specialist (Paragraph D below)

B. Score 45-65, Combination specialist-generalist (Paragraph E below)

C. Score 66-100, Generalist (Paragraph F below)

INTROVERT-EXTROVERT

Paragraph A: Introvert. As someone who exhibits Introversion, you get energy and renewal from time spent by yourself. You can learn to be quite adept at social situations and very skillful at handling interactions with others. You must always keep in mind that no matter how skillful you become, interactions with others will always seem an element of work. Long periods of social or business interaction, no matter how satisfying or enjoyable, will always leave you feeling somewhat drained.

On the positive side, Introverts are able to concentrate on tasks that require solitary effort for long periods of time without undue stress. You can handle social situations by learning to be skillful and adept with them, and this means you can be with other people with very little stress provided you allow yourself enough time alone to regenerate.

Paragraph B. Combination Introvert-Extrovert. You report some characteristics of Extroverts and some characteristics of Introverts. In general, this position on the scale means that you have more choice about your interpersonal environment.

You have a good intuitive and understanding of social situations and you enjoy interaction with other people. You are able to listen well to others and easily guess what they are feeling. On the other hand, you are able to be alone some of the time and enjoy this as well. You are able to concentrate on tasks that can only be done by one person. Obviously, the two sides of the scale are somewhat incompatible. You will probably find that you lean more in one direction than the other. However, your score indicates that you participate to some extent in both.

You will probably need to find a good balance in your life between being with others and being by yourself. If you are around people for extended periods, you will probably get some renewal by being alone. If you are alone for extended periods, you will probably find yourself wanting to be with others.

Paragraph C. Extrovert. You get energy from being with people and you like being around others through a good part of the day. If you were to get into a job that required you to be alone most of the time, or in which your interactions were so stereotyped that you could not really relate to others, you might well find it stressful and unsatisfying. The reason for this is that you would not be having enough contact with other people in the day.

You have excellent intuitive understanding of social situations and you enjoy interaction with other people. You are able to listen well to others and guess easily what they are feeling. Many people who exhibit Extroversion use interactions with other people to help them understand their own thoughts and feelings. Quite often, a thought or idea does not feel "real" to an Extrovert unless it has been shared with someone else. You will always be happier in a position if you have some way to interact with others.

SPECIALIST-GENERALIST

Paragraph D: Specialist. Specialists look at the world in a unique way. The Specialist will always see things somewhat differently from anyone else. This is a clear strength in the right setting, and with the right expectations. If you are expected (or expect yourself) to be part of the herd, or to come up with the "regular" response to problems, you will always be working against yourself. Your strength is that you may have a different slant on things and a different way of looking at things.

Being a Specialist affects how you perceive others and how you communicate. You tend to like the independence and autonomy that come with having total mastery of a body of knowledge or a skill of your own. Specialists often have clear ideas what they wish to accomplish, and work with dedication and personal commitment.

Paragraph E: Combination Specialist-Generalist. You report characteristics of both Specialists and Generalists. Specialists like coming up with original answers to most problems and making unique contributions. Generalists are expert in judging how others in a group respond and contribute. You may well be able to do both to some extent.

You probably enjoy being an expert and having an area of expertise that fascinates you. If you can make this part of your job, it can be of tremendous benefit to you. You are also able to work effectively with teams and groups. This dual characteristic can be extremely valuable in corporations. You can gain a definite position or specialty, but also work effectively in the team atmosphere needed in most business environments.

Paragraph F: Generalist. Generalists like to work with people and through people. The Generalist usually thinks in terms of the overall of the organization, rather than strictly in terms of his or her own specific area or job. A true Generalist can move easily from job to job, and often does, just as long as he or she is furthering the goals of the team. The Generalist does not constantly live and breathe the job, as the Specialist does. For the Generalist, the job is a tool, like a hammer, to be picked up and used for an end, and then laid aside when it is no longer needed.

Generalists like being part of a team. They are able to think broadly about the overall functioning of the organization, and not be so bound to one particular specialty. A Generalist can be willing for others to have their areas of specialty and expertise, because that can help the team. Whereas the Specialist operates through his own particular area of expertise, the Generalist operates through the group.

FOUR STORIES: SKILLS, INTERESTS AND PERSONALITY

Tracy

Skills: "I told a story about organizing a paper-recycling project at my high school when I was a freshman. The school, of course, produced reams of paper every day, and they just threw it into the landfill. I thought, 'We can do something about this.' I got about 10 or 12 people in my class to come over on several Saturdays and we made boxes. Then we got all the teachers to put paper in the boxes. Then we organized collection and got a recycling service to pick it all up. I've always done that kind of thing. I just look around and think, 'What needs to happen here?' and then set out to do it. I could have told a dozen other stories about things I did in high school and college. I think when I really feel passionately about something. I am good at finding other interests, too."

Interests: "I've always been interested in the natural world and the environment. The pictures and articles I cut out to put in my file were about everything under the sun, but they always kept coming back to animals, the environment, nature, science."

Personality: "I am half-extrovert and half-introvert. No surprise. I like people, but I like being by myself to think every once in a while, too. What was interesting was that I am a total specialist. There have always been some things that really interested me. What I enjoy most is going into those subjects totally. There are some subjects I've been interested in for years. I guess that's another reason I don't like my job very much at the law office. I just have to do whatever they tell me to; I don't ever get to have a project or something that's just mine."

Feelings now: "I'm getting more excited. I'm seeing more patterns here. I don't know where it's going yet, but I think it's going somewhere."

Brian and Janet

Brian's Skills: "When I was a kid, my mother would have garage sales. She always liked me to help her because I was so good at getting people to buy stuff. I could always find exactly the right thought to bring someone around who was wavering about buying. I enjoyed the puzzle: What does this person want? Hw can I say it so he will want to buy it?"

Interests: "My interests are mostly in people or sports. I like to read about people who are doing things. I like interesting ideas. It's intriguing to me to see a particularly well-done print ad. I like to scope out how it catches my attention, and then what it promises. I'm always interested in how you 'hook' people."

Personality: "I am a total extrovert and generalist. It's as though I was born knowing people and what makes them do what they do. Put me in a room full of people, and I'm not really happy until I have gotten around to all of them to find out what they think about things."

Feelings now: "Confident. It's amazing how much better I feel knowing how well my job fits me."

Janet's Skills: "The story I told was about doing a senior thesis in college. The school required a thesis for graduation, and most of the other seniors dreaded it. I got interested in the economics of political reform in nineteenth-century England. It was fascinating once I got into it. It combined a lot of different disciplines—history, politics, economics, law—and I had to learn about all of them. Then I had to turn it around and make it understandable to others. I had a great professor. He kept saying that I knew more about some of this than he did. I got high honors, and he said I should publish it."

Interests: "I really love detective novels. I probably read one or two a week. I like to figure them out before the hero does. I also like reading the news. I like to try to figure out what is really going on. When the president or the treasury secretary says something, I like to predict what the reaction will be in the press."

Personality: "I am a complete introvert, and half-specialist, half-generalist. The introvert part is right. I like people, but just one at a time. When I go home, I like to read a book. When I got my scores, I showed them to Brian and said, 'See, that's why I don't like to go around and talk to everyone every time we go out.' I like having one friend, or two. The specialist-generalist score is interesting. Maybe I would like my job better if I weren't feeling pulled in all different directions all the time."

Feelings now: "Very interested. This is fascinating—the same themes keep coming back from the different exercises. Hopeful."

Elizabeth

Skills: "My story was about my senior year in high school. I was president of three organizations and a member of about six others, including cheerleaders. I made good grades, too—almost straight A's. My story really wasn't about all those accomplishments. It was more about how I handled stress. My day was going to meetings, classes, talking to my friends, more meetings, study, talk to my friends, a little sleep. I don't remember feeling tired or stressed, but I can hear my mother's voice, 'Honey, you don't have to do everything.' I guess my life's always been the same. Too much to do. Always on the edge of falling apart."

Interests: "I'm interested in my child. I'm interested in day care. Almost everything in my interest file had to do with child rearing or day care for children.

There is so much that could be done with effective day care, but it is almost a total wasteland. Think of what really good day care would mean to lower-income families. I get so angry when I go to pick up Frederick, my son, because half the time he's just sitting in front of a television. It's not the day care's fault, though. They don't have any budget."

Personality: "In personality, I'm mostly a generalist and mostly an extrovert, I've always like working with people in groups. My managerial style is collegial. I like everyone on the team to take an active part in decision-making. I have to say, though, that things usually go the way I think they should. As a team, we've been working together for a long time. We don't have much wasted effort. We're the top producer in the division."

Feelings: "Hopeful. I feel everything I learn adds a new piece to a puzzle. I just want to see what the next piece will add."

Carl

Skills: "I told a story about volunteering at the Free Clinic at my church after I got laid off. For one day, they had me sorting out donated pills and bandages. Then they put me in charge of organizing the pharmacy. Now I'm organizing the whole volunteer schedule. It has always worked like that with me."

Interests: "I've gotten a lot more interested in my wife and two boys.

I have one son who will graduate from college this year, and another who is married and will have a child soon. Since I've been off work, I talk to my sons every week. I try to go over to see the one living in town. It's interesting to find out what they think about things. I'm also interested in the Free Clinic. I think that's a really worthwhile thing to do."

Personality: "*In personality, I'm a complete generalist and more extroverted than introverted. I like organizations and teams of people. I like working with them and getting them all moving in the same direction. I know I'm good at that."*

Feelings now: "*A little impatient. I am finding out a lot about myself, but it doesn't feel new or different. I still don't know where a job is going to come from."*

NEXT CHAPTER: In the next chapter, we start to give your Personal Vision more coherence. Your natural talents are the foundation. Your skills, interests and personality lend it substance and structure. But your values and goals give real life and direction to your Personal Vision.

WHAT BLOCKED **ANNE** WAS HER
FAILURE TO LOOK INSIDE,
TO EXPRESS WHAT WOULD BE
MOST MEANINGFUL
TO HER.

ALL OF HER GOALS WERE SET UP
BY HER SYSTEMS.

SHE **NEVER STOPPED TO
QUESTION** THEM OR
DECIDE HOW THEY MATCHED
UP WITH HER
**PROFOUNDEST
BELIEFS.**

Values & Goals

"To be able to manage yourself, you finally have to ask, "What are my values?"

— *Peter Drucker, Harvard Business Review, 2005*

While the objective factors of natural talent, skills, experience and personality form the substrate on which to grow a Personal Vision, subjective factors such as interests, values and goals really animate it. In the last chapter, we saw how to begin capturing and using the drive and creativity that come with your interests and passions. In this chapter, we talk about how values and goals give your Personal Vision direction and purpose.

In the process of creating a Personal Vision, identifying your values and goals propels the difficult leap from the Stress cycle to the Balance Cycle. You may remember from Chapter 2 that the Stress Cycle is outer-directed, motivated by wealth and status, focused on short-term issues, and reactive. In the Stress Cycle, you never stop; you just jump through the next hoop before you. To be in the Balance Cycle, you must have an interior sense of who you are and what you want in life. In order to grapple with your values and goals, you must look at your life from the inside and find out what directs and motivates your energy and what gives your life meaning.

With values and goals, you must also look at time. This chapter examines two different kinds of time: the time you live in now and the future time you plan for. With values, the time you spend every day living out your immediate life determines how "in sync" you feel with yourself. When you deal with your goals, however, you need to look into the future—10 and even 20 years ahead.

A Question of Values

Values are one of the most common sources of stress for people between the ages of 38 and 45. Increasingly, as we reach the invisible mid-point of our lives, as we start looking ahead and seeing limits, we start wondering if what we do all day long is worth doing.

Most people do not face this question while they are raising children. The time, energy and money spent in launching children into the world seem well spent to most people. By midlife, though, people can see the end of raising children. The question arises, what now? What will be equally worth my energy and time?

This is a not a trivial question. Answering it can prolong your life, increase your joy and energy, and move you a long way toward meaning—that ineffable commodity that separates the living from the waiting–to-die. Even the business world, ever concerned with the bottom line, has begun to recognize that employees who pay attention to their values are more productive. When people's minds and hearts are involved in what they do, they perform more fully. They are more involved in their lives and work.

Companies that emphasize value-building among their employees are more apt to survive adversity. Also, they are much more apt to avoid the tangles and webs that destroyed such companies as Enron. Corporate values manifest themselves in good customer relations and in care for the company product.

Anne's Story

Anne, 45, was an executive in an international public relations firm. She started with this firm after college and moved steadily upward. She transferred from the New York office to the San Francisco office and achieved a number of prominent successes. She was "second chair" on the new business team—the vital group of high performers that routinely made pitches to new clients. Anne was married, with two children. One would start college next fall, and the other would follow the next year.

"I couldn't imagine doing anything else. Everything seemed to be going just the way I had planned when I was 25. I liked my job. I could see a path upward. I liked the other people I worked with."

Something had been nagging at her, but she could not articulate what, "I basically just wanted to see if I was missing anything or if there were some other way to go about my career. I knew I wanted something, but I didn't know what."

Anne took our seminar to gain a Personal Vision. She quickly discovered why she was so successful in her role in public relations. An extrovert and a specialist, she was a natural performer who liked painting vivid, compelling pictures of the world as she saw it for clients, bringing them in and letting them see it the way she did. With high Classification and high Concept Organization, she was able, in flashes of insight, to understand and overcome a prospective client's objections to a pitch. Then, using an inexorable tide of logic, she turned the client to her point of view. For her, public relations was a perfect fit.

In the course of discovery, Anne examined influences from her family of origin. (We will talk about how to work with your family of origin in the next chapter.) Her mother and father had been missionaries. She had lived a large part of her first 14 years in China. Anne had absorbed an important value as a child, powerfully communicated by both of her parents: *"You should give something back to the world."*

Her parents did not present this value as a mere homily. When she interviewed her mother and father, Anne discovered that her father, shortly after marrying, had spent two or three years working for a bank as a manger-trainee. He was dissatisfied, though, and at age 25 entered a seminary. He was assigned to a small church, but applied to be a missionary because he felt the need was greater. He and his family moved to China when Anne was only two years old. He felt that quitting the bank and embarking on this risky venture that never paid him quite enough, had made his life feel more vibrant and worthwhile.

Hearing her father and mother's story, some of it for the first time, put many of Anne's nagging doubts into sharper focus. *"Public relations was right for me, but I started to see how helping large clients sell more product was not going to be enough. I want to feel that I am contributing more actively to society."*

Some months after completing work on her Personal Vision, a memo came across Anne's desk. An international relief agency was looking for someone to be director of public relations. Pay was roughly half of what Anne took home from her present job. *"Normally, I would ignore a memo like this. If someone I knew were looking for a job, I would pass it along. Otherwise, it would go into the trash can."*

This time she didn't throw it away. "As soon as I saw it I began thinking about giving something back to the world and how important that had become to me. I went home and discussed it with my husband. We thought that with my savings from bonuses over the years we would not have a difficult time putting our kids through college. Otherwise, our two salaries should be fine."

Anne applied for and got the job. She is now director of public relations for the relief agency and routinely travels all over the globe. "I'm now doing work that is inherently meaningful. It makes use of all of my abilities and my experience and skills. It makes everything I've done up to now make sense."

To make values work for you, you must compare your strongest values— what you personally hold most meaningful in life—to how you actually spend your time. That is what Anne did.

Like many people, Anne had never taken the time to articulate clearly her most important values. Articulating values requires a disconcerting shift of focus from the outside to the inside. Anne, like most people her age, had spent the majority of her career jumping through hoops. She had gone after a college degree, a good job, a better position, more pay, a path to the executive suite. Each of these goals had focused her entire attention and energy outside of herself.

Let us be clear. None of the hoops had Anne jumped through were wrong in and of themselves. What had blocked Anne was her failure to look inside to express what would be most meaningful for her. All of her goals were set by her systems. She never stopped to question them or decide how they matched up with her most profound beliefs. She was a victim of the Lemming Conspiracy.

For Anne, the trip inward started when she interviewed her parents. As we shall see in Chapter 7, there are many positive reasons for interviewing your parents. Without question, it is one of the most powerful things you can do for yourself as an adult. Our values originate in our families of origin. We absorb them fully before we even start school. The most important values are the ones our parents live out—not the values they speak to us in words. This holds equally true for yourself—your important values are the ones you live out in the actions of your life.

You can clarify your values initially without your family of origin. The Though Experiment at the end of this chapter will help you articulate the values that most strongly direct your life. Then you can use that information to see how your priorities match up with how you spend your time.

What troubled Anne was that when she did articulate her most important values, she realized she hadn't invested any time in living them out. In working with values, we start by establishing priorities. What is your most important value? What is next?

The critical and difficult question comes next: How do you spend your time? How do you actually live your days? A value, even a clearly held one, feels fundamentally hollow unless you act upon it in real time in your real life. The second part of the exercise in the Thought Experiment helps you compare your most important values with how you spend your time.

Having a fundamental value that inspires you to live a healthy life and take care of your body may be important to living a balanced life. But having this value will do nothing unless you translate it into time and action. If you have health as a primary value, but don't spend any time in exercise, you create a continual disjunction that makes you one of the "hollow men" of the modern world, people who live lives of no meaning to themselves.

In his persuasive article on Managing Yourself, Peter Drucker recommends that we all need to apply the "mirror test" to ourselves when we wake up in the morning. If we are honest with ourselves, the test will tell us whether we are pursuing the values and ethical standards we have set for ourselves. It may also tell us whether the organization we're working for reflects those same values and standards. If it doesn't, we will feel stress and strain during every work day.

Companies that encourage the development of values in their employees perform better. Two recent Harvard studies reported by the *New York Times* showed, for example, that companies that had developed strong relationships with their shareholders outperformed other companies in both sales and profits.

In coming to grips with values, we have begun to accumulate enough objective and subjective information to begin to move from stress to balance.

In the next section we show how goals form the concrete stepping stones leading out of the Stress Cycle and into the Balance Cycle. Goals create this path only if you link them to all of the information, objective and subjective, you have been gathering about yourself. Once again, as with values, time is the medium through which goals move.

Whose Goals? Yours or Your Systems?

The Lemming Conspiracy insidiously blinds us to the difference between our systems' goals and our own goals. In the story above, Anne felt absolutely sure she was charting her own course in life. She had a plan, she was following it and she was on schedule. The nagging doubts she felt at odd moments didn't stop her. In fact, nothing stopped her. As we have seen, stopping is the one thing the Lemming Conspiracy will not let you do. The Lemming Conspiracy keeps you grinding away at the Stress Cycle without ever looking up to see what else you may want to do with your life.

Anne assumed her goals were her own. But when she examined these assumptions, she realized that her goals had nothing to do with her most deeply held values. She had left that part of the equation out. Her goals did not reflect who she really was.

As it happened, Anne's goals were a close match for her natural abilities. They took into account her many skills and interests, as well as capitalizing on her interpersonal style. In many ways, Anne's goals fit perfectly, but in one crucial area they missed. In this section, we will talk about how to match your goals to what you know about yourself. The closer you match your goals to every aspect of yourself and what you want out of life, the closer you move toward a Personal Vision and the Balance Cycle.

We designed the Thought Experiments at the end of this chapter to help you articulate your goals. What do you want to accomplish in the next five years? Ten years? Expand your goals beyond the limits of work. Your life is bigger than work. What do you want to accomplish in regard to your family? Your friends? Your spiritual life? Your physical self? All of these critical elements enliven and enrich your life just as much, or at times more, than work. Later, as you move toward integration, the difference between your own goals and your systems' goals becomes increasingly apparent.

Over time, you may change some of your goals, eliminate some of them, or add others. It is important to start where you are now. Don't expect yourself to get to answers on the first try. We know from experience that you can't create a Personal Vision from logic alone. There are too many competing pieces to this puzzle. Attempting to pin down your goals is an important preliminary step to the creative work of integrating a Personal Vision.

Goals That Can Be Achieved — One Way Out of the Stress Cycle

Goals are the smaller way stations on the path to a Personal Vision. But some goals can keep you fixed in the Stress Cycle, while other goals can move you away from stess and toward the Balance Cycle. As you might imagine, goals that originate in your systems keep you enmeshed in the Stress Cycle. Goals that originate from you create stepping stones toward a more balanced life.

"I want to be comfortable financially." "I want to be healthy." "I want to be a good father." These sound like fine goals; it's hard to argue with any of them. But as stated, they are not goals at all. They are really more like value statements — a statement about what is important to you. As goals, however, they don't work, because they are endless.. They must be more clear to help you. To articulate goals that work better for you, you have to understand: 1) how to know when a goal is reached, and 2) your time frame for finishing it.

SETTING GOALS YOU CAN ACCOMPLISH

For the goals we've begun to identify, what does "comfortable" mean? How much money? When? What does "healthy" translate to in terms of behavior? How many workouts per week? How long? Or what does it mean in terms of blood pressure or cholesterol level? By when? What does "good father" mean for you? Time with your children? How much? How often? How will you know you have succeeded?

Goals are tricky. We tend to feel that once we name a goal, we're done with it. When you deal with goals that may or may not actually be your systems' goals, it is trickier still. One way to recognize a goal that is your systems' rather than your own, is to understand that you won't know when you achieve it.

As an example, look at the goal of being financially comfortable. This is a worthy goal, and an important one for anyone in our society. But what does it mean? For most people, there is no end point to this goal. It just means more:

more money, bigger house, better car, better job. This is a system goal. It pins you to the Stress Cycle.

To make it your goal instead of your systems', you have to translate it into concrete terms for your own life. What are you going to use your money for? Retirement, house, car, education for your children, security? You can allocate an amount of money to each. You can figure out how much and what is enough.

Next, you need to think about when you will need your money. When will you retire? When do your children need educational money? These questions may sound obvious and trivial, but they are not. Most people do not ever bother to figure out what is enough money. As a result, most are like rats on a treadmill, endlessly running and never getting anywhere.

As we saw earlier in Anne's story, a critical piece of her being able to do what she wanted to do with her life was sitting down with her husband and figuring out what money they needed to accomplish their goals. Before she did this, she had never considered the question, "What would be enough?" But without this step, she would never have made the change she made without feeling anxious about it. As it happened, figuring out and agreeing with her husband on what amount of income would be enough for them was an enormously freeing act. It allowed her to pursue her Personal Vision and change her life for the better.

GOALS AND TIME

The second part of making a goal yours instead of your systems' is putting it on a time line. You have to know not only what you want to accomplish, but when. In the Thought Experiment, you will see an example of a time line. There are only two ways to move with time: forward and backward. In thinking about goals, it is often useful to go backwards. Start with what you want to accomplish. Put it on the time line – one year, three years, five years. Then fill in the time to the goal. 'In order to accomplish this, what else will I need to accomplish? When?' Put that on the time line. As you keep working on your time line, it can become an important working document to guide your career. It should never be static. To make it live and breathe, refer to it; update it; add to it. This can become an important part of the written plan for your life.

Systems' Goals vs. Goals That Integrate

Another sure sign that your systems are imposing your goals is that the goals are one-dimensional. "I want to earn $5,000,000 before I'm 50." You know when you want to accomplish it. But is it a system goal, or yours?

It is totally one-dimensional. If a client were to state a goal like this, we would ask, "Why?" The answer might have something to do with power, prestige or things he or she could buy. These are outer-directed goals that leave people in the Stress Cycle. They don't lead anywhere and don't really have anything to do with the inner person, only with his or her systems.

On the other hand, the answer could have something to do with security, children or the ability to tackle a lifelong ambition. This is better. People who answer with these motives are at least thinking about themselves and what they want from their lives. But in that case, the goal becomes security, or having adequate money to educate children, rather than earning $5,000,000 before 50. If you address the motives for your goals, you will go a lot further toward moving yourself out of the Stress Cycle.

We talked to a lawyer once, the founding partner of a successful corporate law firm. He stated his goals this way: "I have spent nearly 60 years amassing a fortune. In a few years, I'll retire, and my goal is to spend it." This lawyer has one of the finest strategic minds in the field. He has made his fortune because he is so adept at keeping his clients out of the very kind of trap into which he has fallen himself. He is a victim of the Lemming Conspiracy. He told us in the same interview that he particularly enjoys working late on Saturday night because no one is in the office to bother him. He is in the Stress Cycle, and his goal will not help him out. His whole universe is defined by his role as a lawyer. If he is not that, what is he?

Truth to tell -- many things. But he won't know them unless he breaks out of the Lemming Conspiracy.

Ideally, all of your goals should relate directly to all or most of the important factors of your life. For instance, as you define what security means for you, how does it relate to your abilities, interests and personality? How does it relate to your skills and experience? How does it relate to your values? To help you see how all of these factors work together with a person's goals, let us tell you about a young woman with a fairly specific goal—she wanted a job within six months.

Ruth's Story

Ruth had been a buyer of women's clothes for a department store chain for five years when a bigger chain of stores bought her company and she lost her job through restructuring. She had not liked her job very much, finding it stressful and unrewarding, so she wanted a job in a new field. She had no idea where or how to start looking.

Ruth had enough money to last for six months without going too deeply into her savings. At the beginning, her goal was simple and straightforward: Get a job, any good job that paid about the same as she had been making, but in a different field, before her savings cushion ran out.

As she found out more about herself, her goals changed. She discovered natural artistic talents of which she had been previously unaware. She also discovered much about her previous job that she liked and that suited her well. She liked the travel and make contact with people; she also enjoyed working with different kinds of fabric and cloth. She had always been fascinated by fabric, and had for a time thought about becoming an artist in cloth and natural fiber. She didn't think she could make enough money with his kind of work, however. One aspect of her previous job she did not like was the boring kinds of cloth and clothing she was required to handle. As you might imagine, she discovered she was specialist, so her interest and fascination with cloth made more sense to her. Her dissatisfaction and discomfort in the large organization she had been working for also made more sense.

So her goal became more specific: she wanted a job in an artistic field, with a small company, or perhaps with an individual, that involved working with specialized cloth, and that made use of the skills and experience acquired as a buyer. This goal related strongly to her Personal Vision, and encompassed several critical factors she had discovered and wanted to express in her life.

Ruth used a process we call Surveying to make her goal real. We will discuss Surveying in more detail in Chapter 9, and we will talk in detail about how Ruth carried out her Survey project.

In Surveying over four months, Ruth received three job offers that fully met her first criteria: good job, decent pay, different field. But she knew they didn't match her goals. They would not satisfy her in the long run. She turned down all three and pressed on with her Survey. She found this surprisingly easy.

Ruth finally connected with an architect who had an interior design studio. He wanted a person to buy unusual and artistic cloth from Italy and France for those clients who wanted something different in their homes. He had been looking for someone to do this for almost a year. Ruth got the job in one interview because she could tell the architect, in detail, exactly how her goals, interests, fascinations, skills, experience and personality worked together to make her perfect for what he wanted her to do. She took this job and is still happily buying cloth.

Ruth's story illustrates several principles we feel are crucial.

1. *The best answers—the ones that lead to the greatest satisfaction in the end— come from inside you.* No counselor – no matter how well educated, supported by no matter how many tests – could have advised Ruth to seek and find the job she ended up with. No one else could possibly know enough about her to give her this advice. Her previous employer could not know; an outplacement service could not know; a career counselor could not know. But Ruth knew. It was always inside her; it just needed a structured process to bring it out and make it plain to Ruth herself. (Although the answers need to come from within you, they will come faster and more easily in an interpersonal environment in which no other participant has a personal investment in your decisions.)

2. *Self-inquiry provides the best definitions and lays out the most direct and efficient route to finding a satisfying job or a satisfying fit in your present job.* Many people feel or act as though looking at themselves would be a waste of time in the practical business of finding the right job or the right fit. Not only is self-investigation the most efficient way to proceed, but it can help you avoid wasting time in pursuits that don't fit you at all.

3. *If you create a clear goal that includes enough insight into yourself, and keep that goal in front of you as a target, you can generally find what you are looking for.* Reread Ruth's story above. Until she articulated a clear enough goal, she couldn't find the right job. Once she had stated her rather definite goals, though, she was in fact able to come up with a job that met almost all of them.

4. *By creating a Personal Vision and using it as a template, you can know clearly which opportunities to accept and which to turn down.* One of the most freeing aspects of creating a clear Personal Vision is to be able to know clearly what does not fit. No matter how attractive a promotion or a project may look, if it doesn't fit you and your Personal Vision, then maybe it's part of the Lemming Conspiracy, the Stress Cycle, and is not something you really want to touch. The other side of this is equally important. With a Personal Vision, you know immediately when you run across an opportunity that you want to jump on.

Ruth's initial goal—find a job, any job—was a product of the Stress Cycle and would undoubtedly trap her in it. By the time she had turned down three jobs that met her first criteria, she knew more clearly what she wanted and how that was different from what her systems would have chosen for her. Ruth's Personal Vision, and the goals she developed out of it, allowed her to break the Stress Cycle and move toward the Balance Cycle.

Thought Experiment E:

Values and Goals

1. YOUR VALUES AND YOUR TIME

How can you know what's important to you? How can you know if you are out of sync?

Go to the values lists below. Read over the entire list.

Start with the Priority list. Think about the importance of each of the values on the list. What are the most important ones from your point of view? What values do not seem as important?

Now number the values, 1, for those that are most important to you; 2, for those that are next, and so on until you have numbered the entire list of 16 values from the most to the least important.

Values List—Priorities

(number from 1-16 according to your own priority)

_____ Security

_____ Monetary Success

_____ Family

_____ Position

_____ Wisdom

_____ Health

_____ Stability

_____ Productivity and Competence

_____ Creative and Artistic Work

_____ Spiritual Fulfillment

_____ Authority and Decision-Making

_____ Excitement

_____ Innovation

_____ Physical Challenge

_____ Friendship

_____ Change and Variety

Now go to the Time list. Carefully go through your calendar for the last two months and count up the hours you spent directly working toward each of the values on the Time list. If you spend 10 hours at work each day, for instance, you might count this toward monetary success, position, authority and/or security, but it would probably not go to family, health or spiritual fulfillment. Now rank the values on the Time list according to your Time, Energy and Focus, with 1 being the value toward which you put the most of your actual time, energy and focus, down to 16, where you put the least.

Values List—Time

(put number of hours spent directly working on each in last month, rank according to time, energy and focus, 1-16)

_____ Security
_____ Monetary Success
_____ Family
_____ Position
_____ Wisdom
_____ Health
_____ Stability
_____ Productivity and Competence
_____ Creative and Artistic Work
_____ Spiritual Fulfillment
_____ Authority and Decision-Making
_____ Excitement
_____ Innovation
_____ Physical Challenge
_____ Friendship
_____ Change and Variety

Compare the two lists—what you consider your priorities versus where you put your actual time, energy and focus.

If your high priority values (1, 2 or 3 on your priority list) are low on your time/energy/focus list (13, 14 or 15 on your time/energy/focus list), this causes stress. This lack of inner direction, of course, is a major function of the Stress Cycle.

In the same way, if your low priority values (13, 14 or 15 on your priority list), are high on your time/energy/focus values list (1, 2 or 3 on the time/energy/focus list) this also signals disjunction in inner directedness, and also causes stress. Again, as you get older, the stress increases.

Stress due to disjunction between what you hold meaningful and how you actually live your life tends to force itself into consciousness for the first time at the Midlife Transition (age 38-45). However, young people feel this stress, too, even if they are not paying attention to it. The sooner people pay attention to their values and work to bring them in sync with their daily routines, the more alive, productive and enthusiastic they tend to feel about their work.

2. PLACING YOUR GOALS IN TIME

First of all, write down all the goals you can think of in your Personal Vision notebook. Near goals, far goals, personal goals, work goals, family goals, health goals, money goals. Don't worry about grouping them yet.

When you have a significant number of goals covering different aspects of your life and career and different times in the future, start grouping them. Connect ones that go together, creating subsets within categories. You may find that you have a few large goals and that many of the others are smaller goals leading to the larger ones.

In your Personal Vision notebook, draw a line. At the beginning of the line, put your age now. At the end, put 100. Now fill in your Turning Points, every 10 years between the age you are now and 100. Mark ages 22, 40, 60 and 80 with heavy lines, as they tend to be major transition points for most people. Some people use a large poster for this exercise; some people tape several sheets of paper together to create a large fold out in their Personal Vision notebooks. Feel free to create your time line in any way that makes it come alive for you.

Place your major goals on the line at the age you wish to attain them. Feel free to be as creative with this as you want—it's your career and your time line. Put pictures on your time line if you want to, draw diagrams, use colors. Your line doesn't even have to be straight. If you want hills, valleys, circles or spirals, put them in.

After you have your major goals on the time line, fill in the smaller, intermediate goals. Again, let yourself have some freedom to create. Fill up your sheet with goals and connect them to a time line.

As you continue with your exploration and work on your Personal Vision, you might find that you want to change some of your goals, add new goals or take some goals out altogether. You may find that after you have done the creative Thought Experiments in Chapter 8, you want to do another time line, taking more of your life into account. The main task is to create a working document that you will be able to use and refer to as you make your Personal Vision real.

FOUR STORIES: VALUES AND GOALS

Tracy

Value: "*The values were interesting. My highest values were productivity, excitement, innovation and change. My lowest were security, money, position and stability. All of my time, though, is spent holding down a job that's exactly the same drudgery day after day just so I can earn enough money to live on. I'm pursuing my very lowest values with all my time and energy. It's no wonder I feel so discouraged.*"

Goals: "*My most immediate goal is to figure out what I'm going to do next. I've given myself three months. I need to get out of my job at the law firm yesterday. Even more than that, I need to be aiming in some direction that will yield some of the excitement and change I want so badly. I want to be involved with what I do.*"

Feeling now: "*Determined. Confident. I know more what I'm looking for.*"

Brian and Janet

Brian's Values: "*My strongest values were monetary success, family, competence and decision-making authority. My weakest were artistic work spiritual fulfillment, physical challenge and health. I guess I would rather watch a game on television with a gang of friends than run or exercise. When I look at my time and energy, it looks about the same, with the exception of family. Family is one of my highest values, but I don't put any time into it at all. That bothers me. The health one being on the bottom bothers me, too. I guess I'm just taking health for granted.*"

Goals: "My goals are these: make the million-dollar club this spring, get at least two older executives to know who I am and be interested in my career, and be in the fast-track pool by next spring."

Feelings now: "Thoughtful, I wonder why I don't want to spend any time or energy toward family."

Janet's Values: "My highest values: family, security, money and stability in that order. I would also put friendship in the highest group. Lowest: position, authority, physical challenge and change. I think family is really the number-one priority for me, but when I look at my time, it's totally different. I don't put any time into family. I just work to make money, so that's in line, I guess. But I don't care at all about promotions and getting more authority. I look at the people in charge, and they seem a lot more stressed than I am. They certainly don't seem happy."

Goals: "Have a family, get a different job or else quit entirely."

Feelings now: "Kind of trapped. Maybe a little confused about what I want."

Brian: "I notice how different we are on our goals. I'm totally focused on work. We both want to have a good lifestyle, and we both feel that family is important. As far as family goes, neither one of us is putting much time into it right now. I don't feel I will ever be able to put much time into it and still reach my goals. So I guess it's nice that it's so important to Janet, because she can sort of make up for me."

Janet: "I'm glad to see that Brian and I have some of the same values. I really see how important family is for me, and how we're not doing anything about it right now. That's sort of worrisome to me."

Elizabeth

Values: "My top values: family, stability, spiritual fulfillment and friendship. I can tell you right now, I'm not putting my time into any of these. They are all pretty much at the end of my time list. My bottom values: monetary success, position, excitement and variety. These are what I put my time into. My life is upside down. I have been working, working, working for all the things that I value least. What I value most barely gets any of my actual time."

Goals: "Change this situation. Now. Immediately. I just don't exactly know how. My only option seems to be to quit, and I am not going to do that—yet."

Feelings now: "Mad, Determined."

Carl

"My primary values are family, wisdom, health, position—in that order. Lowest on the list (but not unimportant, certainly) are excitement, innovation, creative and artistic work and physical challenge. I am spending more time with my wife, and it is very rewarding. I talk to my children regularly. It makes me think about what I missed while I worked so hard for my company. The same with health. I am working out regularly for the first time since college. Maybe this will all make me a little wiser. Actually, the only thing missing from my top values is position, of which I have none, of course. I do work on it every day, but it's discouraging to think that I may have to take less pay and benefits than I had before. One thing I think about is that I don't want to get back into a rat race when I take a new position. I don't exactly know how I would pull that off, but I feel better now than I have in years. I'm closer to my wife, and closer to my children. I don't want that to go away."

Goals: "Get a new job. Soon. I'm beginning to think, though, not just any job I can find. I want it to be one that fits me."

Feelings now: "I can see what I was missing before. I don't want to make the same mistake again. I'm afraid that if I get back into a job, the same force that drove me to work 60-hour weeks will drive me to do that again. To tell the truth, sometimes I don't really want to go back."

> NEXT CHAPTER: In the next chapter, we talk about the final factor you need before integrating all of them into a Personal vision: your family of origin. Just as the Lemming Conspiracy begins in the family of origin, so the family provides by far the greatest energy for breaking out of it. By understanding your family of origin's impact and working with it in a structured way, you may have your best tool for moving your life to the Balance Cycle.

OUR PARENTS'
KEY DECISIONS AT
TURNING POINTS FORM
THE **MODEL** FOR HOW WE MAKE
DECISIONS AT TURNING POINTS.

UNDERSTANDING THE
HOW AND WHY
OF OUR PARENTS' DECISIONS
CAN HELP US START TO LIVE
OUR OWN LIVES INSTEAD OF
RELIVING OUR
PARENTS' LIVES.

Family of Origin

We spend the first 30 years of our lives figuring out the impact of our family of origin and then the next 30 years becoming ourselves.

There is no more powerful influence on our lives than the family into which we were born and in which we grew up. We form our personalities here, largely before age six. We learn our sense of limits here. We learn what work is and how people go about it. So much of what we learn in the family is unconscious that it is sometimes difficult to know the extent of its influence. Most of our learning about systems takes place as children, and as adults we conveniently forget most of what happened before age six. While we may have no recollection of exactly what we learned, the lessons become part of our emotional and social DNA. Many studies have focused on the relationship between the family of origin and personal and career development. What we have added in our work is the recognition that the family of origin is one of eight integrated factors that need to be studied and tied together to reveal the individual's complexity.

Psychologists may sometimes blame parents or families for much of what's wrong. We have never found this approach to be particularly productive. Figuring out what positive things you learned in your family, finding out what makes you unique, and, most of all, asking how your parents made key decisions at Turning Points in their lives – all this moves you into new territory. This new information transforms you and your systems.

Our parents' key decisions at Turning Points form the model for how we make decisions at Turning Points. Understanding the how and why of our parents' decisions can help us start to live our own lives instead of reliving our parents'.

Our parents are the source of the most valuable information we can have about ourselves, but tapping into that information requires particular effort. Normally, a great deal of the most significant information in families is not recognized. It is "understood," or it doesn't seem as significant as it really is. Often, our roles in our families come to take precedence over our individual selves. It may be more important for you to be "father" than to be your own living person, with hopes, fears, inconsistencies, mistakes, ambitions and ambivalence. Families often don't know how to talk about the most important matters because they never get much practice. It's not through any conscious withholding, but merely from force of habit. We have taught thousands of people in our programs how to return to their families of origin and find out some of the most fascinating and significant information they will ever discover. You can go back, too. Remember, you are not out to delve into the deep recesses of a parent's psyche. You don't have to fear the unraveling of complicated relationships. Your prime interest is in the work roles your family members have filled and in their reactions to these roles.

In a recent workshop, we encountered Lisa, a young and successful 29-year old businesswoman. She had been abandoned by her father and raised by a disturbed mother. She rebelled at the exercise that would take her back to this unsettling history. Everything she knew she had taught herself. What benefit could she possibly get from revisiting all that? But forced to draw a family genogram, she suddenly focused on her grandfather, her mother's father, and she was struck by his importance to her life. A simple tailor in the garment industry, his reputation for measuring and making fine men's suits had spread far and wide. His customers were bankers and lawyers. Most of all, he was known for his attention to detail and his meticulous work habits.

To this day, Lisa recalled, her grandfather comments on the clothes people wear. At family gathering, he will tell his nephews and grandchildren that their suits are badly made, that they don't fit, that they're cut badly.

Lisa was now able to draw a parallel between her grandfather's life and her own. She realized that what made her exceptional at her work was her attention to detail and her ability to see fine shadings of a problem. Unknowingly, she had incorporated her grandfather into herself. This new insight turned her dismay and embarrassment at the beginning of the family exercise into recognition, satisfaction and pride.

Families of Origin and the Lemming Conspiracy

If the Lemming Conspiracy exists in the family of origin, the family of origin can also help us escape it. As we saw in Chapter One, our family systems form the model for all future systems in our lives. We learn how to make decisions at critical junctures in our lives, and we learn how to handle such normal aspects of living as work, disappointment, success, the future, balance, and even families themselves. None of this learning is conscious. In Chapter 1 we spoke of the psychological process of identification. We absorb our parents, and they remain part of our social and emotional selves forever. That's what allows us to function and succeed in the world. This unspoken influence on our emotional and social lives is far more valuable and pervasive than all spoken messages combined in terms of our ability to live our lives. But identification with our parents is also what leads us to make errors at Turning Points—decisions about our careers that keep us enmeshed in the Lemming Conspiracy.

Mitchell's Story, continued

We met Mitchell in Chapter 1. He had worked in a large technology firm, but found a much better fit for himself in a smaller, more entrepreneurial company. Before he did his family-of-origin work, Mitchell unknowingly repeated important decisions his father had made 25 years earlier.

When his father was 30, exactly the same age Mitchell was when he felt so dissatisfied, he worked for a large insurance company. Also dissatisfied, his father wanted desperately to start this own business. But he was newly married and had a small child, Mitchell. After much anguish and soul-searching, he decided he could not make this jump. It was too risky. He continued with the insurance company, buried his feelings, and soldiered on.

But the dissatisfaction came back 10 years later, stronger than ever. When Mitchell's father was 41, he decided to start his own entrepreneurial business. Mitchell remembers this time in the family's life. There was never enough money. His father was never home. His mother exuded stress and anger. Mitchell left for college, and his father continued the business for four more years. But it was never successful and eventually failed. To support his family, Mitchell's father went to work in the insurance agency of an old friend.

Mitchell's father never escaped the Lemming Conspiracy. He ignored his feelings when he was Mitchell's age and kept working for the large insurance company. At midlife, he made a precipitous jump for which he was unprepared in terms of capital, experience or personality. It was not quite a disaster for the family, but close. He ended up in a job he did not like, far more stuck than he was before and with an even more limited view of his options.

Even though he didn't know it, Mitchell had absorbed all of this as a child. As a 30-year-old man with a young family, working for a large international company, Mitchell was successful. Thoughts of starting a business of his own also came to him, and he also rejected them as too risky. He felt trapped and stuck—much like his father at the same age.

At this point, instead of swallowing his feelings, Mitchell began to build on the Eight Personal Vision Factors and to create a Personal Vision. He has this to say about his interviews with his father: "It was like a door opening. My father's telling me how he had struggled and suffered with this decision was like looking into my own life. I could see that I was set to make exactly the same mistakes that he had—and regretted. It was interesting because his advice was: "Don't leave your company." But when I asked him to tell his story and describe why he decided to do what he did, it was clear that he had seen only two options: leave or stay. His advice to me was to stay. It was well-meaning and based on his experience of the world, but it was from the same either/or point of view that he had seen in his own life. Once I realized that, the clouds began to clear and I decided that there was probably another middle way that he just hadn't considered. Incidentally, it also helped to know that there were reasons I wanted to leave my company and go to a smaller one. It wasn't just some ego-driven, arbitrary wish on my part. It had to do with my natural abilities, personality and interests. There were some objective reasons why the fit in my job wasn't right. So in that sense, I had an advantage my father didn't."

Mitchell ended up in a smaller, entrepreneurial, technology firm. He could make full use of the skills and experience acquired in his previous job, but expand into other areas of interest and take on more roles than he would have been able to otherwise. He had at least as much security as he had at the larger company. Even though he did not earn quite as much as before, he felt the new company afforded more long-range potential. For Mitchell it was a good compromise. He had beaten the Lemming Conspiracy.

Mitchell's feelings were almost identical to those of his father at the same age. In all likelihood, he would have made the same decision, and for the same reasons, as his father had at that age. And it would probably have been as big a mistake for Mitchell as it had been for his father. Mitchell had absorbed his father's limited point of view without realizing it. If he had not asked his father specifically what life decisions he had made and why, Mitchell would have continued operating from the same point of view.

Mitchell's story exemplifies all of our lives. We take our worldview from one or the other of our parents—even when we consciously want to do anything but. All of us absorb information from both parents. However, we tend to have a worldview and feelings very much like those of one or the other parent—often the parent of the same sex as ourselves. When we change and grow in life, we tend to broaden our behavior and perspective. Often this widening of viewpoint involves allowing information from the other parent to emerge.

When Mitchell took the time to ask and listen to his father talk about his life, many things changed. It was as if he could see his father for the first time. This was not "father", but a person – a person who had been a young man once, just like Mitchell. A person who had been anxious and depressed at times – who had a young family that he wasn't sure he could take care of, who didn't know what the future would bring, and who just took his best shots at life's decisions and hoped they were the right ones.

Just as he was able to see that he and his father were a lot alike and had many similar thoughts and concerns, Mitchell also saw that they were different. One advantage Mitchell enjoyed was that he knew more clearly what he wanted. For another, he saw that he didn't need to be bound any longer by his father's either/or point of view. This freed him to make decisions different from those of his father.

Going Against Systems—How the Family of Origin Helps

We all live in systems and will continue to do so. No system will voluntarily change. It will keep flowing in the same circular channel— and keep channeling its members into the same roles—unless it is dragged, kicking and screaming, into a new channel by someone inside it.

It is obviously difficult to go up against systems and even more difficult to effect any lasting change. But it can be done. Let us tell you more of Joseph's story. Joseph was the lawyer we met in Chapter 4.

Joseph's Story, continued

Joseph decided not to continue as a managing partner. Everyone at the firm thought that he was excellent in that role. But when he became aware of how unhappy he was in the role, he thought about quitting it. But quitting felt cowardly, and he knew that many of his partners would be unhappy. He also knew that his wife would question his decision and be unhappy. She felt his position had cemented her husband's influence in the firm.

Joseph felt stuck. He knew what he wanted to do, and he knew why. It all made sense, but it also felt like too big a leap. He felt the Lemming Conspiracy's pressure to keep him on track. The system had a role for him; the system provided goals; the system wanted Joseph to continue to see its point of view, not his own point of view.

Joseph interviewed his father about his life and his decisions at important Turning Points. His father had been a successful physician in general practice and had done well financially and professionally. He was part of a large group of general practitioners in a city in Texas. He told Joseph that when he was 40, he went through a period of boredom and malaise. The work was always the same. One day he felt that if he saw one more kid with a sore throat and runny nose and his depressed, strung-out, lonely mother, he would scream. He went so far as to think about applying for another residency, perhaps in psychiatry. He dismissed it as impractical. It would cost him a lot of money; he had a child who was getting ready to go to college; he would be giving up a successful practice to start all over again; everyone would think he had suddenly lost his mind. There were a hundred reasons why it wouldn't work. He might not even be able to get into a residency.

Eventually, Joseph's father resigned himself to his career. He told Joseph that it was soon after this that he had his first affair outside of his marriage. It was with a patient. He had others; sometimes he felt that only the excitement of these affairs kept him functioning. Now close to retirement, his practice remained busy and profitable, but he drank too much. He had no plans other than to keep practicing until he died.

Joseph: *"I felt as though I had just had a prophetic dream. I could see how my father had struggled with exactly the same feelings I was having—we both realized our jobs were killing us, even if the reasons were different. He had the same abilities and personality I do, and I could see that he needed the same kind of stimulation in his work that I do. When he gave up trying to get that stimulation from his job, he got it in other ways, ways he regrets now. I don't think he really sees the connection between feeling stultified and trapped at work and starting to have affairs, but I see it clearly. He wanted his life to be more interesting. Well, I do, too."*

When Joseph realized the power of these messages from his family of origin, and when he saw what he knew would be his own future, his vision became clear. He wanted to quit as managing partner—for many good reasons. He wanted to concentrate on work that he enjoyed and that stimulated him, not on work that felt like drudgery. He wanted to be an active presence with his wife and children.

As Joseph became more certain of his ideas, he started letting his wife and partners know what was coming. No one was very enthusiastic, but Joseph's belief and certainty that this was right for him carried him through. At first, both his wife and his partners acted as though nothing would happen—until Joseph turned in a letter resigning his role as managing partner. In two months, the person he had chosen to succeed him (not the person next in line of seniority; rather, the person Joseph felt had the abilities and personality that fit the job) took over. That day, Joseph left early. He didn't work any more on weekends.

Some of Joseph's partners were so angry that they talked among themselves; but when they realized the firm was not collapsing and that revenues were not dropping, everything settled down. Some months later, some of the partners began to realize that the firm was being run better. Some of Joseph's partners started talking about leaving at six o'clock themselves and not working so much on the weekends. The system adjusted to the new perspectives and became more open.

"It was the same with my wife," Joseph said later. "One day I came home around 5:30 and she was trying to get the kids' dinner ready. She *was mad and the kids were hanging on her legs. They were all tired and cranky. I took the kids outside and we shot some baskets while she finished dinner. It was a blast! Sometime later my wife came out and called us to dinner, but she was obviously angry. I tried to find out why, but she wasn't talking. Finally, later, it all came out. She had raised the kids by herself all these years, and now, suddenly, I decide to have a mid-life crisis and come home at a decent hour and have fun with them, while her life is just as boring as ever. Maybe she could have a mid-life crisis and do something different. I thought that sounded pretty reasonable.*

What Joseph is describing is a system's reaction to change. First, the system tries to keep roles and relationships the same. If a person in the system tries to change, the system works subtly to put that person back in line. When faced with the threat of real change, systems work more overtly to return things to normal. Sometimes, systems exert this pressure crudely and powerfully. Often people in the system feel angry when someone challenges the system's rules. Keep in mind that if you decide you need more choices in life than before, you will throw a challenge up to everyone else in your systems. Systems assume the final solution is to reject. Throw the heretic out. Hire someone else who fits. Divorce. Instead, Joseph's systems adjusted.

If a person changes and stays, the system will change. It must eventually adjust to the new conditions. This happened with Joseph's system. His wife and children adjusted to having a more active and present husband and father. His wife started to take better care of herself. She is now planning to do freelance design work—a field she had been in before her marriage. Joseph's firm adjusted to a new manager, but more importantly, it adjusted to the added possibilities Joseph had introduced. His partners didn't necessarily have to work until late at night and on weekends; they didn't necessarily have to face failure in their marriages.

Joseph's systems became more open. That is, they had more options available, and they could be more responsive to new information from the environment. No system is totally open—if it didn't have rules, it would not be a system. Many systems are highly rigid and closed, but all human systems must be at least somewhat open to new information to survive. The most difficult obstacle facing people who want to set their own course in life is the Lemming Conspiracy—the power of systems to control their thoughts, feelings, and actions—even when it runs counter to self-interest. Once a person has gathered and integrated enough information about himself – once he has started to chart a course – it's time to go to the beginning of the Lemming Conspiracy – the family of origin. That is what both Joseph and Mitchell did. This is what you can do.

Going Back to the Family—Why? And How?

Both Joseph and Mitchell learned crucial information, instrumental in standing up to pressure from their systems, by interviewing their parents. How does this work? Why would asking your father and mother about what they did and thought when they were teenagers, or at some other Turning Point, have anything to do with you now? Don't you know that stuff already? And would they talk to you about it anyway?

Interviewing your parents, if you have done the right preparation, can be a fascinating experience. It can help you to see yourself and your systems in a new perspective, one that is outside usual channels.

The most difficult problem you will face in doing your family interviews will be setting them up in such a way that you really move outside your usual interactions. The interactions must be different to be effective in giving you new information to take back to your systems. In the Thought Experiment, you will see detailed and specific instructions for setting these interviews up and carrying them out. Following them closely can help you break out. Otherwise, your instincts will naturally lead you into your usual circle of interactions. They will keep you inside the Lemming Conspiracy.

It is also important to be ready for the interviews. It's tempting to feel "Oh, well, let's just do it and be done with it." But preparation beforehand is crucial to conducting your family interviews. Preparation helps you understand what is unique about you and your career.

In interviewing your parents, your goal is to learn to see them as distinct from what your system has taught you to see, and thereby to see yourself distinctly as well. As Joseph remarked, "It was as though I was seeing my mother and father for the first time."

Thought Experiment F: _____

Interviewing Your Family of Origin

ndertaking family-of-origin interviews can be a mind-opening, enjoyable experience in which you find out a lot more about two of the most important people in your life. But only if you set the interviews up well. We recommend following all these instructions exactly; each one has a definite purpose.

WHOM TO INTERVIEW:

Ideally, you want to interview both of your natural or adoptive parents in *separate* interviews, with no one else present except the two of you.

If you were raised by a step-parent for a significant part of your childhood, you would also want to interview the step-parent. If one or both of your parents is not available for interview, because of death or severe disability, then you should interview a substitute family member. This could be (in order of preference) the deceased or disabled parent's brother or sister, his or her close personal friend or cousin, or an older cousin of your own. Failing all of these, your brothers or sisters can substitute. You would conduct this substitute interview in the same way as with your parent—asking the substitute about his or her own life, not about your parent's. Only after you ask about the substitute's life in detail, should you ask what he or she may know about your parent's life.

WHEN TO INTERVIEW:

Only after you have done all the Thought Experiments leading up to this one.

HOW TO SET UP THE INTERVIEWS:

Call your mother or father. Let's say you start with your mother. Tell her that you would like to talk with her in about two or three weeks. She would be doing you a great favor, and you would like to have the conversation when it would be most convenient for her. You would like to set aside about one or two hours to ask her some questions about her life. You will be coming just to do the interviews, not for any other reason. You won't be bringing anyone else with you.

This sounds simple and straightforward, but it represents a shift out of the family system. Some typical responses to this request, and your answers:

What do you want to ask? I just want to find out some things about your life. Sort of like Roots—a family history kind of thing.

Why wait two weeks. Let's do it tomorrow. No. I would rather plan ahead so that we can be sure we both have the time put aside. Also, I want to make sure that I have my ideas and questions ready. Is this going to be some kind of confrontation? Absolutely not, I just want to find out some more about your life. It would be a big help to me.

Will you be bringing your wife/husband/children? No, only myself.
Are you going to interview Father? Will you interview us together. Yes, I will definitely interview Father, too. No, I want to interview you separately, so I can concentrate on you one at a time.

You should end by saying that you want to be sure you can interview her without being interrupted. Then, talk to your father in a separate conversation and set up the same kind of interview with him.

WHAT YOU TALK ABOUT:

Below are some questions. You should think of these only as starting points. If anything grabs your interest, pursue it. Make sure you ask your parent how he/she felt about each event or occurrence. Also, ask for the reasoning behind whatever your parent did. What was his/her plan? What was he/she thinking about?

Let's assume in our questions that we are planning your interview with your mother. You can follow the same questions and format with your father.

Usually it's best to start with questions about your mother's parents:
1. What did your father do for work?
2. How did he come to do that?
3. What particular skills or abilities made him good at that?
4. What kinds of things came easily or naturally to your father? [not necessarily work-related]
5. Did he have a hobby or avocation?
6. What did your mother do for work?
7. How did she come to do that?
8. What particular skills or abilities made her good at last?

9. What kinds of things came easily or naturally to your mother?

10. Did she have a hobby or avocation?

Next, you would ask about your mother herself, generally following a time line in your interviews.

Take her back to her age at the first Turning Point in her life:

1. What was going on then?
2. Who were your friends?
3. What did you think your life would be like?
4. What did you think you would do with your life?
5. How did you feel about that?
6. How did you decide what to do immediately after high school? Why?
7. What happened then?
8. What did your parents think about your choices?\

For whatever she decided to do after high school (go to college, for instance, or go to work, or get married), ask the following questions:

1. What skills made you good at that?
2. What came easily? What was more of a struggle?
3. What were some of the problems you encountered? How did you respond?
4. Did you ever wish you had done it differently? How? Why?
5. Describe a bad day. What made it bad?
6. Describe a very good day. What felt rewarding about it?

In this way, go through each major Turning Point of your mother's life in the order in which we list them below. Take her back to that age, asking questions about what her life was like, what decisions she made, why she made them, and how she felt about them before, during and after.

- High School to College—age 17-18
- College to the Work World—age 22-25
- Age 30 Assessment—age 28-33
- Midlife Transition—age 38-45
- Age 50 Assessment—age 50-55
- Pre-Retirement Transition—age 60-65

- Age 70 Assessment—age 70-75
- Senior Transition—age 80-85

You may want to tape-record your interviews. They will be a valuable reference for you and your children.

FOUR STORIES: FAMILY OF ORIGIN

Tracy

"I interviewed both my mother and my father for about three hours each. It was amazing. My mother went to nursing school and met my father when he was an intern in the hospital where she was being trained. She never actually worked as a hospital nurse. She worked in a doctor's office to make money while my father finished his residency, and then to make ends meet when he started a practice. It was a stable job with regular hours, and that's what they needed at the time to raise their young family. But she hated the routine of it. She quit as soon as she could, and has never worked since. She's had some problems with depression—especially after the children left home. I sort of knew that was going on, but it felt great to talk to her about it. It turns out, she has been feeling that she should be doing something, work somewhere, but she doesn't know exactly what to do.

"My father has been like a total force of nature. He still works 12-hour days, just as he did when I was a kid. He says he has always loved practicing medicine. He gets angry because he says the profession is changing so much. He was really against my going into psychology because he said I'd never be able to make a living. I asked him about retirement. He said he will never retire. Just work until he dies."

Feelings: "It's a little much to put together right now. I can see myself in both of my parents. When I was going strong in psychology, I was just like my father. But then when I lost focus, I became just like my mother, kind of depressed. I can see some problems with some decisions they made, and I can see myself doing the same thing. I can see that I need to have something of my own to sink my teeth in. But I don't want it to be my entire life, as my father has allowed it to be.

Brian and Janet

Brian: "My father runs an insurance office in my home town. He has always been pretty successful, though not amazingly so. People like him and trust him, and he keeps customers forever. He has to go out at night a lot. He feels it's part of the job; he has to do whatever it takes. He said he felt his major duty as a father was to earn a good living and provide for his family. That was what his father had done. His father had lost his business because of the Great Depression. My father said that his father had never recovered. It had just wiped him out—financially and spiritually. He had found work again but he was never the same. I think that all this had left a profound impression on my father. It was as my father said, 'That's never going to happen to me.' I don't get the sense that he has enjoyed his life very much.

"My mother was a housewife and took care of me and my two sisters. I don't think she was terrifically happy either, but I felt a lot closer to her while I was growing up. She never graduated from college. She met and married my father and then left college to go with him. Her main thing was raising kids. Since we left home, she hasn't seemed to know what to do with herself. She wishes now she had completed college."

Brian's Feelings: "Thoughtful. I'm just like my dad. He worked and worked to get ahead. That's what I'm doing. I feel I'm going to make some terrifically bad mistakes if I'm not careful. I look at my mother, and I think, she could have done so much more. I don't want that to happen with Janet."

Janet: "My father and mother divorced when I was 15. I interviewed my mother face to face, but I had to interview my father on the phone, because he lives in another city. I think my mother's not as angry about the breakup as she used to be. She never remarried, but she's been dating someone for a year now. When my father left us, she got a job with a publisher. She has ideas all the time about books and what books the publisher should bring out next. When she gets an idea, she proposes it to the publisher. She then goes out and gets some expert to write about it. She's very successful. And she loves it. She's like Brian; she would work all the time if she could.

"My father is an engineer and works with one of the Bells. He has *always liked the research work he does, and has published several articles. He remarried a few years ago, and they have two children. He seems to have more to do with that family than he ever did with ours. He seems more relaxed than I remember him when I was growing up—not so removed."*

Janet's Feelings: "Hopeful. I can see in personality and abilities that I'm a lot like my father. I love it that my mother was able to find a job that she likes so much. I also love it that my father has found a happier family life. It gives me hope that I can find that for myself."

Elizabeth

"My father has just retired in the last six months. It hasn't been a great adjustment. He was the king of the hill in his company. He worked for an automobile manufacturing company for almost 40 years and retired as a vice president. Since retiring, he doesn't seem to know what to do with himself. He was the classic executive workaholic. He would do anything for the company, and they rewarded him handsomely. We had to move around the country a good deal because of his job, so most of his friends were business associates. Since retiring, he's gotten more angry—almost bitter.

"My mother just managed the household. About 20 years ago, she got into a lot of volunteer work. She has now worked for years on the executive board of Planned

Parenthood and travels all over the country, giving speeches and talking to political types. She's totally committed to this work. I asked her why she suddenly started doing that. Her answer was interesting: 'I had to do something. I knew your father would never change, and with you kids gone, I needed something else to be interested in. I was lucky that I had the financial security to do whatever I wanted to. I am committed to the organization and to helping young women have more chances in life. It's very fulfilling."

Feelings: "I have always identified with my father. But I can see that, as much as I love my father, I really admire the way my mother has made a life for herself. They seem like a good business partnership. I would probably like more feeling in my relationship with my husband than they seem to have in theirs. More fun, too."

Carl

"My father died two and half years ago. My mother is still alive and lives in an assisted living complex. I've never seen anyone so delighted to do anything as she was to tell me her life story. It was as though she had been waiting years for me to ask. My father was a fairly well-known Episcopalian minister. My mother said that the first time she saw him, she knew they would get married. She played the rather demanding role of minister's wife about as well as anyone could. She never made me or my brothers do anything just to make my father look good. I always appreciated that. She insisted, sometimes over my father's strong objections, that we be allowed to think for ourselves. Before he retired five years ago, he had been depressed off and on for years. He drank too much, too. He and my mother remained together through all of that. I think there was always a good deal of mutual appreciation and respect. My mother always had a wide circle of friends and when my father died, it was really nice for her to have them. A group of them moved into the same complex a few years ago. My brothers and I have remained close to her and close to each other.

"A major change happened in my mother's 'career' when she was 41. She said that up until then she had tried to be perfect —lead all the church women's groups, host teas, entertain my father's guests. At this point, though, she decided that she needed to have a life of her own. She took classes at a community college, took up gardening in a big way, and started teaching in the local high school to add to the family's income. She was different after that. More sure of herself, I guess.

"I interviewed my father's younger sister. She told me an interesting story about their father, my grandfather, whom I barely knew. He worked for the railroad his entire life. He was a die-maker in the huge shops where they build locomotives and railroad cars. He started there when he was 15 and ended as a supervisor. She told me that he was highly respected among the men. His integrity and honesty were above question. He never made a political speech, but he always represented the men in the shop to the Union. The dies he made were patterns that they made tools from. His tools were considered some of the very best because they were so elegantly

and precisely made. My aunt gave me one of my grandfather's tools she had been keeping. It's very precious to me. The spirit that made him make those tools so much better than they had to be, that is what I feel was passed onto my father, and now to me."

"When my mother told me about her change at 41, I started thinking about myself at 41 or 42. That's when I was recruited by a head hunter to be vice president in my entertainment company. It was quite a ride. My whole career changed so much, I had shifted into another gear.

"I feel I am a lot like my father. If I were to get depressed, I could find myself drinking too much as he had. I take care of my health better than he did; I would like to live longer and be healthier."

Feelings: "Moved. Impressed with my mother's and my father's lives. Proud of what I 'inherited' from both."

NEXT CHAPTER: When you have finished your family-of-origin interviews, you will be ready for integration. Your unconscious mind has been working on integration since you began reading this book and working with the Thought Experiments. Now it is time to bring your creative unconscious work to light and use it to create a Personal Vision. Each element of your Personal Vision is important. Each element is also complex. To pull them all together into a coherent focus that can direct your career is a mammoth task. But your creative mind can do it, if you access it. The next chapter deals with the creative process and how to make purposeful use of it in forming a Personal Vision.

MANY PEOPLE THINK OF
CREATIVITY
AS A **MYSTERIOUS GIFT**
THAT SOME HAVE AND MOST DON'T.
MANY ASSOCIATE CREATIVITY ONLY
WITH
PURELY ARTISTIC PURSUITS.

IN REALITY
WE ALL HAVE
CREATIVE MINDS
AND ACCESS TO ENORMOUS
CREATIVE TALENT.
WE JUST HAVE TO **KNOW
HOW TO USE THEM.**

Creative
Integration

To be effective, a Personal Vision should combine all the elements we have been discussing: stage of development, natural talents, skills, personality, interests, values, goals and family of origin. Your creative mind can perform this kind of integration. Your logical mind will not. To make creativity work, however, you still need your logical left brain. In this chapter, we describe the creative integration process we developed for our clients to use with the Eight Personal Vision Factors.

We call this process left-right-left

It uses both sides of your brain, the logical and the creative, to help you achieve useful creative insights and also to make the insights work in the real world. It helps you go from the mental model you have created of your life, based on system oriented perception, to the new mental model based on internal factors you have discovered using the process in this book.

We will show you how creative integration combines all of the critical factors of career decisions into a Personal Vision. We will also give you an example of an actual Personal Vision that one person has used for years to guide his career. You can use the Thought Experiment at the end of the chapter to start your own left-right-left integrative process.

Creativity—Where Does It Come From?

Many people think of creativity as a mysterious gift that some have and most don't. Many associate creativity only with purely artistic pursuits. In reality, we all have creative minds and access to creative talent. We just have to know how to use them.

If you boil creativity down to its pure essence, what remains is simple: A creative insight puts ideas together that no one had thought to put together before. Edison used lamp-black for a filament in an incandescent light bulb. Pasteur realized that invisible microbes in milk cause it to sour. Marie Curie realized that radiation was not a chemical reaction, but a process intrinsic to the element itself. Wilbur Wright suddenly understood that controlling a vehicle in the air, in three dimensions, requires a completely different guidance system than controlling a vehicle on the ground, in two dimensions. Rachel Carson realized that the poisons we spray to kill weeds and insects eventually kill everything else. The sheer obviousness of truly creative ideas often stuns us — after somebody has thought of them.

Consider artistic endeavors — painting a landscape, carving a sculpture, or writing a poem. Each of these activities involves a creative insight; that is, a vision of what the painting should look like, or what the sculpture will be. That sudden connection between previously unrelated ideas springs from the right brain. How do you teach your mind to think creatively? How do you learn to join two unrelated ideas to form a neat, easy solution to an "insoluble" problem? Actually, you don't have to teach your mind to do this at all. Your right brain thinks in that way all the time. You just have to put it to work on the problem you want to solve.

The brain is a complex organism. Different parts perform different functions. To simplify the process of creative thinking we use the term "right brain" to identify the right hemisphere of the brain which naturally thinks holistically. It solves problems by latching on to what it needs—what you remember, what you see, what you hear, what you think. The right brain doesn't know or care about time, and it doesn't have a strong fix on reality, either. Past, present, future, real, imagined, impossible, good, bad, profitable, impractical—they are all the same to your right brain. It doesn't make distinctions like these. The left hemisphere of the brain or "left brain" processes more verbal, linear information.

If you think about your dreams, you'll have a sense of how the right brain works. Your nighttime dreams don't make any logical sense. They are a mish-mash of seemingly unrelated images, feelings and events. Some dream images seem taken from life. They feel so real that you wake up and think they've actually happened. Some seem to have no connection with reality at all. We know now that dreaming is our right brain's way of solving problems from day-to-day life. Psychoanalysis bases some of its treatment on understanding dreams and using them to make unconscious, insoluble problems both conscious and manageable.

Each of the seemingly unrelated images and events in a dream holds a complex meaning. The more deeply you go into a dream, the more profound and multifaceted its meaning. You can have a simple dream about a trip in a car, but the car can represent many layers of meaning. It can be, at one and the same time, simply a car, a symbol for power and control, a representation of your father and an image of yourself. Each time we dream (and experts believe that most of us dream every night whether we remember the dream or not), we create worlds and visions as complex and enlightening as the Mona Lisa or Hamlet.

At night, we are all Michelangelos, Emily Dickinsons, and Mozarts.

Where is all that creativity? Why don't we feel it when we are awake? Our waking minds live in the left brain, not the right. The left brain works through words. It operates somewhat like a digital computer. It lines up facts like parts on an assembly line and puts them together to end in a logical solution. The left brain lives in the present; it remembers the past; it thinks about the future. It makes clear distinctions between real and not-real, possible and impossible, profit and loss, practical and unrealistic. The left brain can plan; it can learn new facts; and it can figure out logical solutions. It's the home of the ego, our adult selves. It is the author of civilizations. If you think about the words on this page—lined up in logical order to express a particular meaning and no other—you have the left brain.

In contrast, look at how words are used in a poem by e.e. cummings

> The fingers make early flowers of
> all things.
> thy hair mostly the hours love:
> a smoothness which
> sings, saying
> (though love be a day)
> do not fear, we will go amaying.

Here you see words created by the right brain. The logic is slippery and the meaning could go down any number of paths. It's not like a digital computer. It's like the colorful images of Georgia O'Keefe, or the dark symbolism of Picasso's Guernica, or the baffling melting watches and clocks of Salvidor Dali. It's playful, subtle, complex, hidden and perhaps a little dangerous. It's creative.

The creative process doesn't just happen in the right brain. The left brain is the unsung hero. While creativity undoubtedly springs from the right brain we don't think of people who live solely in the right brain as creative at all. We think of them as schizophrenic—people who cannot tell the difference between reality and fantasy.

Most people who consult on creativity concentrate on helping people achieve a creative insight. But the power of creativity comes only through attention to three distinct steps involving both sides of the brain. Leave one step out and the whole process fails.

The sequence to any creative work, no matter how large or small, is always the same: preparation, creative insight, execution. Or left-right-left. The left brain prepares the problem for the right. The right brain has the creative insight. The left brain must then translate that insight into the reality that is life. What could Leonardo have done if he had not painstakingly taught himself to draw? Or if he had not taken infinite labor to learn the engineering of his day? His insights and visions would have borne no relation to reality. They would have been the ravings of a madman. Or what would we know of Tolstoy if he had not written draft after draft of War and Peace? Nothing. Edison's dictum that invention is 1 percent inspiration and 99 percent perspiration captures the whole truth.

In *The Mustard Seed Garden,* a traditional Chinese text that teaches drawing with pen and ink, one section deals with the creative process. "First, however, you must work hard. Bury the brush again and again in the ink and grind the inkstone to dust. Take ten days to paint a stream and five to paint a rock. If you aim to dispense with method, learn method. If you aim at facility, work hard. If you aim for simplicity, master complexity. If you wish to draw bamboo, draw bamboo every day for ten years. Then forget about bamboo entirely. When one day you feel inspired to draw bamboo again, its pure essence emerges from the end of your brush." Left-right-left.

The left brain prepares you; it sets up the problem for you. The right brain comes up with the creative insight. The left brain must execute the insight. In our Personal Vision process, we consciously use this left-right-left approach to help people solve one of the most complex and intricate problems imaginable, creating a Personal Vision for their careers.

Creating a Personal Vision—Preparation

Even though it can't come up with the creative insight, your left brain can set up the problem. It can help you prepare. Each of the previous chapters of this book has set up a different part of the problem. Each of the Thought Experiments was part of the preparation, helping you identify and articulate a parameter of the problem. Even though you may not know exactly what your Personal Vision may look like, you can begin to describe it. For instance, "I want to be sure the fact that I am a specialist and an introvert is a positive help to me and that I don't get into a position in which I'm working against myself. That would mean I would be most satisfied working in an environment in which I can spend a lot of time concentrating on one kind of task that really grabs my interest and attention."

Each time you do one of the Thought Experiments, the information is there for your left brain to use in your daily life. But it is also there for your right brain to fold into its creative musings. Doing the Thought Experiments also puts your unconscious mind—your right brain—to work on the problem.

In our seminars participants spend four to five weeks preparing. They learn about each of the eight factors we have talked about in this book—abilities, skills, interests, personality, values, goals, stage of development and family of origin. As we add information and factors, the problem of integration becomes more and more difficult. Participants begin to wonder where the process is leading, or if they will ever be able to put everything together. It can be difficult to see that the models we have built our lives on may not always be true to our internal needs. For most people, some kind of inspiration strikes midway through the process. Each creative exercise produces more "ahas!" and participants start to see a path ahead. They have the beginnings of a Personal Vision.

As we noted at the end of Chapter 5, some anxiety is not only normal, it can be an important part of the creative process. Your right, unconscious brain produces anxiety as it starts to engage the problem. As a general rule, creativity happens where you are most *involved*.

In our process, we are talking about your *life* and what you want that life to be. It's worth getting involved.

Creating a Personal Vision—Inspiration

The problem of creativity is very much the same as the problem of falling asleep. You can't make yourself fall asleep. The harder you try, the more awake you become. You can't force it, but you can set up the conditions in which it can more easily occur. You can't make it happen, but you can allow it to happen.

Once you set up the problem and complete your preparation, you are ready to let your right brain work on it. When you try to make creativity happen, you are using your left brain—the very brain you want to turn off so that the right brain can begin to work. To let our right brain swing into action, we use a three-pronged approach:

- Create an environment in which creativity can happen.
- Put your left brain to sleep.
- Give the right brain a task at which it can excel.

Create The Right Environment

Setting up an environment for creativity is just as important as setting up a problem to solve. For a creative environment, you must let go of your left brain's control for a while. You need to promise your left brain that if it will let the right brain work on the problem, it will eventually get the problem back.

How do you let go of your left brain? One way is by letting go of results — temporarily. Don't demand that the answer be perfect and that you solve all problems *now*. That won't gain you any creative insight because your left brain will not have let go of the problem. Remember, your left brain expects the right answer, the correct solution, perfect results, even the bottom line itself — terms that make no sense whatsoever to the right brain. Your right brain can discover a new way to put the elements of your life and career together, a way that solves several different problems simultaneously. But it will take your left brain to make this insight work in your actual life. If you let the right brain work on the creative insight, trusting that your left brain has the talent and ability to translate that insight to the real world, you will have moved a long way towards creating the internal environment you need to enhance creativity.

Put The Left Brain to Sleep

What is the feeling when we shut down the left brain and work with the right? Most of us know this feeling, even if we don't recognize it as such. In the 1960s, some psychologists were fond of inducing an "alpha" state. A person in the alpha state felt more relaxed, lost track of time, often experienced images and sometimes insights. Today, meditation is the more fashionable term, but the state is the same — inducing the right brain to do the work. In this state, we don't experience conscious thought; the logical left brain stops speaking to us in words. Instead, the right brain produces dream-like images, perhaps with some words thrown in, but not in the logical manner of the left brain.

Albert Einstein once remarked that he had to be very careful not to cut himself while shaving in the morning. Not because he was clumsy, but because an idea often ignited his imagination while he was using his razor. Ideas came to him so suddenly and forcefully that they startled him.

When we lapse into a reverie, when our minds drift without apparent purpose, we are using our right brain. Our left brain falls asleep. We often experience this kind of reverie when listening to soothing music, or watching the movement of water, or enjoying a peaceful walk in a park.

To learn how to put your left brain to sleep on purpose, you need to understand meditation. People who practice meditation every day, create the appropriate scene very carefully. They use a certain room at a certain time of day. They sit in a prescribed position and breathe in and out in a prescribed way. They may say a mantra over and over to themselves. Notice the steps in the routine and preparation for falling asleep: a prescribed room, a prescribed time, rigid steps in preparation (change clothes, brush teeth, put out the cat), or, perhaps, a book to read. Through these steps, we simply bore the left brain until it gives up and goes to sleep.

In the Thought Experiment at the end of this chapter, you will see that the first part of it puts your left brain to sleep. In the second part, the fun begins.

Give The Right Brain A Task at Which it Can Excel

There are some tasks that are difficult for the left brain and quite easy for the right. Driving an automobile would be impossible if you tried to do it logically. But your right brain enjoys this spatial, multifaceted task and does it easily.

As you access your right brain's creative power, you seek an *initial creative insight,* not the final answer. Your right, creative brain can only make the initial connection to a new idea. Your left, logical brain will makes the idea real and practical.

A young engineer had been struggling to design a truck that could be driven through rugged country to search for oil in some of the barren wastes of the West. The many different needs conflicted with the many different functions, and after six months on the project, he was hardly further along than when he started. His boss suddenly demanded that he present the results of his work in just two weeks, but the engineer knew he would have nothing to show. In despair, he sought the help of a psychologist. After listening for an hour, the psychologist told him to come back the following week with the very worst possible truck he could design for the purpose, a truck that would be impossible to use.

The engineer feared he was wasting his time and money, but seeing no alternative, he complied. He returned to the next session with drawings and sketches of the most outlandish contraption imaginable. He laughed so much while drawing the sketches that his wife feared the worst. The engineer had almost decided not to return for that second session. He no longer had any need to worry. He was now working furiously on the sketches for the real presentation. In the middle of creating the horrendous design, an insight had leapt, full-blown, into his mind. "I suddenly knew where everything should go. I immediately started drawing the real designs. It was as though there were a photograph in my head, and I just took the design from the photograph." The oil exploration trucks he designed are still in constant use today in Texas and Oklahoma.

The psychologist had given the engineer a task that had bypassed the left hemisphere. It wasn't a logical task. In fact, the only way to complete it was to heave logic out the window. But in doing the illogical task, the engineer's right brain had gained crucial insight into how to organize the many pieces of the engineering puzzle.

So which tasks use the right brain and bypass the left? There are an infinite variety, but we have discovered several types that are particularly successful in helping people gain an initial insight into a Personal Vision. These tasks make use of the right brain's ability to break with hard reality and think "what if."

The right brain can play with ideas and thoughts; it doesn't require logic or practicality. That's why it can come up with such creative ideas.

Does this mean that any idea the right brain develops will be valuable? Almost any strong image your right brain creates will probably have some meaning for you. Messages from your right brain are never random images. The complexities of your own life profoundly determine each detail. They may be exceedingly difficult to translate, however. Think about the difficulty of unraveling a dream. Your left brain must translate the message.

An accountant did an exercise in which, after relaxing and allowing himself to follow a guided imagery passage, he described an ideal day. He did this exercise after he had done a great deal of work identifying and articulating the pieces of his Personal Vision. That is, he had already set up the problem he needed to solve. His image of his ideal day, as delivered by his right brain, was of himself as a circus clown: funny outfit, greasepaint, big shoes, bulbous nose — making people laugh.

Did this mean he should leave his job and join the circus? No. He lived near a circus training site, and so the repetitive experience of seeing circus performers had probably planted a message which his right brain would use. The accountant understood the message immediately. For many years he had been fascinated by storytelling. His grandfather had told traditional tall tales that had delighted him vas a child. The accountant took every opportunity to seek out particularly good storytellers and record their stories. A strong introvert, the accountant never
thought about what he could do with his interest. It just never occurred to him at first to think of it as anything but a meaningless pastime.

In looking at his natural abilities, however, he discovered that he fit a performer's profile. His personality and thinking style came together in a way characteristic of people who perform in front of others — teachers, presenters, marketing representatives, trainers and actors.

In his image of himself as a clown, he enjoyed making people laugh and enjoyed molding his material in response to his audience. He also realized that as a clown, he was able to hide behind his face paint. The clown can be removed; he is not interacting with the audience, but performing before it. The accountant realized he could hide, a little, behind his stories. And that he would enjoy telling them.

He is actually a gifted performer. He has not stopped being an accountant, but he has added something new, exciting and meaningful to his life.

A Personal Vision

At age 42, the Midlife Turning Point, Edward, a consultant in human resources, went through the Eight Personal Vision Factors we describe in this book. He examined all the factors — abilities, interests, skills, personality, values, goals, stage of development, family of origin — and finally went through a series of integrative exercises. This is how he describes his Personal Vision:

"My Vision came in stages. The first insights came when I got feedback on the Highlands Ability Battery. This was extremely enlightening — even for someone like me. I had been through virtually every kind of development program as a part of my job. I realized that my role at work really capitalized on my natural abilities. I felt much more confident, even though I have always been successful at what I've tried. It said what I had always felt to be true, but now it was there in black and white.

"As useful as it was to know about my abilities, this did not help me make the leap to a Personal Vision. It helped fill in a few pieces, though. More pieces followed: interests, skills, personality. I started noticing a pattern. The same ideas kept emerging. When we did an integrative exercise, my Personal Vision started to take on a definite shape.

"Until that point, most of my thoughts were concerned with the structure of my job. The integrating exercises helped me broaden that perspective. In creating a Personal Vision, I became more concerned with my role at work, but, just as important, what my life would look like as I lived out my career.

"I realized that I would need to hold several aspects of my life in balance. From my family of origin and my subsequent values, I knew my family must still be my overwhelming priority. If this sounds obvious, it was not always so with me. There were times as a young professional when I'd let my family take a back seat. It was only when I consciously thought about values and priorities that I realized the personal importance of time and commitment to my family.

"My interests and talents led me toward art, which surprised me. I had never realized how important this had become to me. I suddenly 'remembered' that my mother had been an artist. Also, I had never thought of myself as having anything to do with design or visual representation. But I uncovered a talent for creative design and words that has been helpful in my job and satisfying to me. I realized I wanted to take a few more risks at work — I could be more creative in consulting with clients.

"I knew from my experience and abilities that I could create the role I wanted at work. I also knew without any doubt or hesitation that there were some roles I might be asked to fulfill that I did not have the experience, the personality, or the inclination to carry out well. I knew people who could and would do that well, but not me. This was a great insight, because I had always felt it necessary to be able to do everything. Realizing there were some roles that fit me well and other roles that didn't was enormously freeing.

"All of these elements came together in the picture I drew of my future career. I drew myself both creating and using a new technology while doing something beneficial for the world. My family was with me, and part of my attention went to them. Off to one side, I was painting, and there were also sculptures that I created. As simple as this picture sounds when reduced to words, its meaning has guided all of my decisions since the day I perceived it."

Thought Experiment G:

Creative Integration

We adapted this series of integrating exercises from similar ones that we do in the course of our programs. If you follow the instructions carefully, you will be able to access your right creative brain — not an easy task to do alone or on purpose.

STEP 1. PUT YOUR LEFT BRAIN TO SLEEP

Find a tape recorder you can use to record the text which follows. You can record it in your own voice, or you can have a spouse or friend record it for you. This will form the lead-in to all of the subsequent integration exercises. Remember that your task is to put your left brain to sleep temporarily. Your verbal left brain can relax and let go of its role in speaking to you and guiding your actions for a short time in order to let your right brain engage a problem for which it is sublimely suited.

Record the following in a slow, relaxed, well-modulated voice. Leave some pauses in your reading to give yourself a chance to picture and experience the images. We will insert the word [pause] where we want you to pause for a second or two. Don't worry about following the script word for word; the important thing is to relax

RELAXATION SETUP

Record: *I want you to take a deep breath and let it out. Now take another, in and out. And as you let that one out, notice how your muscles relax and let go for a few minutes. All of your muscles usually have to have a certain amount of tension in them to hold you upright and help you walk around. But now they can relax for a little while and let go of their usual roles. Let your arms relax. Let your torso relax. Let your hips and legs relax. Let your neck and face relax. Let yourself drift for a little while. Let yourself drift for a moment and just enjoy this feeling of being relaxed. [pause]*

Now think about a place—it can be imaginary or it can be a real place— where you feel utterly safe and secure. In your mind, get a picture of that place. [pause] Now think of yourself there, alone. What do you hear? [pause] What do you see around you? [pause] What do you smell? [pause] What are the sensations you have on your face and arms? [pause] Your back and legs? [pause] Just relax for a few minutes and enjoy the amazingly calm feeling of being in this place and enjoying all of your sensations. [pause] [end].

You can use this tape whenever you want to work on integration. Just play it for yourself, listen to its sound, and follow its simple instructions. This can help your left brain let go for a few minutes and let your right brain work on an exercise that would be difficult for your left brain.

This tape-recorded relaxation device will be the setup for the integration exercises that come next. After the end of the relaxation sequence, wait just a few seconds, and then record the instructions you are given for the exercise you want to do.

After you do any of the exercises, *enter* what you unearth in your notebook. Tell someone else what you discovered, and/or Say what you discovered aloud into a tape recorder. Don't worry if you don't know what an image means right now. Just describe what you felt or thought in words. You may have to do several integrative exercises before you "understand" the message your right brain is trying to communicate.

Make this effort to describe your image in words in order to bring your left brain back into the picture. Remember that the whole process of creative integration is left-right-left. You have done the preparation in the previous Thought Experiments. These exercises help your right brain integrate, but to claim your right-brain discoveries, you must translate and move them to your left brain.

STEP 2. CREATIVE INTEGRATION

We suggest you read the following exercises through first and then decide which one most strikes your imagination. The more you can approach one of the exercises with a feeling of "Let's just see what happens," the more open you can be to whatever your right brain may show you. Don't worry if you can't see the sense in an image or thought right now. Trust your left brain to decipher it later.

In the next chapter on Surveying, you will learn how to make your vision work in a practical way in the real world. For now, you can just let your right brain play with the pieces of the puzzle without getting too uptight about its final form.

Exercise A: Guided Imagery

Record the following after your relaxation setup:

Now, in your imagination, I want you to get up gradually and look around. Again, sense how safe, secure, and comfortable you are feeling. Notice a path leading away from where you are. You don't exactly know where this path leads, but you feel it would definitely be worth your while to find out. You decide to take this path. It winds through some territory that is familiar to you and some that is new. You have a pleasant sensation of moving, feeling your legs step confidently one after the other and feeling your footsteps plant solidly and strongly one after another on the path. You hear the leaves around you stirred by a cool breeze and feel the pleasant and cool air on your cheek. You still feel totally safe and secure. Your feeling is that of exploring a new and fascinating territory and making interesting discoveries.

Finally you come to a large body of water. It is calm, but you can't see the other side. There is a boat nearby. It is exactly suited for the purpose of carrying you safely to the other side. You get in and push off. You guide the boat yourself. You feel entirely in control of it.

Soon you see the shore. Gradually it comes more clearly into view. Finally you feel the prow of the boat crunch gently into the sand. You step out and realize that you are in a different place. It is a place you always wanted to be in, even if you never fully realized that before. You look around and realize that this is a place where you will be living your life sometime in the future. It is the fullest, most satisfying, and most complete life. All of the important elements are here, and all of the important things you want to do are ready for you to take up and do. All of the important people that need to be here are here.

> What is around you? [pause]
> Where do you live? [pause]
> Where do you work? [pause]
> What is the main feeling of your life? [pause]
> Who is here in this place with you? [pause]
> What do you do with your days? [pause]
> What is a typical day like? [pause]
> What is the most important thing you do in a day? [pause]

What is next? [pause]

What are your most important relationships? [pause]

What is the role you play in your relationships? [pause]

Just enjoy this life for a few minutes, and when you are ready, wake up and write in your notebook everything about your image you can remember, no matter how unimportant it may seem. Include your answers to the questions we asked. If you wish, you can also tell someone important to you about your image, or record it on tape. Again, try to describe the image in detail, even if the meaning is not clear to you right now.

Exercise B: Taking Away an Impediment

Record the following instructions after your relaxation setup:

Many people seem to live life habitually as though they were forced to do everything they do. "I have to go to work to earn money to support my children and spouse. I have to put up with work I don't find particularly meaningful because if I didn't, I wouldn't have a job. My boss is abusive but if I don't endure it, I'll be fired."

We find that people have far more choice in life than they think they have. They live life as though forced to endure it, but when they decide what they want, and go after it, they often succeed and are happy.

We designed exercises like this one to give you the sense of choice. If you could choose to do anything, what would you do? [pause]

Imagine that you wake up one morning and find that the life you've been living is actually a dream. Your real life, the one to which you have awakened, is almost exactly like the one you've been living, except for one key difference. You have a bank account that you can draw on any time you want and this bank account has many millions of dollars in it. You realize that you never have to worry about earning money again. You have all the money you can possibly ever need or that anyone close to you can possibly need. You can start each day asking yourself, "O.K., what do I want to do today?" And then do whatever comes to you.

What would your life be like? [pause]

How would you spend your time? [pause]

What would your relationship with your spouse or partner be like?

[pause]

What about your children? [pause]

How about with your parents? [pause]

Who would be your friends? [pause]

What would you talk to them about? [pause]

How would you feel about your days? [pause]

How would you feel about your life? [pause]

Now describe a typical day as you would live it. What would you do? [pause]

Where would you go? [pause]

What would give your life meaning? [pause]

What would be the most important thing you would do with your life? [pause]

Now open your eyes and write down in your notebook all that you can remember of your images and the answers to the questions in your notebook. Write down anything else that seems important from your image. Remember that it doesn't have to make any sense right now. Any message your right brain comes up with may be something your left brain will be able to use. Again, if you prefer, you can tell it to someone important, or record it on tape.

Exercise C: Looking Backwards

Record the following instructions after your relaxation setup:

Now I want you to imagine that you are much older and have lived a very long and productive life. You are still quite healthy and active. You have accomplished the many things you set out to do with your life – not only in your career, but also in your family life and in your personal life. You feel content and satisfied. Your life has been remarkably full and interesting.

A teacher in a local junior high school has given her pupils an assignment: interview an older person about his or her life and find out what advice, ideas and wisdom he or she would like to pass on to a younger generation just starting out in life. One of the pupils, 12 years old, comes to interview you. Here is what the young student would like to know:

What are the most important things you have accomplished?
[pause]

How have you changed over the years?
[pause]
What used to be important to you that isn't so important now?
[pause]
What used to be unimportant that feels a lot more important
to you now?
[pause]
What are your most important relationships?
[pause]
How have you nurtured and maintained them over the years?
[pause]
How have you managed to stay so healthy and vital all these
years?
[pause]
How have you managed to stay so alert and interested in life?
[pause]
What is the most important piece of advice you can give to
someone just starting out about how to live life?
[pause]
What else would you like to say about your life?
[pause]
What other advice would you give to a young person?
[pause]

Now open your eyes and write down all that you can remember about your answers to the questions and about your thoughts and feelings during the exercise. If you prefer, you can tell them to someone or record your impressions.

FOUR STORIES: INTEGRATION

Tracy

"This was fun. I did all three of the exercises and got something interesting from all of them. Science kept emerging. And the environment. Also different cultures. I could see myself investigating interesting problems about the environment and producing something that would be of significant benefit to the world. When I gave advice to the 12-year-old, I was a scientist who had made some important discoveries about the habitats around the coral reefs. I told the young boy that he should find something that was completely fascinating and pursue it like crazy. Don't worry too much about money. Worry more about doing something meaningful that you feel passionate about."

Brian and Janet

Brian:

"When I did the exercise about removing an impediment, I got a rude awakening. If I had all the money I needed to live on — more than I could spend — I wouldn't have anything to do. I could almost picture myself being like my mother: directionless, flat, trying to find something to occupy my time. I did the exercise on giving advice, too. The main advice I gave was, 'Find something worth living for.' Neither my parents nor Janet's parents have had very strong marriages. Unless Janet and I do something different, we could easily drift apart, too. I could see agreeing to have a baby just to give Janet something to do, turning the entire parenting thing over to her, and then endin up just like my mother and father. I'm rethinking this whole deal. Maybe I've been missing something important." Feelings now: *"Very, very thoughtful."*

Janet:

"When I did the exercise on an ideal day, I had this clear image of doing a research project. I would ask people questions about what they wanted and how they liked things, and then figure out from their answers how to make them happier with our service. I could work on my own projects and think about them as much as I wanted to. The whole image made me happy. When I described it to Brian, he said, 'Why don't you do it?' At that moment I realized that's exactly what I could do. I could do detailed research on customers so that the company would be able to avoid some complaints and pitch its services more toward what people already want. Brian said that marketing could use that kind of information. This is all tremendously exciting to me. For the first time, I felt I could do a job that was really me."

Feelings now: *"Very excited."*

Elizabeth

"When I did the exercise about my ideal day, the image I had was of working hard, solving problems, doing something interesting, quitting at 5:30, and going home to be with my children and husband. And I don't mean taking a big briefcase home with me, either. I mean really being with my family. It was a wonderful image. I told my husband about it, and he said, 'Sure, honey. You could no more do that than fly to

the moon.' I started thinking, 'Why not?' "The second image I had was when I did the exercise on looking back. The advice I gave was, 'Find something you're really passionately interested in, and make it happen.' What's interesting was that in the image of myself in this exercise, I was a famous innovator in children's day care."

Feelings now: "Excited. Energetic. I think I know what I want to do. First of all, I'm going to start working more normal hours. I will make that happen. Second, I'm going to look into day care at our company. Maybe there are a whole range of child-related services the company could offer its employees. I know of some innovative programs. I'll find out about them."

Carl

"This was easy. My ideal day was working for the Free Clinic. I enjoy it and enjoy the people there. I feel like I'm doing something for people that they really need. The feeling I get working there is exhilarating.

"When I did the 'taking away an impediment' exercise, I was still doing something like the Free Clinic. I was in charge of it. Which is interesting, because the executive director of the last 12 years is leaving in three months. They've already offered me another job on staff. I'm thinking about looking at that executive director position.

"My advice to the student was this: Do something you enjoy. Do something you find meaningful. Don't wait around until you're old before you realize you ought to enjoy what you do."

Feelings now: "Excited. I haven't felt this enthusiastic about anything in at least a couple of years."

> NEXT CHAPTER: The ideas and images you gain from these exercises may help you start to crystallize a vision—an image of what you want your future to look like and how you want to live in it. As you start to get an image of this future, you are ready to Survey. Surveying is a practical, reality-based, hands-on way to translate your image or picture into substantive reality and into a solid path to get you there. In the next chapter we describe Surveying. The Thought Experiment will help you carry out a Survey interview.

SURVEYING MAKES THE VITAL CONNECTION BETWEEN **YOU AND YOUR DREAMS,** AND THE REALITY OF THE MARKETPLACE.

IT HELPS YOU FIND YOUR EXACT FIT.

SURVEYING

The most difficult part of creativity may happen *after* the creative insight. In fact, lack of attention to this step is probably what sinks most creative ideas. You can have the most imaginative Personal Vision of all, but it won't help you unless you connect it to your real life.

Surveying is a tool we use to help bridge the gap between integrative insight and reality. It is powerful, subtle and remarkably effective. Let's look at how it worked with Jim, a young manager.

Surveying

Jim, a production manager, had a creative idea for tightening production schedules. His idea came to him in a dream. The whole production process could be organized more efficiently with little additional cost and a reduction in total manpower needs. He couldn't wait to get to work to tell his boss.

When he launched into telling her how production should be reorganized, he was surprised and disconcerted as his wonderful idea seemed to melt away. What came out was only a pale shadow of his whole idea, and the more questions his boss asked, the thinner and more insubstantial it became. He finally realized that she was just listening politely and didn't get the power of the idea at all.

Jim did have a creative idea, but he had not done the work that would make it real. The idea had come out of his right brain; it had come from a dream. To explain it to anyone else, he needed to translate it to the left hemisphere. He would have to put it into words.

People generally have the same experience as Jim when they try to put their most creative thoughts into words. What was a rich, colorful idea at the inception becomes one-dimensional, ordinary, and limited. It is only by translating an idea into words that we gain control of it, that we have the ability to use and exploit it.

Frustrated by his first attempt to convince his boss, Jim worked through his idea again. First of all, he drew a picture of his plan to reorganize production. Then he wrote it all down on a flow sheet. The flow sheet detailed every aspect of production affected by the changes. He practiced talking about the changes with his wife, explaining his chart point by point. He told her about the problem his changes were designed to solve, and how his idea would improve overall production. His wife didn't know anything about the production process, but she asked Jim questions that sent him back to his flow sheet to reorganize and solve some major problems in his proposal.

As Jim got more excited about his idea, he became determined to see it through. Then, he noticed an article in a trade magazine in which a manager talked about organizing information systems. The recommendations the manager proposed were structurally very much like those that Jim had conceived of.

Jim called the author of the article. They talked for several hours during four different conversations. Jim felt energized. For the first time since his original conception, he knew his idea would work.

With his boss's permission, Jim then went to other people in the production process who would be affected by change. He talked to a number of them, explaining to each one what he saw as a problem, and then discussed his idea. Each time he did this, he refined his original idea further. He realized that he had not taken into account some important details in his first conception. In some instances, the changes Jim proposed would create new problems.

When Jim returned to his boss, it was with a written proposal for change. He detailed not only exactly what he thought should be changed and how, but also what he projected the results would be. He addressed the kind of real-world detail that adds richness and texture to a proposal. He also addressed potential problems and how to solve them.

At this point, his boss realized that she had only one decision to make. What Jim was proposing would save a great deal in time and effort, cutting out needless redundancies. Jim had thought about it from every angle and the whole plan looked quite promising.

Keep in mind that the basic proposal Jim had described to his boss the day after his dream was exactly the same proposal that his boss later thought was a no-brainer. What had changed was that Jim had made his creative idea real.

The Process of Making an Idea Real

The process Jim had used to transform his original insight into an effective, compelling presentation may seem far removed from the process of figuring out what to do in your career, but it's not. If you are to make any move in your career, you will need to convince someone else that you're right. You will need to make a compelling case for whatever you decide you want to do, whether it is to shift to a new responsibility at your present job, let go of a task that drives you crazy, change jobs altogether, go to graduate school, or jump into a field right out of college. Whatever you want to do, you will have to tell your idea to some critical people and convince them it's a good idea. Even if you realize you want to stay precisely where you are, you still have to make a compelling case for your decision. Otherwise you are trapped.

Surveying makes the vital connection between the reality of yourself and your dreams and the reality of the marketplace. It helps you find your exact fit.

To begin Surveying, you must have an idea. We designed the previous Thought Experiments to bring in all of the important career factors and help you integrate them into a strong Personal Vision. Your Personal Vision can give you direction and focus, or simply a place to start looking. Without this kind of focus, Surveying can't happen.

So let's say that you have an idea about what you are looking for, or what you would like to be doing with your life, or how you would like to be living. If your idea springs from a strong connection to yourself, then it can form the nucleus of your Survey work.

The Steps in Surveying

Step 1: Write it down; force yourself to put the idea, as completely as possible, in words in your notebook. Get the flow and sequence right. Put it on a time line. When do you want to be doing this? What are the intermediate steps? What will you have to do first in order to arrive where you want to be? Put those on a time line also.

Step 2: Tell your idea to someone outside your systems. It has been said that you don't really know something until you can explain it to a reasonably intelligent seven-year-old. A person outside your systems has no agenda or preconceptions about you and your career and doesn't know anything about the issues or the problems with which you are dealing. You will find out a great deal by talking to a person like this about your plans. You can use the insights you get back to revise your original idea.

Step 3: This is the critical step in Surveying: finding someone who is doing the same thing, or close to it. Once you have a clear, written conception of your idea, find someone who is doing something very similar. It may be in a different arena, or involve a different process, but the idea may still be similar. Interview this person and find others to interview. The Thought Experiment at the end of this chapter deals with the Survey Interview. It can save you hours of planning and keep you from going down dead-ends. It can be the most powerful and useful step you take in making your idea real.

Step 4: After thorough Survey work, design a presentation. This should combine all of the elements of your creative conception with how you have molded and modified your idea to work in the real world. The presentation should start with the relationship between your idea and you. What abilities, skills and interests of yours does it utilize? What values and goals does it fulfill? How does your personality help you in carrying out your idea? How does your idea relate to your past or your family of origin?

Then the presentation should shift to the marketplace. You must be able to tell the person you're communicating with how your idea will help him or her. If you were making a presentation for a business, for instance, you would need to have learned enough about the business and the marketplace through your Survey Interviews to know exactly what needs your idea will fill. You will need to know enough to overcome all of the inevitable questions.

So how does it all work? Let's pick up Ruth's story from an earlier chapter.

Ruth's Story, continued

You may remember the story of Ruth, the buyer of Italian cloth, from Chapter Six. She didn't just stumble into the perfect job. She had done all the work of creating a Personal Vision. She had written down what she knew of it. You may remember that the idea she started with, although well connected to her abilities and other personal factors, was vague and ill-formed. She wanted to work in an artistic field. She wanted to use the skills acquired in her years as a buyer. She had a particular affinity for the artistic qualities of cloth and fiber. She wrote down everything she could to describe the position she sought, even though she did not know yet what that position was.

Ruth told her idea to people outside her systems. This is an important step, often overlooked. Ruth first proposed her idea following an integration exercise. "I had this crazy idea of working with cloth. You know, buying special cloth." She was ready to reject the idea entirely and go on to something more practical. The other people in her workshop weren't in her systems, though. They didn't see anything crazy about it. They saw how well it matched much of what she wanted in life. We find in our programs that when people have really creative ideas, they frequently want to reject them at first. But people outside your immediate systems can often see creative solutions as genuine innovations.

Ruth determined to make her idea real. She started Survey Interviews. She started a chart to record her Survey work. Using the interview format you will find in the Thought Experiment, she interviewed people in positions suggested by her description of her ideal career. She interviewed two museum directors and several curators and museum archivists. She interviewed several creative and design people from advertising firms. She interviewed many interior designers and decorators.

Each time she interviewed someone, she found out first about that person as an individual, then about that person's job, then about the company that person worked for, and finally about the whole field in which the person worked. (As you will see in the Survey Thought Experiment, this is a useful order for asking questions in a Survey Interview.) Although Ruth always insisted at the beginning of each interview that she was not looking for a job or asking for one, she was offered three different jobs by people who were impressed with her knowledge and intelligence. Ruth was prepared for this, because it frequently happens during surveys. She knew what she was looking for clearly enough to turn these offers down and keep on pressing. She was not ready to make a formal proposal yet because she didn't know enough about the area of business she was exploring.

Ruth interviewed designers and buyers for design shops. With every interview, she learned more about the tight little circle in which she had become interested, and she found more people to interview. She filled up several posters with her Survey notes. When she understood how difficult it was for upscale design studios to find unusual art cloth, she saw that many had a problem for which she was uniquely qualified to provide a solution.

At this point, Ruth met and interviewed the architect to whom she would eventually make her proposal. Long before this, she had noticed a change in her interviews. She often knew more about what was happening in the field and in her area of interest than the people she interviewed. Often, they asked her questions about what was going on because she was so clearly knowledgeable.

In the course of her interviews, Ruth met a person who had tried to import art cloth, but could never find a ready market. Ruth was sure she had enough contacts to create and sustain a market for this cloth. She felt ready for a presentation. She saw the architect as having the most pressing need, so she decided to start there.

Ruth scheduled another interview with the architect—this would be her third. This time she told him that she wanted to make a presentation to him that would be of interest. She outlined her whole idea, starting with herself, moving to the architect's need for unusual art cloth, to how she would propose to work with him. For the architect, it became obvious. Ruth had known it would be.

Surveying, as a process, is much like a funnel, large at the top, smaller and more focused as you progress. Though her idea was largely unfocused, Ruth was still able to use it to begin her Survey work. In the course of almost 50 interviews over several months, she eliminated a number of dead-ends and uncovered several likely avenues. As she continued to explore, her focus narrowed. As she found out more and more about a progressively narrow field, her idea became more precise and more attuned to marketplace demand. When she made her proposal, it was exactly suited not only to what she wanted to do, but also to what she knew the market needed.

Surveying at Turning Points

At every Turning Point, we need a Personal Vision. At every Turning Point we should Survey. The better the idea we have of the road ahead, the better we can make decisions about our lives.

Starting in 1990, we ourselves were at the Midlife Turning Point. We spent more than two years Surveying. Beginning with an idea for a new business, we interviewed anyone we could find who did anything remotely similar to what we had in mind. We personally went through any program we could find that related to the issue. We interviewed hundreds of potential competitors, potential customers, and business people who used a business structure we might want to use. At each interview we took away invaluable information. Even if it turned out that a particular person did nothing remotely similar to what we had in mind, we focused our thoughts, narrowed our ideas, and became more precise and knowledgeable in presenting our case each time we talked to someone.

Our experience in helping people launch new ideas in their careers—whether they have ideas for whole new businesses or only for a slight shift in job responsibilities—is that they often ignore the need to Survey. The more Survey work you do before your presentations, the stronger your case will be and the more confident and solid you will feel in your presentation.

Let's take the case of Sharon, an advertising director at a large public utility.

Sharon's Story

Sharon went through the Eight Personal Vision Factors and created a Personal Vision. What she found out startled her. She had many more abilities than her staff position was making use of. She had realized before that she was not interested in her job and that it failed to challenge her or push her to grow. Knowing this about her abilities helped her focus on what she wanted. She wanted her job to express more of her unique talents.

Often managers ask us what the company gets out of letting its employees go through a process of gaining a Personal Vision. Some feel that if employees really looked carefully at what they are expected to do, they would quit and do something else. Some feel that their employees are already highly motivated. Our overwhelming experience is that people who create a Personal Vision feel more connected to their companies and their careers because they learn exactly how to position and utilize their unique talents. They also feel less stressed and less burned-out for the same reasons.

Soon after Sharon went through our program, an internal memo came across her desk: The company wanted to hire a national accounts manager. Making that kind of shift would be unusual, but Sharon knew she had the right mix of abilities, talents, personality, and interests for the job. Over a period of two weeks, Sharon pulled out her Personal Vision statement and used it to craft a careful description of how she saw herself carrying out the new job. She then interviewed the person who had just vacated the position, three people who were in similar positions in the company, and five people who would be reporting to her. After each interview, she revised her plan and wrote down what she had learned.

Sharon applied for the job. One of the people who interviewed her was someone she had interviewed about the job just the week before. She had become knowledgeable about the position and the system by interviewing others. She used her Personal Vision to make a compelling and clear presentation for the job. She started with her interests—even her interest in managing detail as a young child. She then went to her natural abilities, her personality and her demonstrable skills, and continued with her strong values. She showed clearly how all these different aspects of herself interlocked and made her qualified, not just for her skills, but for her heart and talents. The case she made was airtight. Sharon got the job.

She would never have thought about this opportunity had she not looked carefully at her career and life to understand more fully what she wanted. Her Personal Vision was like a template. When the right job came along, she recognized it instantly. She is now the national accounts manager. recognized it instantly. By Surveying, Sharon made her Vision real.

Thought Experiment H:

Surveying Interviews, Survey Presentation

Surveying is the most powerful tool we have for making creative ideas real. You can never know enough about a market or a field. Each time you do a Survey Interview, even if it seems that you didn't find out anything new, you force yourself to challenge your ideas against the reality of the marketplace. You become sharper, more focused and more realistic in what you can and cannot do.

The Survey Interview
WHEN TO INTERVIEW

The Survey Interview can serve several purposes in the whole process of career self-management. At the beginning, you can use it to make your Personal Vision more focused and related to the marketplace. So long as you have even a vague notion, you can interview people to find out about them, their jobs and careers, and the fields they are in. Each time you do this, you will narrow your focus by making your Personal Vision more realistic.

You can continue this process of narrowing your Personal Vision almost indefinitely, making it more precise until your idea crystallizes. When you feel more certain about what you want to do, you can continue to use Surveying to gain valuable knowledge about the field and about systems. As we noted in the body of this chapter, when the people you interview start asking you questions because they recognize your knowledge and expertise, you know you will soon be ready to make a presentation. This may take several months, as in Ruth's case, or over a year, as in ours.

WHOM TO INTERVIEW

Let your Personal Vision guide you. Even if it seems ill-formed and unfocused, it can give you clues about whom you should interview. At first, you can gain valuable insight from anyone who does anything even remotely like the things you have in mind. As you do each interview, you will learn more and find other people to talk to. You will also become increasingly precise about whom to interview and what exactly you are trying to find out.

SETTING UP THE INTERVIEW

Setting up the interview lays the tone and groundwork for the interview itself.

Paying attention to details in the setup can insure a successful outcome.

Call the person and state who you are and how you were referred to him or her. Let's say this person is a woman who manages an organization in a style similar to the style you are interested in employing. When you call, tell her that you would like to meet for 30 minutes or so at her convenience. You are not selling anything. You are not looking for a job. You are only interested in learning how she manages her organization. Explain how you found out about her. Make very effort to accommodate her schedule and time.

CONDUCTING THE INTERVIEW

Start with the person herself. How did she decide to get into her present career? What were the decisions she made at Turning Points? What was her reasoning at each?

> College to Work (age 22-25)
> Age-30 Assessment (age 28-33)
> Midlife Transition (age 38-45)
> Age-50 Assessment (age 50-55)
> Pre-Retirement Transition (age 60-65)

How did she move into her present position?
What does she like about it? What does she dislike?
How did she come to adopt her present management style?
How would she describe it?
Describe a recent day that she felt was productive and that she enjoyed.
What made it enjoyable?
What made it productive?
Describe a recent bad day or one that was unproductive.
What made it bad?
What made it unproductive?
What does she see for her own future?
What does she see for the future of this field (industry, company)?
What has helped and guided her most over the years?
What advice would she have for someone just starting out?

Again, just as with the family interviews, use these questions to give yourself a springboard for the interview. If anything strikes your interest, pursue it.

Remember, you are asking this person, as a favor to you, to talk about the most fascinating subject on earth—herself and her opinions. You don't have to agree with everything she says; just listen. If you approach it openly, you will learn a great deal, even from interviews in which you thoroughly disagree with every point your subject makes. Your job is not to change this person's mind, but to learn something that will be valuable to you in making your Personal Vision real.

When you have done enough Survey Interviews to be thoroughly knowledgeable about the field and what you intend to do in it (to recognize the best fit for your abilities, personality, interests, values and goals; to understand others' needs that your Personal Vision can contribute to; and to plan how you want to go about implementing your Vision), you are probably ready for a presentation.

YOUR PRESENTATION

Start your presentation with yourself. Ideally, list what you have learned about your talents, interests, personality, skills, experience, values, goals and even family of origin and stage of development. This is the most effective way to communicate who you are, what you have to offer, and why. Next, talk about what you know to be the needs of the organization or the person to whom you are presenting. Your Survey work will pay off here – it will enable you to speak knowledgeably and cogently. Link yourself to the company's needs by means of your Personal Vision, showing how the sum total of your personal career factors contributes to fulfilling a need in the company. (If you find you can't make this link, or that it appears weak, this may be a signal that you need to do more Surveying.) You should have a clear vision for this job—what it entails, how you would work and with whom, what the potential problems may be, and what factors will make you successful. Your job in the presentation will be to communicate the essence of this vision, to be able to answer any questions that may come up, and to transmit the enthusiasm and passion that you can bring to the job.

FOUR STORIES: SURVEYING

Tracy

"I have interviewed about 10 people so far. I started with a microbiologist

at the university. He was interesting and let me tag along with him for a day to see what he did. I knew from that I wasn't interested in pure science. I need to see some result that is closer to the real world. He pointed me in the direction of a friend of his who is a behavioral biologist. Her work is almost all theoretical. But it was interesting to talk to her about how she sees it being useful to people—eventually. After her, I interviewed a biochemist. He introduced me to some people running a primate research lab. That was more like it. I interviewed several of their research people and talked to them about their projects. I liked the whole feel of the place, and I was interested in what they are doing. After I had had two or three interviews there and spent a day with one of the researchers, one of them told me to apply to be a tech assistant there. So I did. And now that's what I'm doing, working full time. I am also planning on taking a graduate course in primate biology and evolution at the university. I am pretty sure I will go to graduate school in the next couple of years, but I feel the experience I'm getting now in hands-on research is wonderful, so I'm not in a crashing hurry. The scientists I'm working with have connections all over, and I'm sure they can help me get into a good graduate program when I'm ready. I don't think I'll spend my career in primate research, but I know I will go to graduate school in some area of biology. Lately, I have become fascinated with marine mammals."

Feelings now: "For the first time since I quit psychology, I feel like I know what I'm doing. I know I have a long way to go, but that's OK, because I have this clear image of doing something interesting and meaningful."

Brian and Janet

Brian:

"My first question was, whom do I interview? I'm already doing what I like. Then, as I got to thinking about it, I realized that the real question for me was how to have a life besides work. My father never has. When I put it this way, I thought of a story someone had told me about an older guy in Human Resources. He had refused some assignments because it would take him away from his family. At least that was the story. I found out who the guy was and called him up. When I said what I wanted,

he immediately suggested we have lunch. It was fascinating. He decided early in his career that he would not let his work take him from his family and that he would not ask his family to move around unreasonably. I asked him if he felt it had hurt his career. He said, in the short run, yes, though not as much as you might be afraid it would. In the long run, he's accomplished much of what he wanted to do in his career and has ended up in charge of a major portion of Human Resource services nationwide. I would like to end up like him. He gave me the names of two other executives in different departments who have done the same thing. I called them and talked to both of them a long time. The more I talked to them, the more I realized that it is more possible to have a family life than I had thought. It's going to be rough for the next five or six years, but if I don't start making room for a family now, I could wind up divorced like about half the people I know.

"Next, I took my boss to lunch and set out the whole deal to him. I went through my abilities, interests, personality, values, goals—even what I had found out about my family. After that I told him what I wanted to do and why, and asked him if he could help. He was actually very sympathetic and quite helpful. He likes my work a lot and feels that I have real promise with the company. He said I would have to set limits on my time myself, but that he would help by making sure I got some good projects. He doesn't know what effect this will have on my being chosen for the fast track."

Brian's feelings now: "Determined. I feel I am sort of sailing into unknown territory. The company would like it if I worked 24 hours a day. To tell the truth, a part of me feels I should work around the clock if the company needs it. But I need a whole life, too. So does Janet. If we are going to have a family, we have to make it a priority for both of us."

Janet:

"I did some research and found out there is a company in town that does market research. I called them up and got to talk to one of their senior researchers. He was very happy to talk to me when I explained what I wanted. We met and talked probably two hours about what he did. This was fascinating. It was like doing a research project for your work. He gave me the names of two other people in the field, and I interviewed *both of them. One of them gave me the name of someone doing market and customer research in a large corporation. This would be more like my own situation, so I was eager to interview her. She helped, because, as it turned out, she had started her own little unit of customer research in this company about 10 years ago. She had been able to show tremendous benefit to the company over that time for very little outlay. This would give me a strong case to my bosses. She offered me a job there, but by this time, I was already feeling I could get my own show going in my company. Over the next three months, I continued interviewing. I also started some preliminary talks with some people in my company about what I had in mind and why. I wanted to get an idea about what roadblocks I would probably run into. I finally wrote up a proposal in which I showed what other company's experiences had been with ongoing customer/market research. I made a formal pitch and they are going to let me proceed on a trial basis. This whole project is the most exciting thing I have ever done."*

Janet's feelings now: "Tremendously happy and proud of what I've accomplished. Brian and I are planning to have a baby after next year. I want to get his project rolling. I am finding out something new every day, and I couldn't be happier."

Elizabeth

"The first thing I did was go to my boss and tell him that I was out of here at 5:30. I was not going to travel, and I wouldn't work at night. That was rash, I know, and I was holding my breath after I said it. He looked at me and said, 'OK.' I didn't know whether I'd be able to stick to it or not, but mostly I have. I've had to travel some, but I have also been able to turn down some travel. I do leave between 5:30 and 6:00 every day. My family responded immediately. Things have been much less stressed at home. I have had to force myself to be more organized and to be clearer about my priorities. I also delegate better. I think I am actually working so much more effectively that I get everything accomplished that needs to be done.

"The second thing I have been working on is company-sponsored day care. I've probably interviewed 50 people, from day-care operators

to consultants to human-resource people to architects. This has been interesting. I know we'll win eventually.

I have my own team of people from all over the company who are now working on this project—all on our own time. The company hasn't quite understood the idea yet; nor do they see the benefits. Other companies are sponsoring day care for employees' children, and we will have to solve a number of significant problems to bring it off, but I am sure we are right. Anyway, the whole project is very exciting."

Feelings now: "Excited. Creative. Alive."

Carl

"I started right away and interviewed the executive director of the Free Clinic. It is very intriguing. Resources are quite limited, and a large part of the role is fund-raising and public relations. I have a lot of contacts in the business community, and I think I can build some corporate sponsorships. The only thing holding me back is the pay. It would be a lot less than I had been making. On the other hand, my wife and I are pretty well set for retirement, and college for the kids is nearly over; so I think we could make do with less. I am pretty sure from talking to the Board members of the Free clinic that I would have a good shot at the position, and I think I will ask them to consider me for it.

"I feel I could always go back into business somewhere, but I realize I would be disappointed to do so. The opportunity to work at the Free Clinic is much more exciting to me, even if it won't pay as well."

Feelings now: "Happy."

NEXT CHAPTER: One of the biggest problems facing people who create their Personal Visions and then set out to make them real is creating boundaries. Elizabeth had to create boundaries in the story above; Richard did the same in Chapter 5; and we saw it in Joseph's story in Chapter 7. The first step in creating boundaries is the hardest one—figuring out what you want. That is what this book has been about up until now. The next steps in creating boundaries involve stating what you want your boundary to be and then making it stick. That is what the next chapter is about.

SETTING A BOUNDARY GIVES
YOU THE OPPORTUNITY
TO MAKE
AUTHENTIC STATEMENTS
ABOUT **YOURSELF**.

IT GIVES YOU
THE **OPPORTUNITY** TO SAY
"THIS IS WHERE
I START AND THE
CORPORATION ENDS."

Creating Personal
Boundaries

A very successful manager in one of the fastest-growing high-tech companies in the world spent about forty to fifty hours going through all of the exercises in this book. How he came to do that is an interesting story in itself.

"My work has always been rated 'Excellent' by my managers. I have been with this company for five years, which is generally considered to be two or three lifetimes because of the stress level here. At each career juncture, I was offered a promotion to more and bigger managerial responsibilities. I don't really know how many hours a week I was working, but there were many nights when I slept on a cot in my office. The reason I read this book and took the trouble to go through the exercises in it was an insight I had one (rare) day when I was actually at home. I was watching my young daughter and her friend play with their Barbie dolls. My daughter took the male doll and tossed it over her shoulder into a box. 'Dad's at the office sitting in front of his computer,' was her explanation. I knew then that something would have to change in my life. I just didn't know what. It was very soon after that that someone gave me this book."

After going through all of the exercises and creating a Personal Vision, this manager realized something important: "I knew what I wanted to do, but I felt that the only way I could do it would be to quit my job and start somewhere else. I desperately wanted to follow through and create the life I had envisioned—a forty-hour work week, a job I felt I could actually manage and enjoy, no nights, no weekends—but the culture at this company views a job like that as a vacation, not an actual job."

Systems and Rules

What the manger had come up against was what everyone who goes up against a system eventually faces—how to make his own reality stick as opposed to the system's reality. His system had a clear, simple, but unstated rule that covered engineers' time: You will be available at any time and all times to answer the needs of our customers. If you're on vacation and a customer needs you, then you will come back. If the customer needs you to work 24 hours a day for three for four days in a row – well, that's why we have sleeping cots at the office.

Almost every story we've told in this book involved change by someone. And those changes almost invariably involve systems that do not want anything to change. Furthermore, part of what makes a system a system is that it has built-in self-correcting mechanisms. If one part of a system (you, for instance) strays too far out of line, then the system reacts. It will try to pull the errant element back into line. If the straying element doesn't respond, the system will up the ante, finally getting to the point of rejecting the rebel altogether.

As we discussed in Chapter 1, all systems have rules, and this includes all work systems. The rules that are easiest to manage and deal with are the ones that are clearly and overtly stated: All employees will wear white shirts and ties (men) or conservative business suits and stockings (women) every working day. You may not like this rule, but since it's so clearly stated, you can decide whether you want to live with it or not before you sign on.

The rules that lead to far more stress and binding anxiety are unstated, covert, 'implied' rules. These are legion—a good example of one is provided in the example of the engineer's company. These rules control our behavior, but they are hard to fight or even understand very clearly, because they are never overtly stated. If you were to look up the company's policy in the HR manual, you wouldn't find the rule that requires engineers to be available 24 hours a day. But everybody in the company behaves as though that rule is absolute.

What this means is that in order to fit in, you have to submerge yourself. You have to allow the company to take over some of your life. You have to give up some of your decision-making power and sense of control. The net effect is to give up something of your personal identity.

Whenever you are involved in a system, you have to give up part of yourself. The important questions are: How much of yourself and what parts of yourself do you want to give up to stay in the system? The flip side to these questions is equally important: What are you *not* willing to give up about yourself in order to be in this system? Having clear answers to these questions is an important part of your Personal Vision.

Boundaries

Boundaries are the means by which we create our identities in the first place. The setting of boundaries starts when we are young, in our families of origin. They help us create our identities as individuals and teach us how to form groupings and set limits in our relationships with others. When our parents set a limit for us—"No you can't go out after dark, because you're too young"—we have a clear and definite response to it. Limits set by others can make us angry. We know what we want; we just can't have it. In the process of having a limit set and having a definite response that is our own, not our parents', we create a boundary. We gain a sense of who we are and what reality is. I want to go outside. Reality says that I can't. As we get older we take over setting our own limits, so instead of letting our parents set limits and make boundaries for us, we have to do it for ourselves. By setting boundaries for ourselves, we carve out a clear and continuing sense of our own identities.

The reverse is also true. When we *don't* set limits and *don't* create boundaries, we begin to lose our sense of identity. In corporations, that is another way of saying that we fall victim to the Lemming Conspiracy. The Stress Cycle involves taking our direction from outside and submerging ourselves in the direction our systems want us to pursue. It usually means that we are caught up in spending our time and energy pursuing goals and ends that ultimately don't matter very much—to us. As adults involved in corporations, all of us get caught up in systems and start to feel the stress of being a System Self instead of an authentic True Self.

The Balance Cycle involves taking our direction from the inside, planning ahead for our careers, finding worthy values and principles to guide ourselves and making decisions from a Personal Vision. We can create a win-win situation for ourselves and our companies by recognizing how and where we can make our best contribution.

When you create a Personal Vision, it becomes a picture of your True Self operating within a system. But to make it real, you have to impose a boundary.

It's not enough to have your Personal Vision in your thoughts. Your system will never be able to respond to your True Self unless or until you say, "This is my limit, I will do this, but not that." The question is, how do you get to the point where you can create a boundary in a corporation or system, and how can you be sure that the system won't turn around and throw you out because you broke the rules?

We have found that setting boundaries is one of the most important hurdles people face after they create their Personal Visions. A manager at IBM realized that he was most interested in and worked best in environments that were a bit chaotic. He liked to be assigned to brand new teams with lots of problems to solve because that was how he could use his natural talents most fully. When management asked him to take over a unit that was doing well and that had a long history of making its numbers, he realized there would be trouble.

> **"Boundaries define us. They define *what is me* and *what is not me*. A boundary shows me where I end and someone else begins, leading me to a sense of ownership."**
>
> **–Cloud and Townsend, Boundaries**

"I knew from doing the work on my Personal Vision that the fit would be bad. Even though the new assignment would be a promotion, I was very hesitant to take it because I knew it wouldn't interest me. Eventually, I would get bored. Finally, I told them no, I didn't want it. I used my workbook from my Personal Vision seminar to explain my decision to my boss. And his boss. It ended up working in my favor. They could see the truth of what I was saying about myself. They could see that I wasn't being capricious or uncooperative. I was just telling them an authentic truth about how I work best and what was the best fit for me in the company. Later, I got another assignment from them that was much more in line with who I am and what I have to offer to the company."

Exerting a boundary gives you the opportunity to make an authentic statement about yourself. It gives you the opportunity to say, "This is where I start and the corporation ends." If you look at your Personal Vision as a complete, authentic and true statement about yourself, then when you exert a boundary in order to make the Vision happen in your actual life, you are taking a step to establish a clear personal identity in relation to the corporation or the system.

Setting a boundary can also make you feel vulnerable when you go up against a strong and seemingly unified culture. Questions arise. Is it fair for me to assert a boundary that no one else has? What if my boundaries are totally unreasonable? What if they are perceived as unreasonable? What are my choices then? Am I then faced with caving in or quitting? What if they just think I'm too much trouble and fire me?

These kinds of questions and anxieties are fairly normal when you take on a system at work. Let's look at some practical ways to deal with boundaries that can help you know when you want to assert some boundary for yourself and how to go about it.

First, Know Yourself

The first and most important part of setting boundaries is to know what boundaries you want to set. This is an important goal in creating your Personal Vision. In our seminars with corporate clients, the participants spend time creating their Personal Vision, but they also examine how they can work most effectively within their teams and corporations.

You may think that people in corporations who go through our seminars end up with extreme Personal Visions that couldn't possibly work in any rational company environment. In fact, we don't find this to be true. We do sometimes have participants who, through the Lemming Conspiracy, have strayed far away from their True Selves and are living out a System Self that does not satisfy their needs—like the executive who went through our program a couple of years ago and who routinely worked 95 hours a week. When participants do the work of creating a Personal Vision, they often find that they want to make changes. But the changes people generally want to make are specific and focused.

The executive who was working 95 hours a week—Lauren—was completely amazed when she did the Values portion of the seminar she attended. "I realized that the values I was living out were exactly at opposite poles from the values that I hold to be most important. I was putting the most energy and time into my least important values—money, position and power—and the least energy and time into my most important values—my children and my marriage. I knew that something had to change."

Before I started the seminar, I thought, "I'll just keep working at my present job for another year or two, and then quit. I felt so much stress that I was beginning to doubt that I would even make it six more months. I also felt that my company did not really care about me or about what was important to me."

"In the seminar, though, I realized that I didn't want to quit my job. I like it. I'm good at it. It really uses my most important abilities. I like the people I work with. Many of my life goals are definitely related to my job. What I really needed to do was make my work more manageable—more human, I would say."

A year after Lauren finished the seminar, we talked to her about what she was doing. She was still working at the same company and in the same job, even though there had been at least two major reorganizations. "I work about 55 hours a week now. And I'm still hitting my numbers. In the last week I have been told that I am a better manager, better executive, better parent and a better wife than I was nine months ago. You guys saved me before I crashed and burned."

Interestingly enough, the story doesn't end there. We talked to Lauren again about nine months later. We got some inkling about what was going on when we called her office to make an appointment with her. As it happened, we called about 5:25 in the afternoon. Her secretary told us that she would take a message, but Lauren wasn't there; she always walked out the door at 5:00. We thought this probably boded well for her life. It was obvious that she had set and maintained a clear boundary.

When we did catch up with her, she had this to say: "I work about 40 to 45 hours a week these days. I can't remember the last time I took work home. I almost never travel. The thing I'm proudest of is that I have not paid $1.00 in overtime childcare in the last six months. I am still on my numbers. I work more efficiently now than I did before I developed my Personal Vision. I use my real talents better, and I delegate better. I think a lot of what I was doing before I went through the seminar was spinning my wheels and wasting a lot of energy. I have a lot better feeling about my company. I feel that they care about me here. I'm not thinking about quitting any more. I can see staying here and moving up in my organization."

The company she works for is a global technology company. We have had a number of people tell us—in earnest—that you have to work at least 70 hours a week at this company in order to keep your job. So how did this executive do it? Was it luck? Was this some special case?

No, it was not some special case. Lauren went through the process that we follow in this book. Part of the answer for her had to do with her natural talents and abilities. She saw that she never got to use some of her strongest talents because she wasted so much time in tasks for which she had little talent at all. These tasks absorbed 90 percent of her energy and creativity and gave her little pleasure or satisfaction. She also saw that her priorities were out of whack. When she interviewed her mother and father, a lot of her choices began to make sense to her; she was duplicating the life her father had lived. He had been in sales and traveled a great deal when she was growing up. Her memory of him was that he was gone a good deal of the time. "I always hated it that my father did not participate much in my life when I was growing up. You can imagine my shock when I realized that my own kids would probably say the same things about me."

Second, Be Clear About Your Goals and Priorities

After creating her Personal Vision, Lauren figured out goals that were specifically related to that vision. As she set her goals, she took everything she had learned about her values, priorities, talents, interests and family of origin into account.

One of the best ways to identify the boundaries you want to set—at work, home or in your personal life—is to look first at how you spend your time. One of the basic boundaries that we all deal with in life is that we have only a limited amount of time—in a day, in our waking hours, in our lives—and no more. How you apportion that time makes a simple, powerful statement about how you live your life. Most of us who are caught in the Stress Cycle and the Lemming Conspiracy find that our time is sucked away from us in tasks that don't seem to matter. Tasks that do matter don't get their fair share of time. A critically important part of moving away from the Lemming Conspiracy is to take charge of your time. A basic law of systems and human relationships is this: Everyone else will control your time unless you take active control of it yourself.

After you look at your time, the next most basic and important factor to control in your life is how you apportion your energy. When we are young, we tend to think (or at least, we act as though) our energy is endless. If we need to exercise, we'll just get up earlier. If we need to finish a project, we'll just stay up later. But just as with time, energy is not endless. We have limits. Our bodies have limits. Putting energy into one set of activities means that you don't have energy for something else. The more careful you are about controlling your energy and putting your energy into projects that are meaningful to you, the more productive and satisfying you will find your career. This means setting boundaries. One writer we know finds that he writes best in the morning. By the afternoon, he has a hard time coming up with anything creative. By setting and maintaining a clear boundary that he can't be disturbed or have appointments in the morning, he is much more productive in his writing, and a lot happier.

Once you have control of your time and energy, other boundaries become possible. If you're not spinning out of control in the Stress Cycle, you can begin to think about the quality of your relationships at work. You can begin to think abut your role at work and how to move into roles and tasks that use your abilities better or that are more rewarding. You can even begin to think about internal boundaries, such as how you want to act with co-workers or how you want to speak to them.

Lauren looked at several boundaries for herself. "The first thing I did was to be clear about my goals. After I worked on my Personal Vision, this was easy. Some of my goals were work-related. Some were family-related. Some of my work goals were about how I work. I knew I wanted to use my talents better and spend less time on tasks that had nothing to do with what I do best. The main goal, though, was that I wanted to spend less time at work. It had pretty much taken over my life. Though I enjoy most of it, I don't enjoy it *that* much. This, of course, dovetailed with my personal goals. I definitely wanted to spend more time with my kids while they were still young, and I wanted to have more time and energy available to be with my husband. I knew I couldn't do it all at once. So I figured out some reasonable intermediate steps."

Lauren knew that her ultimate goal was to manage her career in a different way than she had been doing. She felt it would put too much stress on her and on her systems—work and family—to try to move immediately to her final destination. After gaining a clear sense of her ultimate goals, she thought backwards to create a few intermediate way stations. Lauren's goals were complex. Her goals for work related to and involved her goals for her family.

A Note on Systems

Perceptive readers may have noticed something interesting about the last paragraph. Lauren felt that a sudden, drastic change in her work schedule might put too much stress on her job and her family. One might logically think that if it were a good thing for Lauren to spend more time with her children and husband, then the best thing would be just to do it. The truth is that systems don't change very much or very fast. Even family systems. Lauren felt that if she started showing up at home at 5:30 every day expecting that everyone else in the family would adjust his or her schedule to hers, she might be setting herself up for disappointment. She felt that if she eased her schedule in stages and discussed it beforehand with her family, then everyone might be able to accommodate the changes better.

Every system is different. And the steps for imposing changes in systems are different. Sometimes it's better to introduce changes into a system all at once. Other times, it works better to introduce change so gradually that no one is really aware that anything new is going on. One constant, however, is that if someone in a system changes—that is, changes the rules of the game—then everyone else in the system has to adjust to those changes. Or else the system must expel the member who is trying to change the rules.

Third, Identify Your Internal Points of Resistance

When faced with creating change in a seemingly monolithic corporation, we all tend to think that resistance to change will come from the corporation itself. In fact, however, many of the most important barriers to change will come from you, from your own thoughts and feelings. These are your internal points of resistance.

What are these barriers? Here are some typical thoughts that will almost certainly result in non-action:

- My boss would never go for this.
- This will result in more work for my co-workers.
- Everyone will be mad at me.
- No one has ever done anything like this before.

- What right do I have to do something different from everyone else?
- I'll feel guilty if I have it better than everyone else.

The common denominator in all of these statements of internal resistance is simple; they are all externally focused. They say, in effect, "I can't do what I want to do and what I feel is right for me because someone else would feel unhappy about it." Remember from Chapter 2 that this is also the hallmark of the Stress Cycle. As long as your concern is primarily with what others think or will think, you will indeed be stuck. [At the same time, concern for others is a sign that you are approaching your decision with maturity. You are not a free agent and what you do will affect others. Depending on your stage of life and career development, the web of your inter-dependencies may be small and simple or large and complex. To be a responsible person, you must respect the interests of everyone who is dependent upon you or who works with you. In helping you to develop a Personal Vision, our programs will help you to balance your own true interests against the interests of the other people in your life.]

Our experience in helping thousands of people create Personal Visions and then take action on those visions is that as long as you are only externally focused, you won't be able to see most of the real options available to you. On the other hand, the clearer you are about your goals and priorities and the more clearly you can state them—to yourself and to others—the more options you will see.

Find your own points of resistance. Find the statements you make to yourself that keep you stuck. In most cases, these will be statements that are focused outside of yourself, as in the list above. It may well be that your most powerful internal points of resistance to change come right out of your family of origin. As we discussed in Chapter 1 and Chapter 7, all of us learn how to work in systems from our family systems. When we grow up, we join systems that fit us, so it makes sense that we would resist change using tactics that we learned in our original family systems. A simple and useful way to find out what kind of influence your family of origin may have on your resistance to change is to complete the Thought Experiment at the end of this chapter.

You will probably start encountering internal resistance almost as soon as you become clearer and more specific about your Personal Vision. Your resistance may be in the form of simple statements like the ones above, or it may be more nebulous and complex. If you do the Thought Experiment at the end of this chapter, you may become aware of resistance that you didn't realize you had.

As you become aware of points of internal resistances, write them down in your Personal Vision notebook. Don't let them just circulate in your mind. When you write them down, you start to gain some insight and control over them, and they will stop influencing your behavior and decisions so much.

The more you pin down your points of resistance, and the more you write them down in your Personal Vision notebook, the less power they will have over you. The central key to real change is to create your Personal Vision in the first place. When you learn to focus on it to guide your decisions rather than focus on what you think others want you to do, you will be on your way to the Balance Cycle.

Fourth, Develop a Plan—'As If'

This step may help you if you feel you would like to set some boundaries but wonder if you can really do so. If you feel that you can go ahead and create all the boundaries you need to make your Personal Vision real, you may not need to worry about this step. However, if you find yourself clear about the result you want, but you can't figure out how to make it happen, of if you find that the thought of creating a boundary (like Lauren's above—"At 5:00, I'm out of here.") makes you feel anxious, then this small exercise may help.

Start with your Personal Vision. Whatever your Personal Vision is, ask yourself, "If I were going to make this vision real, what would I have to do? Whom would I have to talk to? What points would I have to make stick? What behavior would I have to carry out?" Notice that none of these questions implies that you would actually do anything. You just want to think about what you *would* do if you were going to carry out your Personal Vision.

What boundaries would you need to set and keep *if* you were going to make your Personal Vision real? Remember to think of the larger context of your career, not just of the job you are doing every day. What will you need to change at work? Think in terms of time, energy, relationships, and tasks. How do you want to use your time? How do you want o use your energy? What kind of relationships do you want to develop at work? What tasks do you want to do; what do you not want to do? Write the answers to these questions in your Personal Vision notebook.

What about your personal life? What boundaries will you need to create in your family—even perhaps in your extended family? Remember to think of your goals in terms of your family, your marriage, and your personal and spiritual self. The more you can write down in your Personal Vision notebook, the better.

Remember that you don't have to do anything. Just because you write something down doesn't mean you have to do anything about it. You can help yourself by letting go, for a while, of any sense that you have to translate your boundaries into action. This will help you play with the idea and play with the thought of setting boundaries and leading a different life.

The next part of this imaginary exercise is to pick out one boundary to concentrate on. If you were going to start with one new boundary, which one would you choose? Don't choose a large, far-reaching boundary for the first one. Rather, choose one that is small and relatively easy to translate into action, like reducing your overtime. Now pick the other "as if" boundaries you want to create and put them down in order on a list. List them from the easiest and smallest all the way up to those that will change great parts of your life.

This list is your action plan. The important thing to keep in mind is that you don't have to implement your plan all at once. As an example, if you want to set a boundary to leave the office at 5:30 every day, when you are now leaving at 7:00 every night, it may seem too difficult to achieve that all at once. But if you let everyone know that you intend to leave at 6:30 every night from now on—and then do it—you will be surprised at how much better you will feel. The world won't come to an end. In fact, you may find that you can move relatively easily to your next step, 6:00. And the next, 5:30.

Fifth, Setting Boundaries

The most important and significant part of setting boundaries is that you are the only one who can do it. You cannot expect anyone else to set boundaries for you. You can't even expect anyone else to be happy with boundaries that you set for yourself. If and when you set a boundary, it will be up to you to maintain it. If you want to leave work at 5:30 every day, you are the only person who can make that happen. In fact, there will be some days when you feel that you have to fight everyone in the office to make it happen. There are ways to go about setting boundaries that can help, though.

The main tactic that can help is this: Talk to the people involved. If you want to set a boundary at work, for instance, if you want to take on this kind of task but not that, then talk to the people that this boundary most affects. Don't just talk to your boss; talk to your co-workers and subordinates. Talk to anyone on whom your boundary will have an impact. Tell them how you came to think about this boundary and why you came to the decision you did. Go into as much detail about your whole Personal Vision as you want to. The more people understand why you seek change and exactly what changes you plan to make, the more willing they will be to accept the changes—and they will even cooperate with you to make them happen.

The manager in the high-tech company at this chapter's beginning created a Personal Vision. He spent a good deal of time doing the exercises in this book and putting together a whole picture of what he wanted his life and career to look like. When he finished, it looked as if the only answer for him was to quit. He didn't see any way he could work at his company and live even close to the kind of lifestyle he envisioned.

But he decided nothing would be lost in trying. One of the first boundaries he wanted to impose was around the kind of work he did. It was clear from his work on his Personal Vision that he was not suited by talent or personality to be a manager. "Being a manager drove me crazy. There were so many different problems to take care of all at once. I never felt that I could keep track of everything I should do. It made me anxious all the time. The other part of it was that I really enjoyed working on the tech side. I liked to take on a really interesting tech problem and just work on it until I figured it out. As a manager, you never get to do anything like that, and I missed it.

"Beyond my role as a manager, I wanted to take control of my hours. I wasn't going to work every weekend and I wasn't going to work at night. It was clear from my values that my family comes first in my mind. I was determined to carry out those values in action.

"I talked to my manager first. I took him through the whole story— including watching my daughter throw the Ken doll in the box. I showed him the work that I had done on my Personal Vision and showed him what specifically my Personal Vision looked like. We started developing ideas about how it could work in the company.

"We didn't solve all of the problems at once. The first time I talked to him, we didn't get very far at all. But as we continued talking, I could see that he really wanted to try to make things work. He could also see that I wanted everything to work for him and the company as well.

"It turned out that the hardest boundary to set was to stop being a manager. I am actually still managing people in a very limited way, but I mostly get to work on the kinds of projects that I like. It seems as though every month or so my big boss wants me to take over some management position or other, and we have to go back and forth on how I don't want to be a manager and I'm a lot happier working where I am.

"Setting boundaries around my time has gone a little easier. I talked to the other people on my team about what I had in mind. They were amazingly supportive. I had felt that if I left at a reasonable hour I would feel guilty and feel that I was increasing the work load of everyone else. That has not turned out to be true, but I've had to work at doing parts of my job more efficiently.

"The logic finally became clear in my mind, and it has stayed with me: if everyone worked late and on the weekends without setting any boundaries, then the management of the company would not get the feedback that they need to hire more people or restructure the job. I know that management does not want to be abusive to people. On the other hand, they are not going to change anything unless people set boundaries and let them know what's really going on.

"I work about 45 hours a week. I don't work at night. I don't work on the weekend. Every few days something comes up that makes me think that I should just keep working past the time when I need to be home with my family. I just keep this image in my mind of my daughter throwing the doll in a box, and it helps me set a limit on my time and maintain my boundaries.

"I am still working for the same company and I am still rated well by my managers. I have just been offered a management job that I refused. I don't feel like quitting any more, and I feel that my company cares about me as a person. I feel that my job fits me and that I deliver the best work I can do for my company. And I feel that it is appreciated."

Boundaries in Systems

One of the main reasons that systems react so strongly when people set boundaries (and why co-workers often seem to undermine any boundaries that people do set) is that when one worker sets a boundary or a limit, that same boundary becomes an option for everyone else in the system. In effect, when you set a boundary, you give other people in the system more choices.

This can be a positive thing if others are ready for those choices. But if other people are not ready to look at their own lives and are not ready to see their own choices in life, they can react strongly to your efforts to take control of your life. You may find, however, that as you yourself begin to function more effectively, you will provide both the attitudes and the impetus for others to perform at their best. One of the most significant contributions you can make to your family and your employer is to manage yourself. Effective self-management reduces anxiety and builds self-confidence. Our programs have proven repeatedly that developing and implementing a well planned Personal Vision increases personal effectiveness at work and at home.

If you want to create boundaries at work, taking other people through your whole thought process in creating the boundary—even enlisting their input—can help a great deal in pulling in their cooperation. The more you have worked on your Personal Vision and the more of that work you share with others, the more they can feel a part of the boundaries you set.

Thought Experiment I

Resistances To Change

Much of our internal resistance to change originates in our families of origin. It is here after all that we learn how to deal with systems. Our sense of what is 'normal' and 'right' to do in systems comes right out of the families in which we grow up. It makes sense that when we start thinking about doing something differently, our first reaction may be to think, "I can't possibly do that." You can start to find out the sources of some of these internal points of resistance with the following simple exercise.

In order to complete this exercise, you will need to have already done some work on your Personal Vision. You will also need to have done some work on identifying appropriate boundaries as described in the body of this chapter.

1. Once you have figured out what boundaries you would like to establish, write them down in your Personal Vision notebook. For example, you might write: "I want to leave work by 6:00 every day." You might have a list of a dozen or more boundaries you are interested in enforcing.

2. For each of your boundaries, whether work-related, family-related or personally related, answer the following question: "How would my mother react to this boundary?" The best way to answer the question is to write your answer in your Personal Vision notebook as though your mother were writing it. Don't assume that you already know what she would say and that there's no need to write it down. Try to write what she would write as her answer. You may surprise yourself with what your unconscious comes up with.

3. You can increase the sophistication of this exercise by considering your mother's response at two different times in her life. How would she have responded to this boundary when you were about twelve? How would she respond to this boundary now?

4. For each of your boundaries, answer the question: "How would my father react to this boundary?" Again, you can increase the sophistication of the exercise by answering the question at two different times in your

father's life. Once again, write the answers in your Personal Vision notebook as though your father were writing them.

5. If you want to take another, very interesting step in this exercise, then call your mother and father and schedule times to go and talk to them individually. When you talk to them in individual interviews, tell each the situation at work and the boundaries you intend to put into place. Listen to how each one responds to your proposed boundaries. How do their responses differ? Does one think it's a great idea? Does it make one nervous? Does either parent discourage you or encourage you? Which parent mirrors most closely your own internal responses?

6. You may find that as you try to come up with reactions from your parents, you uncover some resistance—and perhaps some encouragement. Some people even find that the very words they use to resist change in their minds are the same words they imagine their parents using. Writing down these words will help you gain some distance from them and guide your choice about whether to proceed or not.

> NEXT CHAPTER: We created Eight Personal Vision Factors for individuals. However, in the new economy—the Knowledge Economy—corporations are increasingly recognizing that the path to thriving or even surviving involves helping individuals do what they do best and find the right fit in the company. These are exactly what research has shown that our program accomplishes. A program that helps individuals can end up helping the corporation to be more profitable.

WHEN **INDIVIDUALS** HAVE ENOUGH INFORMATION ABOUT THEMSELVES, THEY CAN BE **PROACTIVE** AND **INFORMED PARTICIPANTS** IN THE MANAGEMENT PROCESS — MAKING THE **WHOLE CORPORATION** RUN MORE **EFFICIENTLY** AND **EFFECTIVELY.**

Corporations &
The Personal Vision

A few years ago, McKinsey and Company published the results of a two-year study of talent in U.S. businesses. Their conclusions were somewhat sobering. Over the next fifteen to twenty years, there will be an increasing talent gap. The economy will try to expand at its usual rate, but the supply of young people to fill increasing numbers of positions will actually dwindle. This talent shortfall has already begun to affect companies in the high-tech arena. You can check it out in any major city by just driving down the freeway. Billboard after billboard advertises websites dedicated to helping people move up into high-tech professions. In Silicon Valley, the billboards are more direct—"If you're tired of your present job, call this number."

In our Knowledge Economy, success or failure depends on talent: the talent that a company can bring to bear on a key problem or process, the talent that creates the new ideas that change how business is done, the talent to organize and manage increasingly complex elements of global money-making. McKinsey's numbers are cold and emotionless, but the statement they make is compelling: There won't be enough talent to go around in the next twenty years. The immediate corollaries are obvious: Make better use of the talent you already have—and above all, don't lose it.

A number of recent books have been published whose purpose is to help business use talent more effectively (Jeffrey Pfeffer, *The Human Equation,* 1998; Heskett, Sasser and Schlesinger, *The Service Profit Chain,* 1997; Kaplan and Norton, *The Balanced Scorecard,* 1996; Edward Gubman, *The Talent Solution,* 1998). One of the most interesting of these is by Buckingham and Coffman, *First, Break All The Rules* (1999). Buckingham and Coffman, of the

Gallup Organization, report on a number of studies that included over 80,000 managers in 400 companies. They sought to identify those attitudes in the workplace that led companies to be more productive and more profitable.

The authors didn't look at company strategy. They didn't look at product advantages. They didn't even look at technological innovation. They looked at people. What were the attitudes of people in teams, divisions, sections, units, and companies that were more productive and profitable, and what were the attitudes in units and teams that were less profitable?

"Talent will be the most important corporate resource over the next 20 years. It is also the resource in shortest supply."

–Ed Michaels, McKinsey and Company, The War For Talent

Two points stand out in Buckingham and Coffman's conclusions. First, people in more profitable companies and business units reported that they get to do what they do best everyday. Second, people in more profitable companies and business units reported that they felt a connection between themselves and the mission of the company.

The conclusions Buckingham and Coffman drew were that the path toward a better-functioning company or business unit must begin with two critical steps. First, companies need to place people in positions in which they can use their talents—where they can do what they do best every day. Second, companies need to insure that there is a good fit between the company and the individual.

Buckingham and Coffman concluded that the critical difference between the more profitable business units and the less profitable ones had to do with their managers. Highly talented managers put people in positions in which they can use their best talents. In addition, they somehow help people to feel a better fit between themselves and the company.

We feel that our program has implications for these conclusions. By driving information down to individuals, corporations have the ability, for the first time, to have a meaningful dialog between individual and manager about talent and fit. The effect of this dialog will be to make any manager function as one of the Great Managers mentioned by Buckingham and Coffman. As we will see, some companies have already seen that this highly profitable dialog can improve team functioning and the bottom line results of a variety of business units.

The Knowledge Economy

Peter Drucker started talking about the implications of the Knowledge Economy almost ten years ago. Here is what he said in one of his articles in the Harvard Business Review:

> *Most of us, even those of us with modest endowments, will have to learn to manage ourselves. We will have to learn to develop ourselves. We will have to place ourselves where we can make the greatest contribution. And we will have to stay mentally alert and engaged during a 50-year working life, which means knowing how and when to change the work we do.*

Drucker draws the clear, logical conclusions you have to draw when you start thinking about knowledge workers and the Knowledge Economy. The name for this economy stems from the fact that economic value no longer lies in things; rather, it lies in the special knowledge and talents that each individual brings to the job. 'Human capital' is a phrase we encounter more and more. But just because people describe it as "capital" doesn't mean that this kind of capital is the same as the more traditional capital of machines, buildings and rolling stock.

Frederick W. Taylor once said to factory workers: "You are not paid to think. Other people are paid to think around here." Now, even in factories, there is an increasing expectation that everyone will be responsive to what is happening around him or her and make decisions accordingly. Now, almost everyone in corporations is being paid primarily to think and respond to a constantly changing business environment.

Increasingly, to compete effectively, all organizations need people who make decisions. Not just executives. Not even just managers. To deal effectively with a work environment that changes daily, everyone has to be alert to changes and react appropriately.

The fundamental fact about the knowledge worker is that he or she is not merely one among many interchangeable machines humming day after day on the factory floor. The knowledge worker is an individual with his or her own individual talents, experiences, connections and history. As corporations increasingly discover, these workers can always take their knowledge, experiences, contacts and relationships and simply go elsewhere.

In the Knowledge Economy, the company and the business are contained in the heads of the people who work there. Our point of view is that it cannot be left to Great Managers alone to place those people in the right positions so they can use their strengths. It cannot be left solely to Great Managers to make sure people feel a good fit between themselves and the company. Our point of view is that when individuals have enough information about themselves, they can be proactive and informed participants in the management process—making the whole corporation run more efficiently and effectively. Each person can be a Great Manager of himself or herself.

Success In The Knowledge Economy

Peter Drucker has some ideas about what is needed for success in the knowledge economy:

First and foremost, concentrate on your strengths.

Put yourself where your strengths can produce results.

Figure out how you work best.

Figure out how you learn most effectively.

Figure out how your values impact what you do.

Figure out how your career will change over a 50-year span.

Mr. Drucker, writing years ago, seems to have foreshadowed our commitment to the understanding of abilities. A knowledge of abilities tells you what your strengths are. It also tells you how you learn best as well as how you make decisions and solve problems most effectively. By working through the elements of the Eight Personal Vision Factors and integrating them creatively, you can come to amazingly productive conclusions about how you work best, what your values say to you, and the best fit for yourself in the workplace. An important part of our insights concerns how your career changes through your life cycle. There are predictable ways, points and issues that you can plan for and take into account before they become crises.

As if to emphasize the importance of seeing yourself as a whole person, not just a collection of skills and functions, Mr. Drucker has recently begun to stress the importance of the spiritual side of people in business. The implications of Mr. Drucker's thinking are clear: in our Knowledge Economy, people will be more effective, more productive, more satisfied, and they will last longer in their jobs, if they can see themselves in a bigger way and see what they do in a bigger context. As Mr. Drucker is at some pains to point out, figuring out all of this about yourself is not a matter of filling out a few personality tests and attending a class or two. He describes a process that takes years.

The process that we describe in this book is an entire structure. It helps you to see all of the important factors that will impact you and your career at any given time in your work life. It allows you to be proactive in an economy and business environment that changes constantly. It allows you to concentrate on your strengths—as opposed to trying to be everything to everyone.

Above all, our program is a tool to help you articulate your highest and most important contribution to the company, to your family and to your own life. It allows you to articulate and deal with the truth about yourself. What you find out when you go through our program is not something that someone else tells you or that you make up. It comes out of you. It is you.

We have found that if you can say with complete conviction, "This is how I work best, and here is where my values lead me; this is what I am really passionate about and this is what I see as my highest contribution" – you will open and create many opportunities for yourself.

Why? Because there is enormous power in dealing with the truth. The Eight Personal Vision Factors lead you to the truth about yourself. It's an objective truth that you can describe to your spouse, your children, your co-workers, your subordinates and your boss.

Our Program in Corporations

We have been using our program in corporations for many years. When we first created it, we didn't think of it as a corporate program. We thought of it strictly as a tool for individual development. Many of the most important aspects of the program – and of other corporate programs we have developed since – actually came out of that original conception.

- **We wanted our program to be complete.** Since we weren't trying to please any one manager – e.g., a manager who may want a program done in a half-day – we felt free to put in all the elements we felt necessary for an effective program. This means that we design each program to fit the needs of the corporate client and the participants.

- **We wanted our program to be inside out, not outside in.** The program would not be a series of lectures delivered by an 'expert.' It would be a guided self-discovery by the real expert—you.
- **We wanted our program to be practical and useful.** There would be no reason for people to undertake a program like this unless there were a direct and palpable benefit—one that they could feel and experience. This held us to a rigorous standard.
- **We felt strongly that the individual should own the information about him- or herself.** This is a program for the individual, not for anyone else. Only individuals can make decisions about their careers, and everyone should be able to have and manage the information about him- or herself.
- **We are not invested in the outcome.** We care deeply that people who go through program should receive the best and most complete insights we can deliver; however, we do not base the success of our program on the extent of the discoveries people make about themselves. It's not because this doesn't matter to us; it is because we would not presume to know what is right for any one person. Instead, we presume that if people approach the program honestly and go through it with an open mind, they will find the right answers for themselves.

There were some pretty big obstacles for using the Eight Personal Vision Factors in corporate settings when we started out. Managers who were used to traditional training programs assumed we would share any data that came out of the programs with them. They assumed that they could use the data to hire new workers or to shift workers to new responsibilities. We explained that an important component of the success of the program is that the individual participant owns the information. Our point of view has always been that the individual, armed with enough information, can ultimately make the best decisions about his or her own career. We feel that when individuals take responsibility for their own careers and enter into a dialog with management, the results will represent the most positive outcome for both.

Managers often wanted to know whether the trainers who delivered the program could make it entertaining. This was an interesting point. The managers knew that their people were used to motivational shows and energy-inspiring hype. They knew that if the speaker was dull, their people would simply drift away. Our response to this was "Don't Worry. If there is one subject on earth that you— along with everyone else—will find fascinating, compelling and endlessly absorbing, that subject is you." This is what our program is all about – helping you to develop knowledge about yourself

How We Got Our Start In Corporations

A young man who worked at IBM was so disgruntled with his job that he decided to try our program. His idea was to see what else he could do instead of what he was doing – deep down, he had come to hate it. He was making a good salary and was named to the pool of young talent being groomed for the executive ranks, but his heart was not in his work. He did not understand why he was so unhappy, but he felt that if things didn't change, he would quit.

When we first started doing our programs, we thought that one way we could measure the success of the program would be by the number of people who quit their current jobs and got into whole new jobs in whole new fields. We found out quickly that that particular measure did not tell us anything. Instead, we found that in the vast majority of cases, people did not switch jobs. Even people, like the young man at IBM, who were markedly unhappy with their careers almost always tried to figure out how to make their present jobs work better for them, rather than quit and start all over somewhere else.

The young man did go through the whole program, and it was a life-changing event for him. He was so excited that he went to his boss with his notebook in hand and took the boss through everything he had learned about himself: how he worked best, where his real strengths were, and what he saw as his best fit in the company. The young man was not thinking about quitting any more. He knew what he was looking for at IBM and felt that with his boss's help, he could find it.

This was one of the first examples of the kind of dialog between individual and manger that can happen when people have solid knowledge about themselves. We have seen a great many since.

The young man's boss was so impressed with the result that he asked us to develop a corporate version of the same program. We did develop this program using the same concepts you see in this book.

Research and Outcomes

From the very first seminars we delivered in corporations, we wanted to demonstrate what was happening as people went through the programs. We decided to develop a series of research scales covering significant measures related to profitability, retention, satisfaction and productivity. In addition, we determined to measure long-term outcome results rather than just immediate post-seminar results. Our thinking was that the program should demonstrate an impact on significant business measures and that only long-term gains were really meaningful.

We developed a questionnaire of some 220 items. From these items we derived nine different scales:

1. Ability Match: The perceived match between the person's natural abilities and talents and his or her major roles in the organization. There have been many hundreds of studies over nearly 70 years confirming the importance of Ability match in productivity and job satisfaction.

- When the match is <u>low</u> (weak match), it is related positively to stress
- When the match is <u>high</u> (strong match), it is related positively to:
  Optimism
  Internal locus of control
  Connection to company.

2. Stress. The person's own report of how much or how little stress he or she is currently experiencing on the job. Stress has been studied by researchers for decades.

<u>High Stress</u> is related to:
- Poor job satisfaction
- Poor company connection
- Poor personal satisfaction
- Poor health
- Poor retention
- Poor overall productivity

3. Optimism: The person's report of whether he or she sees a positive future. Martin Seligman has spent much of his career in psychology studying the effects of optimism and what leads to optimism.

<u>High Optimism</u> has been positively linked to:

- Higher Productivity
- Lower Stress
- Better Management Decisions
- Higher Retention
- More Effective Sales
- Better Health

4. Internal vs. External Locus of Control: A measure of how much or how little control people feel they have over their own decisions and how these decisions affect what happens to them in life.

<u>Internal Locus</u> of Control has been positively linked to:

- Higher Productivity
- Higher Satisfaction
- Better Management Decisions
- Better Long Term Health

5. Connection to Company: A measure of the person's sense of his or her connection to the company and of the company's care and concern about him or her. Connection to Company has just begun to be studied in detail in the last ten years or so. Nevertheless, there have been valid and confirmed findings in this area.

<u>Higher Connection</u> to Company results in:

- Greater overall job satisfaction
- Better retention
- Higher Productivity

6. Vision: A measure of the specificity, completeness and objectivity with which a person looks forward to the future. A complete, specific vision for the future that you arrive at with some objective information is more predictive of both success and satisfaction than any other factor researchers have ever found.

7. Balance: A measure of the kinds of factors a person takes into account when figuring out personal and career goals. When people create career goals with some attention to job, family, and personal aspects of their lives, and when they fit these into an overall scheme or vision, they are much less likely to burn out, derail or make precipitous career moves.

8. Satisfaction Index: An overall rating drawn from all of the previous scales of the person's present sense of satisfaction with his or her career.

Strongest determinants:
- Role satisfaction
- Optimism
- Balance

9. Productivity Index: A rating drawn from all of our scales of the person's overall present productivity. Strongest determinants:
- Role Match
- Internal Locus of Control

Our questionnaire was administered before corporate participants started the programs and immediately after they finished, and then administered again after six months. This resulted in pre-, post- and six-month follow-up scores on all nine scales. A total of 165 corporate employees participated in the research over a two-year period.

The following chart shows the results:

Long Term Gains From The Highlands Corporate Program

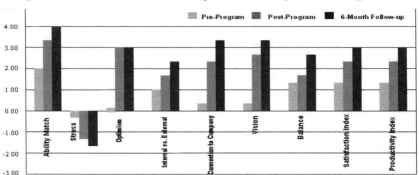

These results are also shown in the following table:

	Percentage Gains		
	Pre- to post-	Post- to 6 mo.	Total Gain
Ability Match	19%	7%	26%
Stress	-20%	-12%	-32%
Optimism	56%	-1%	55%
Internal vs. External	11%	8%	19%
Connection To Company	40%	11%	51%
Vision	47%	8%	55%
Balance	11%	13%	24%
Satisfaction	19%	10%	29%
Productivity	19%	10%	29%
Average	27%	9%	36%
Average	27%	9%	36%

Note that Stress is reversed—if Stress goes down, that is good. All changes pre- to post- are in the positive direction and statistically significant. All changes pre- to follow-up are similarly in the positive direction and statistically significant.

The interesting thing about this research is that a program we created and designed to be used by individuals — to help them lead more fulfilling and balanced lives — is now actively being used by corporations to help increase productivity and profitability.

Using The Program In Corporations

We have worked with a number of corporations over the last five years. Our program is a basic framework that different organizations have used for a multitude of purposes. By starting with the individual and how that person uses his or her talents, companies as diverse as IBM, GlaxoSmithKline (GSK) and Chase Bank of Texas have used our seminars to deal with such critically important issues as diversity, team functioning, retention and organizational vision.

TEAMS — GLAXOSMITHKLINE

At GSK, our program is being used as a tool to help improve productivity and profitability in an increasingly competitive and crowded marketplace. A former Director of Corporate Learning and Development was quoted as saying: "I had my entire team go through the program. We measured both job satisfaction and performance pre- and post-. I'm convinced that participation in the seminar can lead to improved job performance and satisfaction at the individual level. I believe using the process with an intact group can be a powerful way for a team to gain a better understanding and appreciation of one another, improve the manner in which they communicate, and adjust job activities to take full advantage of each individual's talents."

Post-program analysis indicated that the individual productivity of people on the team had improved an average of 8%. The overall productivity of the team had improved 7%. And the individual job satisfaction of people on the team had improved an average of 17%. Changes due to participation in the seminar were isolated from changes attributable to other influences.

In the course of completing the seminar for this study, it became obvious that two people on the team were in roles that did not match their abilities and personalities well. The fact that this team was composed of experienced human resources professionals pointed out the difficulty of matching people with roles without objective information to go by. By carefully moving through the structure of the seminar, the two people involved became aware of the role discrepancies involved. This realization resulted in the kind of open dialog that often characterizes systems that work well. Both team members ended by radically redesigning their role assignments.

The difference in attitude and performance was startling. Both team members had performed well in their previous roles. In their new roles, they showed the kind of spark and creativity that managers wish for. One of the team members has completely redesigned the structure of the programs they offer to eliminate redundancy and to follow a more logical path. Both team members have performed so well in their new roles that they are now in line for promotions and wider responsibility.

This team's story is an example of a phenomenon we see over and over again. Talented people in the wrong roles can usually perform satisfactorily, even quite well. But the enormous effort required to do that means they're not going to enjoy their roles and are certainly not going to be very creative in them. From the outside, though, there may be nothing particularly striking about the picture.

When people are in the right roles, however, we are in another universe. In this universe, people fit their roles by utilizing talent, interests, values, personality, skills and goals. In this world, people are happy; they come up with creative new ideas all the time; and they are hugely productive.

DIVERSITY— CHASE BANK OF TEXAS

The Chase organization is well known for its work in diversity. A Vice President of the Diversity Group at Chase Texas first heard about our program during a conference on diversity in the work force. "As a part of Chase's diversity strategy, our aim is to attract, nurture, challenge and reward people who have a wide range of talents, experiences and perspectives. Vigorous and effective career development is integral to that goal, so our employees have access to an extraordinary array of development tools and resources. Yet the Highlands assessment instrument and discovery process outlined at the conference appeared to offer something unique. It seemed to provide a missing link, one that would enable Chase employees to clarify and articulate their natural talents and interests and then match them to the organization's mission and goals.

"I was spurred to try a pilot program by a comment from a participant in our Leadership Mentoring Program. This is a mentoring program in which high-potential mid-level African-Americans are paired with Chase Texas executives. He said he was unsure of his next career steps at Chase. I realized that until he could create and envision his own direction in the bank, he could not achieve the success of which he is capable, nor could Chase benefit fully from his talents.

"We completed a pilot program with a group of Leadership Mentoring protégés. Many have told me that it was a life-changing experience. And six months afterwards, their stories are even more powerful. Already Chase has benefited from participants' enhanced loyalty, productivity, communication skills and satisfaction. We are currently considering additional ways to offer the program in conjunction with succession planning, top talent development and intact team initiatives. By helping individuals know themselves better and clarify and communicate their vision, we have helped them connect with Chase, and this will result in tremendous long-term benefit to the organization."

ORGANIZATIONAL VISION—MATRIX RESOURCES

Matrix Resources is a fast-growing IT placement firm with headquarters in Atlanta, Georgia. A Vice President of Corporate Services led a team that managed all aspects of operations except for sales. "We've experienced 900% growth in four years. My management team consists of me and seven directors. We've been together as a team for about three years and I feel that as a team we were pretty tight before we ever did the seminar. My goals for the seminar were for me and my team to gain a better understanding of ourselves and a better understanding of each other.

"We had three definite steps in our growth—each one significant. The first was when we went through The Highlands Ability Battery™ together. It made a huge impact almost immediately. I noticed a new level of self-awareness and a new level of self-confidence in the members of the team. I attribute this to two factors. First, individuals could see objectively that they really were good at some things. Second, and this is a little more subtle, people could see that they were not well suited for other things by their natural talent. It meant that you don't have to pretend you're great at everything. What a relief!

"The second step happened when I made copies of my Ability Battery report for everyone on the team. People found this so helpful in understanding how to work with me that each person on the team ended up making copies of his own report for the other people on the team. Communication opened up. We reached a level of support and acceptance that we had never reached before.

"The third step happened in the seminar that followed. We did a number of modeling exercises and ended by creating a Vision Statement for the team. We came up with eleven principles that would be our vision for the leadership team. After the seminar we realized that this Vision Statement was pivotal and we began to flesh it out with examples and statements about how to carry it out. It is now a one-page document listing the eleven principles and their supporting statements. The seven directors are now in the process of taking this Vision Statement to each of their teams to form the basis of their team visions. The vision that emerged from the seminar will ultimately be the basis of a statement of principle for our entire company."

RETENTION AND MOTIVATION—MARRIOTT INTERNATIONAL

The Alliance Accounts Organization at Marriott International was responsible for strategic accounts management. Their clients were the top 31 global corporate customers of Marriott, and they were responsible for over $700 million in sales. A member of the Alliance Accounts team first became aware of our program when she read the previous edition of this book. "It's evident that self-development is important. This seemed different from the many other things that Marriott offers. It seemed far more complete. It also seemed more powerful because it was self-discovery, not some expert telling me about myself. My thought was that our group has been together for three years. It is a very close and well-functioning team. If we could go through an experience like this together, it seemed to me that we could have a better chance of staying together as a team and have less chance of people moving off into a different career path just to do something different. I took the idea to my boss."

The "boss" was Vice President of Alliance Accounts and leader of the team of 15 relationship managers. "When Carrie brought this idea to me, it seemed different. I wanted to see how we could be a more effective team. I wanted to raise the overall level of performance and I wanted to revitalize the group. For three years, this organization has been on the front of a paradigm shift at Marriott. This is sometimes frustrating work."

"I wanted the members of the group to be able to know each other individually and for the team to be able to draw on each other's strengths. The members of our team never see each other for most of the year, and our experience with the seminar was intense and very open. I feel we understand each other at core level. The team is more focused and energized.

"Every member of the team has been at Marriott for many years. One always has the question, is there a better place to work outside of Marriott? The program helped bring this question from the back of our minds to the forefront: Is there alignment? And what exactly attracts and keeps people on board? With the war for talent out there, people can always go out and make more money. But maybe that's not the most important thing. One person on the team, as a result of the seminar, realized that she could not find a fit with her career and life goals at Marriott. The other members of the team completely understood her position and were very supportive of changes she wanted to make. All of the other members of the team felt more clearly and positively aligned with Marriott and with the team. This was an exceptional use of our time and exceeded my expectations."

COACHING AND THE LEARNING ORGANIZATION—PRINTPACK

Printpack is the largest privately held flexible packaging converter in the United States. It has about 4,000 employees in 18 domestic plants, and has about $1 billion in revenue. Tom Brown was the Director of Organizational Development for Printpack. Tom has been interested in creating a coaching model for the development of front line leaders for some time. "Printpack is a manufacturing company. We wanted to create a program to develop our plant-level leaders that would take people off the floor as little as possible but that would allow us to grow a learning organization from the very lowest levels. Our model would depend on the development of talents by people that we are training as coaches. We call it the Frontline Leadership Development Program.

"The Highlands Program turned out to be the glue that holds the whole thing together. It made us consider vital learning issues such as: How does this person learn? How does she solve problems? By understanding individual differences in learning and problem-solving channels, our coaches can go out to the plant floor and meet the people on their own ground. They can work from the point of view that starts with the individual. We call the Eight Personal Vision Factors an indispensable part of the program we call Leadership From Within. There is no question but that it is extremely beneficial for the Frontline Leadership coaches to have this tool. These coaches will be the delivery mechanism for development to our production supervisors. The Eight Personal Vision Factors provide a gymnastic-like floor mat—a platform from which to take off and land."

SUCCESSION PLANNING—BELLSOUTH CELLULAR

Roy McAllister was Vice President, Human Resources, at BellSouth Cellular Corporation. He became interested in our program when he went through the ability battery himself, "I learned things about the way I work and how I pace myself. I understood better that not everybody works in the same way. As a senior manager, one of my most important jobs is the identification and development of the future leaders of BellSouth Cellular. I had noticed before that our most talented young people go about things differently. Partly that is a difference in generations. But another important difference is simply how they are uniquely wired.

"I felt it would be valuable for the young people who will be leading BellSouth Cellular to have the benefit of learning what things they can do easily and well, and what things they will have a hard time with. I also wanted them to be cognizant of how people are different. I wanted them to be able to become observers of how other people work, so that the program could help them as managers and prepare them better for leadership roles.

"The participants in the program have been uniform in their appreciation. One interesting sidelight was that they all felt more responsibility for their own development after the program. One person, after going through the program, realized why a current assignment was particularly frustrating for her. With the knowledge gained from the program, she could talk to her boss clearly about what was frustrating and what kinds of assignments would be more in her line. For several others, you could tell that the light bulbs went off when they started to understand why they worked the way they worked. I feel that this is extremely valuable knowledge for these young people to have in their development as leaders."

LEADERSHIP—IBM

Bob Gonzales is Vice President of Human Resources Operations at IBM. His focus is North America, with some global responsibilities. He leads a team of 20 people, all of whom are leaders and managers of other teams. "I was interested in your program because 70 percent of my team members are new to their jobs. I wanted the team to do something that would bring us together as a team. I think the program helped us deal with our own talents as individuals. More importantly, it helped us see and appreciate and value our differences. Diversity does not have to pull us apart. By valuing our differences and the differences we see in others, our diversity gives us more strength.

"The experience was emotional and memorable. It has stayed with us. We have a better understanding of our individual strengths, but also the strengths of others on the team. It helped us see what we as individuals bring to the team that others don't. I think it has helped us use the strength of our diversity of styles and work types. It has helped us personally, but also helped out leadership skills and how we work together as a team."

Motivation In The Knowledge Economy

Researchers have known for at least fifty years that pay and benefits—beyond a certain baseline—are not particularly effective motivators for people in corporations. In spite of this, managers have up to now almost exclusively relied on pay to motivate people—probably because this is what they felt they had control over. In the past, this worked—or at least it worked well enough. In the Knowledge Economy, managers are increasingly faced with trying to motivate people for whom pay has ceased to be the most significant motivator.

What does motivate people now? If you ask people what they want, they fall back first on the one answer our society teaches everyone — pay. The problem is that most individuals haven't fully engaged the issue of motivation. In Silicon Valley, where companies desperately try everything to keep people from jumping ship, the answers they come up with are frequently bizarre: valet laundry, for instance, or on-site dentistry. As one HR manager pointed out, the effect of many employee-generated suggestions is actually to keep people at their desks working without so many interruptions. One company motivates executives by letting them use the company Humvee for the weekend.

But if you dig a little deeper into the problem, you will find a more substantive answer. Generally, what people really want is success, along with a more balanced life, less stress and more time to enjoy their leisure. The wish for more pay and more perks, on closer interview with the individuals themselves, translates into a wish for a better lifestyle.

To quote Jeffrey Pfeffer:

> *Creating a fun, challenging and empowered work environment in which individuals are able to use their abilities to do meaningful jobs for which they are shown appreciation is likely to be a more certain way to enhance motivation and performance—even though creating such an environment may be more difficult and take more time than merely turning the reward lever.*
>
> *—The Talent Equation*

The experts all point to similar conclusions. If you want to succeed, if you want to make your company profitable, you have to structure things so that people can do what they do best, feel a good fit between themselves and their jobs, and enjoy and feel engaged by what they do all day long. The Eight Personal Vision Factors give corporations a way to accomplish all of these goals. The only caveat is that they first have to think outside the dots of traditional skills-oriented, outside-in management and system-driven programs. They have to be willing to trust their employees with enough information about themselves to create a meaningful dialog between management and individual. This will enable the employees to gain their goals individual by individual. When enough individuals are doing what they do best and bringing their entire selves to work every day, then the system has changed, and everyone benefits.

> The next chapter helps you pull the information in the book together. It lets you see how the creation of a Personal Vision based on the Eight Personal Vision Factors becomes not just an interesting exercise, but a guide for life.

PEOPLE ALMOST ALWAYS HAVE MANY
MORE CHOICES IN LIFE
AFTER THEY CREATE A PERSONAL
VISION THAN BEFORE.

WHY?

IS IT BECAUSE PERSONAL VISIONS
CREATE MORE OPTIONS?

NO, ALL THE OPTIONS
WERE ALWAYS THERE.

RATHER,
PERSONAL VISIONS HELP THEM
FOCUS ON WHAT THEY REALLY WANT.

WHEN YOU **KNOW WHAT YOU
ARE AFTER,** YOU CAN ALMOST
ALWAYS FIND IT.

Personal Vision as a Guide for Life

Your Personal Vision is a way to see into the future and link yourself to a future that makes sense to you. It points the way, it works as a template for making decisions, and it draws you forward. One of the primary characteristics of happy, productive, successful people is that they see themselves in a future that feels positive and attainable.

The opposite is also true. A defining characteristic of people experiencing stress, anger, depression, boredom, ennui and burnout is that they do not see themselves in a future that feels positive. Any positive future they see feels too distant or too difficult to attain. They don't like the way things are going, and they don't see things changing. They are caught in the Stress Cycle.

When people don't have Personal Visions they confuse their systems' goals and interests with their own goals and interests. The goals they seek are actually their systems' goals. They move toward a future that is not really their own, but one imposed by their systems

Some Thoughts about Personal Vision

The more objectively connected your Personal Vision is to you, yourself, the better it can guide your career. Your Personal Vision must come from inside to be effective; no one can hand it to you. If you don't follow a structure to create your Personal Vision, you run the risk of leaving out key aspects of your life that may prove critically important later. You also run the risk of viewing yourself and your options through the distorting lens of your system. The more solidly and objectively your Personal Vision is grounded in your present life, the more surely it moves you into the future.

No matter how accurate the Personal Vision you create now, change will inevitably occur. Our lives all move in regular cycles from Turning Point, to periods of stability, to Turning Point. No matter how satisfied we have been with our career, there will be times when we long for change. No matter how dissatisfied and unhappy we are during periods of stability, we continue along the same path without changing – until we arrive at another Turning Point.

The work you do to create a complete and viable Personal Vision will not only help you at the next Turning Point; it will also continue to help you at future Turning Points. Opening options at one Turning Point can give you more options at the next, just as shutting down options at a Turning Point can easily limit your options later.

As we move through our lives and careers, each Turning Point builds on the strengths and weaknesses of the process we used at the last one. Knowledge about your abilities, skills, interests, personality, values, goals and family of origin, as well as ideas and answers for putting them together, helps you every time you face a decision. If you make career choices enlightened by a clear Personal Vision, these decisions can help you grow and experience your life more fully. When you get to the next Turning Point, you not only have a useful structure for figuring out what you need to do, but you also have several years of fuller, more successful, more enthusiastic experience under your belt upon which to draw.

If, when faced with change, you ignore increasingly negative feelings, you can certainly survive a Turning Point intact. But you will not have found out any more about yourself. You will have missed one of the most powerful opportunities in life to figure out who you really are and what you really want.

The same can be said of ill-considered, radical or catastrophic changes at Turning Points. These sudden changes usually occur only after years of unrecognized and unexpressed unhappiness. The consequences of catastrophic change usually mirror closely the consequences of having done nothing at Turning Points. Great, sweeping changes may ignore the many advantages of long experience. Starting over from scratch may mean that you spend your time and creative energy getting back to the point at which you started, rather than exploring new territory. No new learning takes place. And an opportunity to figure out what is productive and satisfying and what can create more meaning in your life goes to waste.

When people limit their options at Turning Points, it becomes more and more difficult to open new options later in life. Not because new options aren't available, but because it becomes increasingly difficult to see anything outside the Stress Cycle. By using the Eight Personal Vision Factors we have described in this book, you can create an ongoing guide that you can reshape and update at Turning Points in your life. You've learned the variables; now, you just have to update them to meet your present needs and goals. By looking at the changes that have occurred in your interests, values, skills, etc., since your last Turning Point, you can more easily adapt those changes to your current Personal Vision and thus move into the Balance Cycle.

Creating the Balance Cycle

The nature of humans and systems is such that balance doesn't just happen. We have to create it consciously. We learn how to fashion our lives from our parents. Obviously, if our parents live stressfully, we learn to live stressfully, too. Any life outside the Stress Cycle would seem unnatural.

But what about those parents who are able to balance work and family, productivity and connectedness – parents who grow and change throughout their lives, adapting effectively to changes in their environments and in themselves? The example set by these parents is incalculably valuable for the child who is to become an adult. Parents like these have held steadfastly to an interior sense of themselves and what they want, and they have consistently seen this interior sense of self as more important than the self their systems see.

The children of these parents learn to create an interior sense of self, too. They also learn that this interior sense is more important than the self the system sees. But these children will need to be just as active in creating and retaining a Personal Vision as their parents were. They will have to move purposefully into the Balance Cycle—it won't just happen for them any more than it did for their parents.

Children in these families learn that they are not one person now and forever. Rather, they constantly learn, grow and change. Our systems, including our schools, colleges, corporations, and families, seize on one view of us—usually a fairly simple, one-dimensional view— and maintain that view despite all manner of evidence that the person has changed and grown.

We must constantly assert our own view of ourselves, based on an interior understanding of who we are and what we want out of our lives. If we don't, our systems will define us, and our systems will determine our goals. And our systems will suck us inevitably into the Stress Cycle.

The tool for creating the Balance Cycle is a Personal Vision. Derived from a close objective and subjective structure for understanding yourself, a Personal Vision gives you solid ground to stand upon, a secure fulcrum to help you move your life, and a way to be sure it is your life you are living, not someone else's. As parents, we can give our children the tool of our examples, to help them understand themselves and separate their True Selves from System Selves. But they must step out in their lives and create their own Balance Cycles for themselves. No one can do it for them. Their lives will be different from ours. The Balance Cycles they create will of necessity be different from the ones we created for ourselves. The underlying certainty, though, is that the more and sooner we create balance in our lives and understand ourselves, the more powerful will be the tools we hand our children to do the same in their lives. Any option we open for ourselves automatically becomes a possibility for our children.

Personal Vision through the Cycle of Adult Development

"Change is the only certainty." This wisdom comes to us from the past, but its lesson often eludes us. In any case, the cycle of adult development regularly alternates between change and stability.

Just as we must of necessity continually create and recreate the Balance Cycle for ourselves if we are to live in it, so must we periodically reassess our Personal Visions throughout our lives. A Personal Vision we create at age 17 before leaving for college can include certain areas of knowledge, like a knowledge of our abilities, which don't change through our working lives. But a 17-year-old cannot create a Personal Vision that will work for a 25-year-old or a 30-year-old. The areas of experience that the 17-year-old cannot know are too many and too vast. Having a Personal Vision does not exempt us from the cycles of change; it just gives us a method for handling change more effectively.

We tend to make major changes in our lives and careers approximately every 20 years, starting in our early twenties. We tend to make minor changes and adjustments at 10-year points. As noted by Gail Sheehy, Daniel

Levinson and others, women may delay a mid-life change comparable to men's Mid-Life Transition for 10 years or so, effectively delaying the kind of change associated with mid-life until their fifties. However, we can usually look at our life spans as a series of 20-year cycles, with mid-point assessments and adjustments.

The jumps from the security, structure and support of our families to the way station of college, and the independence of the work world, are some of the largest we will ever make. But the forces of change at mid-life are almost as great. Many people at mid-life literally set about recreating their careers from scratch, and many more wish they could. At the Mid-Life Transition, men and women have some advantages that younger people don't have. They know a lot more about themselves for one thing. People at mid-life also have a huge wealth of experience to draw upon, and they are often socially and financially more stable. On the other hand, people at mid-life often feel trapped by these same factors. They feel they shouldn't just throw away all the experience and stability they spent twenty or more years building.

At the Pre-Retirement Transition, we are once again faced with creating a new life. The lessons of the Mid-Life Transition continue to be important here. This Turning Point is just as inevitable as any other in our lives, and yet many people pretend it's just not going to happen. They think that if they have enough money saved up, that's all they need to consider.

As a general rule, the more gradual and continuous, and the less sudden and catastrophic, the change in your life, the better you will come out in the end. This is true even of inevitably great changes such as the shift from being a student to entering the work world, or the shift from work to retirement. If a young person's first job after college builds naturally out of college courses, internships and work experience in college, chances for success and satisfaction increase dramatically. At the Mid-Life Transition, if changes build naturally out of interests, plans, experiences, and values, then you are no longer dealing with a crisis; you are dealing with a natural time of transition and change. Plans for retirement can build out of relationships, interests and activities already in place long before actual retirement. Retirement can be an opportunity to express passions and values or play out major themes in your life, but in a different way or in a different environment. Continuity in life helps lend it substance and meaning.

The Senior Transition is yet another inevitable focal point of re-creation. As the balance of your life shifts gradually from doing to being, the sense that you have focused on themes that are important to you enriches your moment-to-moment existence.

A Personal Vision in Your Present Career

Most people who do the work of creating a Personal Vision and making it real find many good reasons for having chosen the career path they're on. For most people, many parts of their careers fit them well. As we have seen, when people start out in new careers, their roles may initially fit well. As people progress in their careers, however, changes in themselves and rigidity in the system may cause this fit to deteriorate. Feelings of stress, anger, boredom and loss may follow. Despite these negative feelings, however, a relatively small change in what they are doing or how they go about their careers can often make a very great difference in how they feel. A highly-focused 10 percent shift in their work roles — adding something new that they find meaningful or interesting or letting go of something they find tedious or difficult —can make a 100 percent difference in their feelings about themselves.

Moving from the Stress Cycle to the Balance Cycle does not usually or even ideally mean that you have to shake up your life. Carefully assessing and integrating all of the important aspects of your life to arrive at a Personal Vision, and using your Personal Vision to make forward-looking and considered changes, can lead much more directly to balance. Unless you have done the work to create a Personal Vision, it is next to impossible to know exactly what to change to direct you toward balance.

Failing to create a Personal Vision leaves you vulnerable. Without a Personal Vision, over time your various systems will almost certainly pull you into the Stress Cycle. When you arrive at Turning Points without a Personal Vision, you are highly susceptible to the two Big Mistakes: doing nothing, or making sudden, catastrophic and ill-considered moves that turn your life upside down. Both of the Big Mistakes can lead to notoriously unsatisfactory outcomes. Having a Personal Vision gives you a tool of incalculable value to use now and in the future as you navigate through a change.

Let us look at those Turning Points at which we construct or reconstruct our careers to see how a Personal Vision can impact them.

A Personal Vision to Create a New Career

Young people are usually forced to decide upon a direction and a career with very little information to go on. Considering that this is one of the most significant decisions anyone can make, it is surprising how little attention schools, colleges, institutions, or the young people themselves pay to it.

Research has shown clearly that young people who have a positive vision for themselves in an attainable future are more likely to complete college on time and less likely to drop out or transfer. They make better grades, get more out of their college experience, and feel happier, more satisfied and more enthusiastic about college. Later, they get better jobs that are more related to the work they did in college.

A Personal Vision begun in high school can frame and define a student's college experience. By figuring out what areas to explore in college—not an objective pulled out of a hat, but a real objective created and discovered within—students can know with a great deal more certainty what courses to take, what jobs and organizations to pursue on campus, which professors to contact, and what internships or summer jobs to attempt. Think of those 18-year-olds who arrive on campus with no idea of what they will do or what they want to accomplish in school— and our research indicates that this is the majority of students. Taking one course after another with no idea how this work will relate to their lives; declaring majors for more or less random reasons; or deciding upon a career with virtually no knowledge of what that career involves – it's no surprise that the majority of these students do not finish in four years. The wonder is that any finish at all.

These students are all victims of the Lemming Conspiracy. Unless they work purposefully to create a Personal Vision, they will continue to be victims throughout their lives and eventually add their lives to the statistics concerning stress, burnout and boredom.

The rare student who has a plan—one carefully constructed from self-discovery and from first-hand experience of life—stands out from the common herd. More focused, more energized, more confident, able to benefit fully from what college offers, these students appear to cut through life more easily than most. Perhaps as a result of family encouragement, or through instinct or intuition, they have created something like a Personal Vision without really planning one. But this does not have to be an accident or a chance development. Anyone can create a Personal Vision. And a Personal Vision can transform everyone's life.

Personal Vision at Midlife and Retirement

To some extent, we create new careers every 20 years. The 41-year-old at mid-life is in just as much a quandary about what to do as the 20-year-old college student or the 62-year-old facing retirement. At these major bends in our lives, we need some connection to the territory ahead. We need a vision that connects us as we are now to a future that makes sense. This is the job of a Personal Vision. There is no short cut. The process for creating a Personal Vision merely helps it emerge and helps make it useful to you.

One of the most interesting aspects of Personal Vision is its benefit to corporations. The next section describes how corporations can use the idea of the whole person to create more human—and more profitable—organizations.

Personal Vision in the Workplace

Stress pervades most people's working days. The higher they go, the more stress takes it toll. The workplace does not usually encourage families to thrive, nourish values or produce people who live full lives.

Employees grow and change. They arrive at Turning Points and seek more meaning. It is no accident that executive derailments, transfers and loss almost invariably happen at Turning Points. Corporations cannot provide Personal Visions for their employees, but they can provide conditions in which employees can create their own.

As we have seen, some businesses are beginning to see that the interests of their employees are in some ways the same as the bottom-line interests of the business itself. In all cases, though, the responsibility for living a fulfilling and satisfying life rests with the employee, not the corporation. Recently, however, some researchers have documented that there is a strong and replicable connection between satisfied customers and satisfied employees. Businesses have found that by retaining more key employees, they also retain more of the vital relationships between the business and its customers. Even small increases in customer retention translate into very large gains in profitability and business health.

Investors pay attention to these connections. It has become apparent that satisfied employees mean increased efficiency and profitability for the company, and this fact has assumed greater importance in investment decisions.

So what makes an employee fulfilled and satisfied? Money? Prestige? Power? No – none of these makes it into the top seven factors that influence employee satisfaction and retention. The key to retaining key employees? Balance and meaning.

People want to have whole lives. They want families and communities, and they want to feel productive and useful. When they don't have this balance and don't see any prospect for attaining it, they hit Turning Points and leave. Or they become less involved in work, or less satisfied with it.

Companies can't fashion and mold the lives of their employees. There is no set of commandments they can lay down, no matter how liberal or enlightened, to insure that employees achieve balance. In the end, only individual workers can examine their own lives and decide what they want to do.

But companies can help. In those rare cases in which companies actively encourage employees to do the work of creating Personal Visions, effectiveness, efficiency and profitability increase. Even middle performers – who make up 70% of the typical work force – can become high performers by developing a knowledge of themselves and how they work, especially if they are given the tools to create a Personal Vision and to become responsible for their learning and career development. Experience based on thousands of corporate participants shows that employees who create a vision of their futures don't leave their jobs, but instead make a 5-10% shift in direction, enabling them to make greater use of their abilities and achieve greater effectiveness and satisfaction.

In the traditional corporate hierarchy, responsibility resides at the top. Orders and direction pass down the pyramid to the bottom. In this paternal model, if you do as you're told, you don't have anything to worry about. Daddy will do the thinking and Daddy will take care of you. This old model for corporations produced massive inefficiency, abuse and excess. Fortunately, the model is changing

The new corporation is more efficient. It engages in a dialogue with its employees. The corporation says, in effect, "This is what we need you to do, and this is what we're willing to pay to get it done." The employee says, "This is who I am, and this what I can do well and in a way satisfying to me, and this what I am willing to do." The new element is employee choice, an element so powerful and effective that it transforms the corporation. What employee choice creates is the difference between someone who comes to work and just does a job and someone who likes to go to work because it creates meaning in life. "My work expresses who I am."

The Lemming Conspiracy and Leading a True Life

The positive power of systems makes civilizations possible. All of the advances in culture, comfort, productivity, security, longevity and health that civilization contributes were made available to us all through systems. However, individuals do not thrive in systems. They exist for themselves. They play a role. They provide a function. But the real life of a person happens individually, on the inside.

Creativity, energy, passion, wit and life are produced by individuals. The more we can express these elements of ourselves, the more fully human we become. We do not see the choice as either/or: "either you express your true self, or you exist as an automaton within the system." Like most black-and-white statements, this is not a true statement of the choices.

It is possible to express your True Self and to fulfill your function as a member of systems. The difficult part is attending to the whole person. That is why we created the process in this book. Once you have delineated your "True Self" and figured out a Personal Vision to express it, it becomes entirely possible to find a place for that Personal Vision within your systems. People almost always have many more choices in life after they create a Personal Vision than before. Why? Is it because a Personal Vision creates more options? No, all the options were always there. Rather, a Personal Vision helps people focus on what they really want. When they know what they are looking for, they can almost always find it.

The Lemming Conspiracy keeps you from seeing yourself, and it keeps you from seeing the true options for your life. By keeping you focused on a System Self, believing that this is all there is, the Lemming Conspiracy limits you and causes you to waste your true talent. A Personal Vision is the most productive way to find and express your True Self and fully use the talents you were born with. Once you can communicate your Personal Vision to others you have the option – the real choice – of expressing your True Self every day in the life you lead.

> *"I have learned this, at least, by my experiments; that if one advances confidently in the life he has imagined, he will meet with a success unexpected in common hours."*
>
> — *Henry David Thoreau,* Walden

About the Highlands Company
& the Highlands Ability Battery

For information about the Highlands Company, to order the Highlands Ability Battery, or to arrange for a corporate program or workshop:

- **Visit us on the web at**
  www.highlandsco.com or
  www.highlandslifeandcareercenter.com

- **Call us at:**

  Larchmont, NY office   Atlanta office:
  (800) 373-0083   (877) 872-9974

- **E-mail us at: info@highlandsco.com**

- **Write to us at:**

  New York Office: Atlanta office:
  1328 Boston Post Road   P.O. Box 76168
  Larchmont, NY 10538   Atlanta, GA 30358